UNBOUNDED

UNBOUNDED

A MEMOIR

SEARCHING FOR IDENTITY BEYOND THE ANCIENT WALLS
OF THE DESERT

BY
HUDA AL-GHOSON

Medina Publishing

Medina Publishing
50 High Street
Cowes
Isle of Wight
England
PO31 7RR

www.medinapublishing.com

First published in 2022
2nd printing

Cover designed by Maya Smadi
Printed and bound in the UK by Clays, Elcograf

ISBN Hardback - 978-1-911487-59-3

CIP data: A catalogue record for this book is available at the
British Library.

CONTENTS

For my mother

I want to sing like the birds sing,
not worrying who hears
or what they think.

—Rumi

INTRODUCTION

I was forty-seven years old, with twenty-five years of dedicated service to Saudi Aramco, the national petroleum and natural gas company of Saudi Arabia and the largest oil producing company in the world. One by one, my male peers had ascended to the decision-making level of the corporate ladder, while I was left dangling in place. I was on a high rung, to be sure, but only in the company's eyes and as far as women are concerned. From my perch as a consultant in Saudi Aramco's compensation division, I knew my skills and intellectual capabilities exceeded the requirements of my job, and I aspired for positions with higher responsibilities and influence. The obvious next step was a directorship.

For a quarter of a century, my performance reviews had been uniformly outstanding. My motivation and work ethic were held in the highest regard. The top brass continually expressed their respect for me. Yet, as I awaited the slightest hint of an advancement, nothing came.

Admittedly, I was never one to make noise about rewards or payoffs. Perhaps that was my problem. I thought it more dignified to let my work speak for itself. Other than my gender, what reason could there possibly be that was preventing my otherwise perceptive bosses from coming up with an offer? We were an international company, fast-acting and forward-thinking, but here I was, mired in the same old sand trap of traditional thinking: Women must remain subservient. We are nothing.

"Your silence gives consent," Plato said.

I no longer gave consent to be sidelined. It was time to make noise like the men did. They never had a problem giving voice to their egos. Perhaps that's why they were successful!

When I took my case to my boss, Yosef (not his real name), his knee-jerk response was, "Management wants to protect you." I thought that was the dumbest thing I had ever heard. Only, he wasn't finished.

"Being a leader is extremely difficult," he went on. "It requires a very thick skin if you expect to survive among the tough characters the rest of us have to deal with." If that wasn't patronizing enough, he said, "We appreciate your good work. Be patient. Good things happen to those who wait."

Examples of my thick skin had been on display a multitude of times, and he knew it. So, why the timidity? Was it a matter of keeping up Saudi Aramco's masculine image? Were company leaders afraid that, by appointing a woman to a position of power, they would be criticized for acting against tradition? Or may be accused of not having enough strong men around to carry the load? Was it painful for them to acknowledge that women are as capable and courageous as men in facing and overcoming the challenges?

"Thank you for your concern," I told Yosef. "In case you haven't noticed, I've had no problem dealing with difficult men before, in or out of an unforgiving environment."

I let him know that the real question had to do with the leadership of the company.

"Do they have the backbone to make tough decisions?"

A year later, in the spring of 2006, Hamed, vice president of Employee Relations & Training, called me into his office to say I was the new director of Employee Relations Policy and Planning, a name I later changed to Human Resources Policy and Planning. The current occupant of the office was switching to another organization, Hamed said, and my selection was decided from a short list of qualified candidates, all the others men.

My hard work was, at last, recognized.

I was now entrusted with the design, development and maintenance of Saudi Aramco's remuneration policies, which covered fifty-three thousand employees throughout the corporation, both domestically and internationally, and in charge of fifty professionals within my own department. By the time I retired, twelve years later, the employee count had increased to sixty-seven thousand.

"Congratulations, Huda. You did it," Hamed said, also wishing me luck. He conveyed Saudi Aramco's appreciation of my achievements but warned the road ahead could be treacherous. He did not have to spell out the most significant stumbling block. We both knew.

"You will be overseeing sensitive people and sensitive policies," he said. "Some of the men will resent you, others might fight you, but we are confident you have the strength to face these challenges."

One of the first casualties was a former boss who was expecting to fill my new slot himself. When he heard that the job went to me, he requested an immediate transfer to another area. We never saw each other again.

Hamed further said, "As the first woman to have the job, you will be under a spotlight, so let us know if there's anything we can do to make your life easier."

Then, in a sentiment I greatly appreciated, he added, "We are both making history."

As a little girl, I believed God "the compassionate and merciful" created all people equal, no one has superiority over others. And I silently rejected and was repulsed by the ancient doctrines that tried to convince women that they were weak creatures and would always need the protection of men.

Growing up, I had no choice but to watch silently as women collapsed before men who controlled them and denied them their simple right for self-determination. I witnessed fear and insecurity as women tiptoed around the men in their families, including their sons, to ensure every male need was met; unable to object, complain or protest their oppression, just to preserve peace and protect their safety. Force-fed the backward teachings of our elders, our self-images were shattered. Not that such concepts as a husband is entitled to beat his wife ever found a home in my soul.

It pained me to see every woman in my circle stripped of her identity. Their aspirations had been severed long ago, as they crossed the threshold to womanhood.

They never stood up for themselves; they were taught this was their destiny, and they accepted it without a trace of doubt.

I was taught this, as well. Call it bad luck, call it bad timing. It wasn't a bad upbringing. This simply was the way things were done. I was raised in an ultraconservative culture during a repressed era when women were considered property. I suffered sexual abuse at an age when I was just opening my eyes to a world that I thought had been entrusted with my protection. I was packed off to an arranged marriage at age fifteen, then had to deal with the repercussions of being a divorcée, which left me with no standing in the community. My society saw no place for an unmarried woman as it was. When I did follow my own path, and assumed an independent life, I was harassed for not projecting the image of a submissive female. And when I ascended the ladder of an already alpha-male-dominated corporate system, I was met with freshly hatched prejudice from within. Many of the men believed women were unfit for leadership positions.

Despite the odds, I succeeded on my own.

My progressive—some might even have said radical—new executive rank a few years later provided me with the opportunity to elevate women within my circle and help them claim their long-overdue rights. At the same time, the Fates also played an amazingly helpful hand; our national government was in the midst of affecting major changes to improve the status of women. One such change was enabling our full participation in the Kingdom's economic growth. Everyone, finally, acknowledged that marginalizing half the population is not good for business. That game-changer delivered enough of a jolt to make headlines around the world.

The new mood in the country encouraged me to establish educational- and career-development programs for young girls and adult women so they could deal with their roads ahead. The exercises were designed to foster self-assurance and allow the women to embrace their empowerment, unlock their capabilities, and show themselves that they mattered. The programs proved remarkably popular—and effective—and literally bolstered the confidence levels of thousands of women in the company and within the community, in women's high and lower-level schools, and in women's universities. Any advances were minor in the beginning, but as I established my credibility and expanded my influence, so did my impact grow.

At nearly every juncture, I seized the opportunity and ended up devoting the better part of my career to seeking equality and recognition for women within the Aramco domain, and then working to help share that experience with the wider community. I did this by participating and speaking in local and international conferences about women's empowerment and encouraging women to take hold of their destinies.

I do not wish to give the impression that I am an activist or public figure in the fight for women's rights. I am not. While I proudly possess a warrior spirit, I also have a peaceful nature that quietly leads me to take small steps to improve my circumstances. It was, also, not my intention to be in the public eye. In many respects, it was my worst nightmare. It wasn't only that I did not care to be scrutinized. I thought the social tendency was not within my makeup, and I preferred my solitude over socializing. Then again, sometimes your worst nightmare can turn out to be your greatest gift.

I worked hard and reached the highest executive position ever to be assumed by a woman in the long history of our company. My new status was not a gift. This was an achievement I had aimed for since childhood; although little did I know what hurdles would be thrown in my path. But I did sense that something positive I could not yet fully grasp would happen to me one day as a result of my convictions.

My story is about the life experiences that shaped my independent identity, an identity unbounded by place or time.

My story is about that journey, not the destination.

When my promotion was announced, I thought of my parents. If only Mother were alive to witness what had transpired. My late father would have been impressed and proud too, I would like to believe.

Because let me tell you, he was much tougher than any character my former boss Yosef ever encountered.

1. BEGINNINGS

My parents married in 1953 and lived in the Eastern Province of Saudi Arabia, where my father, Mohammed Al-Ghoson, served as the assistant head of the Coast Guard. My mother, Shaha Al-Dughaither, was his second wife, and the two were cousins living in separate countries until they met for the first time at their arranged marital engagement. Both their families originally came from Qassim, one of the thirteen administrative provinces of Saudi Arabia. Qassim, which in classic Arabic means a flat, sandy terrain where desert trees germinate, is in the heart of the Kingdom, northwest of Riyadh, and home to many renowned families engaged in commerce and government. It is also one of the most conservative and traditional regions in Saudi Arabia.

My mother's family hailed from Unaiza, itself a prominent city in Qassim. Her grandparents migrated from there to Iraq in the nineteenth century to escape the harshness of the desert and seek a better life and source of income, something her grandfather and father would find as merchants buying and selling with the passing trade caravan.

Mother's family settled in Basra, which is where she was born. The city, which dates back to the year 636, is located on the Shatt-al-Arab waterway (formed by the confluence of the Euphrates and Tigris Rivers), and it remains Iraq's main port. Among Basra's other distinctions are its location, about seventy miles north of the Arabian Gulf; its heat, which consistently registers the highest temperatures in all Iraq; and its legend, as a port of call where the fictional Sinbad the Sailor landed on one of his fabled seven voyages.

Traditionally, Basra projected a free-wheeling atmosphere of culture, religions and social customs, which, combined with its winding canals and flower-decorated gondolas, earned it the nickname "Venice of the East." Lovers and newlyweds were among those who flocked there for its beautiful backdrop, romantic music and poetry, and vibrant nightlife. Sad to say, this was entirely abolished by conservative Islam in the aftermath of the 1990 and 2003 Gulf Wars, which, along with the 1980-88 Iran-Iraq War, destroyed the landscape and left brutal physical and psychological scars on the city.

Mother grew up in a prosperous, cultured atmosphere, rich in art, literature and music, although, like all females her age, she was told her future life would be devoted to marriage and motherhood. Her formal education might have ended at the sixth grade, but that did not stop her from developing a lifelong passion for knowledge. She was a stalwart, independent woman—charitable and compassionate, with an extraordinary sense of humor, a gift she skillfully deployed whenever a situation grew tense. We called her "yomma," which is, essentially, Arabic for mama. Father we called "yoba," which means papa.

Despite her many strengths, Mother firmly believed, as did most women of her age, that members of her sex had a built-in limited capacity for self-determination and could not survive without the support and protection of a man. Men were therefore idealized and treated with absolute obedience and submission.

This unquestioned acceptance flew directly in the face of one obvious fact.

Many of the elder women in Mother's world, including her own mother, were widows living and thriving on their own.

Unlike my mother's prosperous upbringing, my father's childhood was shaped by the rigors of a primitive tribal life in the desert and conservative religious teachings. He was born in the early 1900s in the agriculturally rich capital of Qassim, Buraida, and, like my mother, into a family of merchants. His teenage years were spent with the "Oqaylat"—camel caravans—which, to avoid the hottest months, traveled from autumn to spring across the northern desert into Iraq, Syria, Palestine and Egypt as they traded dates and local goods. It was a harsh life made up of months on the road, exposed not only to the unforgiving desert environment, but also to roaming brigades of bandits. As told in stories I would hear from my family, the exclusively male domain of caravans provided learn-as-you-go lessons in organization, survival and chivalry to the up to one hundred fifty traders with their camels, horses and sheep—along with their tribal chief, council of elders, guards, medicine men, poets, cooks, servants, and star readers to steer navigation. Despite a clear division of labor based on an intricate political, economic and social structure, everyone worked together as part of a team. No wonder so many early trainees ended up as major players in politics and commerce later in life.

Father joined the caravans when he was fifteen, and his education was confined to schools run by clerics. Despite such restrictions, he nurtured an inherent curiosity about the world beyond his modest village. This inspired him, when on trade expeditions, to spend a good share of his earnings on books about history, politics, philosophy, theology and literature. Eventually, he amassed an impressive library that I would later raid once I realized my early passion for reading.

Father married his first wife, Nora Abdulaziz, when they were in their late teens. She was the daughter of a prominent merchant family in Buraida, and she and my father had three children, two girls and a boy: Fatema, Aljohara and Fahad. As the years went on, my father, through a forceful combination of intellect, sophistication and charm, reinvented himself, from a desert vagabond into an elegant, eloquent presence. At the same time, his past had left an indelible imprint, making him rigid and antagonistic to anything that might threaten his boundless sense of self-importance. He believed that men should be harsh and heartless. To him, compassion and kindness were signs of weakness.

As a father he was very tough, and, by the time I was born, he would often criticize Mother for the care and sensitivity she would show the children.

The caravan trade began to decline after World War II and all but ceased by the end of the 1940s, when modern transportation took over commerce in the region. At that point, Father moved to Dammam in the Eastern Province of the country to find new work, leaving behind his first wife and children in Buraida. Life in the Eastern Province was beginning to flourish in the 1950s thanks to the oil business and the arrival of Americans attached to Aramco, the Arabian-American Oil Company, later officially known as the Saudi Arabian Oil Company. Here, Father held a series of high-profile positions in the Coast Guard and, eventually, as head of the Port of Ras Tanura. Ras Tanura was also the name of the city that housed one of the gated communities and refinery operations for Saudi Aramco.

Given his new station in life, Father decided to take a second wife, one whose background was compatible with his new stature. In Islam, it is legal for a man to be married simultaneously to a maximum of four wives. Should he wish to have additional wives, he must first divorce the same number, so that at any single time he never has more than four. To find a bride, Father sought the counsel of his maternal uncles in Iraq, with the aim of marrying one of their daughters. Father's first wife, meanwhile, remained in Qassim with her children, who by now were already grown.

Despite being twenty years younger than my father, my mother was chosen to be his new wife. She had been raised an only daughter, with both an older and younger brother to whom she remained close their entire lives. Early on, she adapted to playing big sister to both of them. And while Mother was happy to be marrying an established gentleman—and, it was hoped, a caring relative—there was also the lingering question about a total stranger removing her from her familiar surroundings and resettling her in a place alien to her upbringing.

To start off the marriage on the right foot, my father took her to Beirut—at the time, a jet-set playground—for their honeymoon.

Not to be wicked, but when I look back on my mother's marriage, I think of a line from the Austrian philosopher, Ludwig Wittgenstein.

"I don't know why we are here, but I'm pretty sure it is not in order to enjoy ourselves."

By the time my parents wed, Father had developed an amicable relationship with King Saud, the ruler of the country. In all likelihood, the two had met during royal visits to the Eastern Province for inspections of the Coast Guard and the port's facilities. The king admired the smooth manner in which my father presented himself. This, along with the astute negotiating skills Father had acquired in the caravan trade, fueled the king's decision to appoint Father Emir of the Neutral Zone territory, an as-yet untapped, as far as oil was concerned, tract between Kuwait to the north, Saudi Arabia to the south and west, and the Arabian Gulf to the east. (Until a demarcation agreement to partition the area took effect in 1970, the governments of Kuwait and Saudi Arabia shared equal rights in the Neutral Zone territory.)

"Emir" is an Arabic term meaning prince or a ruler of a district, bestowed to indicate status and allegiance to the country's ruling family. Grand as the title of Emir may sound, it was strictly a temporary position whose salary ended when the job did—unless you were born with the title as a member of the royal family. In my father's case, it was a job title only, not one from birth. There were no grand palaces or lavish accoutrements that came with it, and when Father left his post, he had to use the little savings he had amassed in order to make a living and start his business.

King Saud had a sense that Father would be the right person to work with the Americans—primarily the Getty Oil Company, still run by its founder, J. Paul Getty, who in 1949 had secured a 60-year concession in Saudi Arabia's half of the Neutral Zone by paying King Saud $9.5 million in cash and another $1 million a year in rent, whether or not oil was discovered. Father also worked with the Japanese, to whom the king had granted rights for the Japanese Commercial Oil Company to form the Arabian Oil Company. Getty's investment did not pay off until 1953, when enormous quantities of oil were found. One field alone produced in excess of sixteen million gallons a year, making Getty, by 1957, the richest man in the world.

The time Father spent with these companies as they explored for oil deepened his appreciation for foreign cultures and the pleasures of life. Ultimately, this would lead him to settle for a lengthy time in Cairo.

As for Mother, her world narrowed. The Neutral Zone in the 1950s offered no roads, no hospitals, no schools and no modern industry of any kind. Its residents had to travel to Saudi or Kuwait to shop and find household necessities. Every time Mother was ready to have a baby—within ten years there would be six of us, two boys and four girls: in chronological order, from the eldest, Muntaser, Ateka, me, Mazen, Asma and Mona—she would wait out the last few weeks of her pregnancy in Basra with her mother and aunts. She would then give birth in the Royal Hospital of Basra, although Mona was born in Kuwait.

Why so many children? Because each one is viewed as a blessing from God.

And they grow up to support each other and become providers for their elderly parents.

Father's nearly twenty years' experience with the caravans left him vigilant to all tricks of the trade, especially where imported goods were concerned. He employed experts to inspect every delivery to see it was up to the agreed-upon specifications. Those who tried to cheat were not treated mercifully—and the scam artists were many. They somehow mistook the Saudis' lack of formal education for stupidity. They were wrong.

One particularly memorable case involved a top-ranking overseas oil executive, whom I'm still not free to identify, accompanied by an entourage of his company's staff, who brought expensive equipment to the territory. Upon inspection, the Saudi experts found the apparatus had not only been previously used but was also rusted. Father was furious. He summoned the executive, who showed up only to have Father's guards arrest and take him to court in Dammam. The oilman was handcuffed and thrown into the back of an open pickup truck for the three-hour drive across the desert.

Arriving in court, the culprit was shocked to discover that the judge found the legal complaint incomplete—as Father knew he would. The executive then had to suffer another torturous three-hour drive back just for Father's signature, all part of Father's intended lesson in defense of Saudi interests.

By the time the truck once again returned to court, the oilman was writhing from dehydration and sunstroke, which sent him into a coma, with no available medical staff to see to his care. The judge surrendered the man to his company's entourage, which informed its federal government, which, in turn, arranged for a private plane to transport the sick man to a hospital in Beirut. Luckily for my father, the man survived. But it cost my father his job.

Foreign officials lodged a complaint with the Saudi government, at the time represented by Prince Faisal. Embarrassed by the incident, the crown prince issued an order to detain my father in order to appease the foreign government.

Father had close and strong relations with the Emir of the Eastern Province at that time, Prince Saud ibn Jalawi, who had much respect for Father and held him in high regards for his loyalty and diligence to protecting Saudi interest. So instead of following Prince Faisal's instruction to arrest my father, Prince Ibn Jalawi sent a covert messenger to warn Father of his imminent arrest and advise him to leave the country. Father knew he would not be able to plead his case and succeed against foreign power. As it was nearing the end of his five-year tenure as Emir, Father immediately resigned, packed us up, and moved us to Kuwait. It was his plan all along to relocate there. It just happened sooner rather than later.

As a postscript, in 1964 Prince Faisal became King Faisal. Following tradition, he issued a pardon to all those who had committed minor political offenses. This included Father.

However, Father decided to remain in Kuwait—that is, until he found solid reasons for us to move to Saudi Arabia.

At the time of our great escape, Saudi living conditions were rudimentary at best, and economic and social conditions still underdeveloped. In comparison, by the 1960s, Kuwait was considered the most advanced country in the region. Father's main motive in our moving, other than his escaping incarceration, was so that his children could secure the type of quality education he never had. Moreover, girls' education in Saudi was still in its gestation phase, with the first state school not yet open. Socializing with the American families also enhanced Father's desire that his daughters have a solid education of their own. He realized that the day would come when women would claim their appropriate place in the Arab world—just like in the West. In that regard, especially for his time and place, Father was a visionary.

Kuwait was still governed under the British protectorate until 1961. With its liberal attitudes, social freedoms and a democratic system of government, the country was also considered a pioneer in the literary renaissance of the Arab world. With that came a thriving theater scene, a free press, and first-rate schooling. There were civil rights, too; women were not required to wear the hijab. Women could participate in the labor market, become educated, and practice personal freedoms—up to a point. They could travel on their own and drive cars, although they still had to answer to male guardians when it came to adherence to community customs and Islamic traditions. As such, they had to dress and behave modestly, not socialize with foreign men, not party in public—in short, not stand out. In an odd way, the parameters were useful for Mother to raise a family as large as ours.

The proximity to Iraq also allowed her mother and aunts to visit us frequently and lend a hand in our upbringing and with the chores around the house. It was not the tradition to hire strangers to perform household tasks because people wanted to protect their privacy from outsiders. Usually, women from the extended family, or women relatives in need, lent a hand in exchange for money, food and clothes.

Believe me, Mother needed such assistance.

Our father was away the majority of the time.

Father opened a small enterprise in Kuwait as a supplier of automobile spare parts, but his chief goal was to build a lucrative business with the Saudi government and establish a base in Riyadh. This had him frequently traveling between Riyadh, Europe and Kuwait, seeking out opportunities to build his fortune. As a result, those few times he was home, for only a few days before he disappeared again for months, he was treated more like an honored guest than a patriarch. When he showed up, Mother would insist we children be on our best behavior: polite, clean, cutely dressed and, above all, quiet. She knew that Father, being highly complex and difficult as he was, would become easily agitated by children noisily running around the house.

It was times like these that I could sense a distinct shift in my mother's mood. She herself would become edgy and easily agitated when Father was home, already being stressed out by his presence and that of six generally rambunctious children. (She knew better than anyone that this is how children act when they are between the ages of one and ten, but Father's demands came first.) Not a single neighbor or relative dared visit without an appointment when Father was home. It was like living in lockdown with a twenty-four-hour curfew. As such, we children eventually grew to dread Father's visits, even as adults—always having to sit in silence while he read his books or watched television.

Mother, on the other hand, overflowed with affection and warm-heartedness. Not that she spoiled us; indeed, she enforced strict discipline on the six of us to prevent her life descending into chaos, but the only time she would raise a hand to us was to deliver a slap if she ever caught us lying. A timetable as exact as a Swiss watch clocked every aspect of our young lives: homework, recreation, meals, naps, showers, cinema, friends, the park. And should we lag behind, we risked losing precious time for singing, dancing, picnicking, shopping, and visiting one of our many relatives.

In short, Mother mothered us, and the simple fact was, other people also delighted in being in her company. Being funny and bright, Mother had a wide circle of friends in Kuwait City, including those from other countries and cultures. Once a week, at teatime, she would invite over her cousins and friends (women only). The activities were generally the same: records by the Lebanese singer Fairouz or Lebanese folklore songs, accompanied by handclapping and singing along to the Dabke, a line dance performed on happy occasions. We children would sit on the floor and giggle, and sometimes dare to join in, until it was time for homework. Then came Mother's marching orders.

Mother fastidiously followed fashion, as evidenced by her wardrobe of the latest silk and satin dresses. When Father came home after several months, Mother would dress up for him every night, whether they were spending the evening at home or going out on the town with other couples.

How we loved watching Mother prepare: perfect coiffeur, ruby red lipstick, silk stockings (adjusted for their seams), sleeveless short silk gown, high heels, and Chanel No. 5. Those nights she and Father were home alone, she would make a movie-star entrance as Father sat in his favorite chair, already indulging in his drink and the mezza spread on the coffee table.

After Mother allowed us to witness her dressing ritual, she would take us to our bedroom, tuck us into bed, turn off the lights, then leave the door ajar, wanting to make sure she could hear our voices in case we called for her.

This also allowed me to hear, ever so faintly, the sultry voice of the Egyptian singer Om Kulthoum or the lively rhythms of Fairouz coming from the phonograph.

Between the music and my parents' voices and laughter, I would doze off.

Despite my youth, I often wondered why Mother worked so hard at playing obedient wife, though it was a role she filled magnificently. Perhaps this was her way of seducing Father into longer visits or having him miss her when he was gone. "Happiness," Immanuel Kant said, "is not an ideal of reason, but of imagination." In the case of my parents, Mother knew Father's devious nature and must have suspected he was cheating on her, although, in a legal sense, it really was not cheating.

We learned that Father had taken on a third wife in Riyadh, where he spent the majority of his time with his business in the late 1960s. Father and this new wife, named Hakema, had a son, Nasser, with whom, like with his other children, Father maintained a halfhearted relationship. Granted, he preferred daughters over sons—I was his favorite, for what that was worth—but he was never one to show his affection publicly.

When I think back on my parents' marriage, the thought of Father having two other wives did not stop my mother from devotedly waiting upon him, keeping up a beautiful home for him, raising well-mannered children for him. As was the case with Mother's contemporaries, theirs was not a union of equals.

But I suppose, for some mysterious reason, my parents' souls had made a prior agreement to travel this life together.

As Father grew older and traveled, he severed his relationships with his first and third wives, whom he continued to support financially, although he never divorced them. Over time, my siblings, step-siblings and I developed a close bond, something we keep up to this day, despite being scattered geographically.

Father, who had suffered no health issues throughout his life, died of old age in 2005. He was somewhere between ninety-eight and one hundred; there were no birth certificates when he was born. For years, up until his demise, his relationship with the rest of us remained cool.

After all, it was difficult to build a warm connection after several years of separation. Besides, we had all moved on with our lives.

Mother's death, which turned out to be years before his, would be a different story.

2. INNOCENCE

I was born on November 19, 1957, at the Royale Hospital in Basra, and while I have no clear memory of our time in the Neutral Zone, my childhood in Kuwait City, the country's capital, vividly lingers in my mind and plays out as a colorful tableau scented by rose water, henna, saffron and musk. We lived in a sprawling, traditional Arabic-style house made up of two stories and eight rooms. A large courtyard, surrounded by our communal quarters and a spacious kitchen, stood in the center. The children's bedroom and our playroom took up most of the first floor. I loved our house. And, despite its open design, I quietly managed to disappear into any of its many corners whenever I needed to escape the constant clamor that pervaded the rest of the place.

In those days, we did not have air-conditioning, television, or any type of communication technology, other than a radio and gramophone. Electrical power was sporadic, and streetlights few and far between. On the plus side, no human-created distractions were around to intrude upon the resonance of nature or the simple enjoyment of life.

As children, we were seldom bored, given our wild imaginations and our adventuresome surroundings. By the time I was five, my curiosity led me to begin marveling at the various mysteries of life, from the enormity of the universe to the spindly legs on the tiniest of insects. Most of the time I spent outdoors with my four siblings (the youngest Mona was not born yet) was devoted to playing treasure hunt. Even if we embellished our findings—such wonders as marbles, offbeat-looking stones, the occasional baby bird that had strayed from its nest, butterflies (they seemed almost mystical) and locusts (when in season)—we managed to make discoveries wherever we looked: under rocks, inside the cracks of the walls, between our toes. Nothing escaped our careful analysis, not even the smell of rain.

Roaming the dirt roads of the neighborhood with the bigger children—seldom venturing more than a block away, all that Mother would allow and far enough for us—we would peek inside our neighbors' houses, where the doors were never locked. This was an era when no one questioned safety and security. Those residing nearby were mainly merchant families with small children but, unlike in our house, the fathers were around practically all of the time. That sense of permanence added to the solid nature of our community, with neighbors acting like second families to all the youngsters, as if we had several sets of parents, all with eyes watching out for us.

During the prolonged summer months, bedtime moved outdoors to the cooler rooftops. Up there, we would place the thin cotton mattresses one next to the other and assemble a gigantic bed that allowed all the children to snuggle together. This way, no youngster was left alone to be afraid of the dark. First, though, we would sprinkle drops of water to cool the sheets before we entrusted our tender bodies to their embrace.

For parents to preserve their privacy, the adults would arrange their mattresses at the far end of the roof, distanced from their children.

The roof at night became my favorite playhouse. Lying on my mattress, I could detect hushed laughing and murmuring from the tops of nearby houses, until it gradually grew fainter, and it seemed the entire world had fallen asleep. That was when I could have the spectacular night sky all to myself.

Brilliantly illuminated, given the lack of intrusion by city lights, the stars became my faraway friends. Some traveled so fast you would have thought they were late for a date. That explained how they so quickly disappeared. The spectacle allowed my imagination to run wild, and I would fantasize about what was playing out above me. One story I told myself was, "The great show gathers momentum with all the divine guests greeting each other with gentle laughter so not to disturb the sleeping humans below. The party gets going with the soft sound of music as the stars with their glittering costumes start dancing in groups of two, three, four, or more—or in solitude, just like my soul." (Mind you, I fancied myself a poet.)

Sometimes, I pretended our lives were a movie, with each of us responsible for playing a certain role, and the stars and planets gazing down at our performances.

Many times, too, I would ask, "What is my role in this movie?"

That was when I would tell myself with a surprising sense of self-assurance, "Whatever I want it to be."

As children, we were warned never to point a finger at the stars, because they would leave a blister on our finger. That was all I needed to hear. "If you would be a real seeker after truth," Descartes said, "it is necessary that at least once in your life you doubt, as far as possible, all things." I started doubting at a young age. Every time no one was looking, I would point at the night sky, daring the stars to leave a blister on my finger. I desperately wanted their attention so they could answer my questions: Could they see me? Could they hear the whispers inside my heart? Why was it forbidden to point a finger at them? Why would they want to hurt us simply for wanting to connect with a power so far away?

Every morning on that rooftop, the second I opened my eyes, I'd carefully inspect my fingers for blisters. And, to my astonishment, I would find . . . nothing. How I would smile at having conquered a silly superstition that was handed down for generations. I habitually tested tales that adults would utilize to frighten us—until, as I got older, I came to question everything that did not align with what I felt inside me.

There were other rooftop riddles to solve, and their answers, even if provisional, seemed to come just as soon as I fell into the spell of my sleepy imagination. The starry symphony of the night would then sing me its lullaby and my soul would take leave, for she had a date to dance among the heavens. Her partners were other divine souls. Angels would drape a protective veil over my eyelids, and sleep would unfold its wings to caress my world. Yet my youthful mind kept inquiring. Who else is inhabiting space? Is God out there, singing and dancing in a festive universe? Where did God come from? Where does God live? What was God doing before the universe and life came into being?

These questions would arise for years through different stages of my life, until one day I came to realize that God dwells in the heart, not in houses of worship, not in the heavens, and not in some mysterious place. God abides here and there and everywhere. God is in you and in me and in every pulsating atom of the cosmos. The great fourteenth-century Sufi master, Hafiz, provided me the perfect explanation, writing, "When no one is looking/and I want to kiss God/I just lift my own hand to my mouth."

I don't know how or why I came to this conclusion, but it has evolved and echoed within me far more than any of the teachings from my schooling.

During Father's months-long absences, my grandmother, Lulwa Al-Zuhair, and great aunt, Latifa, would come from Iraq and stay. We called our grandmother "Bibi" and our great aunt "Habayeb," which means lovely. We loved them both. Bibi had lived most of her life in Iraq, having married my grandfather, Rushaid Al-Dughaither, when she was young and then given birth to three children in quick succession. My grandfather died shortly after the arrival of the youngest, my uncle Ahmad, leaving Bibi to fend for herself on the trade money he had left her. A proud woman, Bibi never asked for help—late in life she remained independent, rejecting repeated suggestions that she live with one of her children—and she was as proud of my mother's family as they were of her.

In addition to singing to us as they combed our hair or painted henna on our hands, Habayeb and Bibi helped Mother take care of us, and during summer school breaks, if we were not headed to Lebanon and Syria for a holiday, we routinely went to spend time with them in Iraq. The trip there lasted nearly three hours. Mother would hire a driver who tended to the wheel of the large station wagon while she tended to us, keeping us entertained with stories about the aunts and uncles we were about to descend upon. She also reminded us to be on our best behavior once we got there.

In Iraq, we stayed at Bibi's house amid the mud houses and narrow alleys in Zubair, a town that predates the Ottoman Empire and takes its name from a companion of the Prophet Muhammad, Zubayr ibn Al-Awwam, who is buried there. The older houses of Zubair were squeezed next to one another and distinguished by their carved wooden double doors—one large, to accommodate supplies and heavier items, and within that one a smaller door for people. Some houses had connecting doors inside, so families who lived together could come and go and never step outside.

Bibi lived alone in her house, which was roomy and had in the center of its courtyard a prickly tree that yielded nabq, sweet green and amber fruit the size of grapes. Most of my aunts and uncles lived in Basra and some in Baghdad. Bibi would not move to Basra because she was attached to her neighbors, friends and maternal relatives. Also, Uncle Ahmad, her younger son, had already moved to Zubair with his young family to be near his mother. So, when we visited, we split our time between Basra and Zubair.

Coming from Kuwait with its slightly sterile modernity, I found Bibi's town, where roosters crowed at dawn, utterly charming. At times,

I was convinced I could hear Zubair's ancient inhabitants muttering their blessings to me from the shadows of the village, through the walls, through the windows. I was smitten with everything about the place, from the boys playing marbles on the dirt paths to the old women carrying vegetables in straw baskets on their heads. The aroma of bread wafted deliciously from the bakeries, as did the pungent kitchen fragrances of the stews, whether they were made from dolma (tomatoes, green peppers, vine leaves or eggplants stuffed with meat, rice and spices), sabzi (another mixture of vegetable), or okra.

Then there was the breathtaking display of stars at night.

My siblings and I each started school at a private educational center from the age of three. It seemed we were never out of school. Those summers we were not traveling, Mother enrolled us in extracurricular clubs that offered music, sports, drama, and the English language. She, meanwhile, attended adult-education classes in the hope of completing high school. That proved an endless journey for her; not only did she leave school in the sixth grade, but when she resumed her education, she had to repeat several grades because she lacked certificates of completion. She also took driving lessons right before we moved to Riyadh but never bothered to apply for a license, knowing that women were prohibited from driving in Saudi Arabia.

My favorite subjects were math, music, and gymnastics, in no particular order, although I did take special joy in being light on the pommel horse and balance beam. Even for only a few seconds, defying gravity meant the world to me. I approached music with the same dedication, hoping one day to become a composer. I genuinely liked the thought of contributing beautiful melodies to the world. The two instruments I was assigned to learn were unconventional and, now that I think of it, polar opposites (perhaps I was unconsciously trying to test my range to its fullest): the accordion and the xylophone. (Even their

24

first letters are at opposing ends of the alphabet.) Next, I was supposed to learn the piano. But, alas, we left Kuwait before my fingers got the chance to dance on those magical keys. I never practiced at home, only in school. In my household, music was not perceived as a dignified profession for either boys or girls. My siblings really didn't care, and, as it was, none of us made a big deal of accomplishments or talents. We were taught to be humble and never brag about our advantages.

One inclination of mine that needed no encouraging was reading. The time I spent with a book also meant time away from the children who would taunt and take advantage of my quiet nature. As a child, I was a loner who was constantly teased, despite Mother urging me to speak up for myself. Too timid to fight back, I preferred the solitude of a book to a scuffle. I would hide myself at home and devour every escapist title I could wrap my hands around: *Alice in Wonderland*, *Around the World in 80 Days*, *The Adventures of Pinocchio*, *Tarzan of the Apes*, *Gulliver's Travels*. I also loved mystery stories and used to revel in my brother Muntaser's collection of Arsène Lupin's stories. When I was eleven, someone—I don't remember who, but I am forever grateful to this individual—gave me a biography of Madame Marie Curie. It astonished me to learn that this French-Polish woman, born in the late 1860s, cleared her own path, breaking down barriers to study science at the Sorbonne and becoming the first woman to win the Nobel Prize for physics and chemistry. "Nothing in life is to be feared, it is only to be understood," she said. "Now is the time to understand more, so that we may fear less."

Now, in 2020, as I recall my excitement over that first exposure to this greatly accomplished woman, two women, Dr. Emmanuelle Charpentier, from France, and Dr. Jennifer A. Doudna, an American biochemist, have been awarded the Nobel Prize in Chemistry for pioneering work allowing scientists to alter the DNA of animals, plants and microorganisms. "What started as a curiosity-driven, fundamental discovery project has now become the breakthrough strategy used by countless researchers working to help improve the human condition,"

Dr. Doudna told the press. She and Dr. Charpentier are the fifth and sixth women to win the chemistry prize, and the first pair to be so honored together.

Hooray and thank you, Madame Curie, for leading the way.

And for being the first to show me that a woman can become whatever she wants, regardless of the roadblocks.

No one ever asked what I wanted to be when I grew up. Only boys got attention when it came to their talents being nurtured. This approach wasn't merely confined to the home, but was repeated in school, the mainstream media, and the general attitude surrounding us. Doctors, engineers, lawyers, politicians, economists, business leaders, all men, were conditioned to follow their proclivities from birth. Teachers, nurses, secretaries, all women, were equally conditioned; that is, if they dared poke their heads above the crowded field of wives and mothers who habitually cooked, cleaned, and sewed in what I called the silent brigade. Dividing lines between the sexes were not only respected but heavily enforced. Such stereotypes went completely against my grain. I wanted the same freedom to have a career as the characters I admired in my books.

My independent streak was something I was born with, not simply something I picked up from reading; it served to reinforce my autonomous spirit. Never would I ask for help, even when sick. I never allowed an emotion to show. I never cried in public. When stricken with a stomachache or diarrhea, as was so common among children in those days, I walked myself to the clinic and requested medication or an injection directly from the doctor. My stubborn pride would force me to conceal my feelings. Never would I give others the satisfaction of thinking they might have control over me. I would never surrender. I would never be helpless or defeated.

Because Mother did not have the time to pamper us individually, she would only be affectionate when we were obedient. That might also have been her secret weapon to keep us in line. Seeking the extra attention, I went out of my way to show how good a girl I was. I excelled in school. I did my best to be perfect at home. By age seven I was Mother's sous chef, at her side to make the yogurt, clean the rice, roll the grape leaves, wash and pare the fruit and vegetables. My fondest memory is of the two of us in the kitchen, listening to her hum the love songs of the Iraqi crooner Nazem Ghazali.

I loved those times with Mother. Truth to tell, I was jealous of the time and affection she spent on my brothers and sisters.

I wanted her exclusively to myself.

For a variety of reasons, Mother grew tired of our house. A chief factor was the central courtyard, which exposed the entire residence to severe weather, especially sandstorms. The grit would seep into every crevice, from the closets to our ears, and wreak havoc on our lungs. The sheer size of our house also hindered Mother's ability to keep track of all six children. One solution was to gather us in whatever room Mother occupied and not allow anyone to leave except to go to the bathroom, which we very often did, if only to escape her vigilance. (Hide and Seek was not her favorite game.)

Finally, enough was enough. Staying within Kuwait City limits, Mother, with Father's approval, moved us into an apartment that was brand new and extremely comfortable. By then, it was the mid-1960s, I was nine, and we had TV, air-conditioning and dependable electricity. The apartment was on the first floor of a luxury three-building complex, with a balcony overlooking the fountain in the large courtyard, which instantly became our new playground, perfect for riding bikes around. Any difficulties with the adjustment were further alleviated because neighbors from our former house, the Al-Qadhi family (likewise, Saudis from Qassim, with four children), also moved to the same complex.

Notwithstanding the new comforts, I was unhappy about the move. The new place felt constantly crowded and offered nowhere to hide. Mostly, I was homesick for the rooftop and my intimate tête-à-têtes with the stars. The air-conditioner had wiped out the need to sleep outdoors.

Social butterfly that she was, Mother quickly got to know most of the families in the compound. My brothers and sisters also made new friends easily, provided the other children met with Mother's approval. Personally, I had little interest, being perfectly content to keep to myself and walk around the buildings, or sit beside the fountain, watching the other children at play. Even better was letting my mind wander and imagining the life dramas playing out in the other apartments.

Only, somehow, they seemed less compelling than my visions of the stars.

3. WOUNDS

I was five when it first happened. But my memories of sexual abuse are still vivid and continue to fuel a painful and familiar rage every time I hear about a child's ordeal. I no longer feel the shame and guilt that overwhelmed my childhood, thinking that somehow I was responsible for provoking grown men to inappropriately touch me and exploit my innocent and powerless little being.

Wahid (not his real name) was a trusted relative. Everybody in the family loved him, children and grownups alike. He was free to come and go in our home as he wished. He was 30 years old, educated and considerate, with an endearing humility. Most of all, he was great fun. I looked up to him and enjoyed his humorous stories. One would never suspect that his good nature was nothing but a veneer shielding his inner demons. They were only looking to strike the right victim.

One day, Wahid paid one of his usual social calls. As we children did every time, the five of us (Mona had yet to be born) ran up and started rummaging through his pockets for treats. Mother was on her way out to run errands, and as was routine, entrusted him to watch us. Father was off on his usual travels. Wahid was busy regaling us with magic tricks when, all of a sudden, he privately whispered into my ear, "You and I are going to play a special game." Leaving my sisters and brothers to play among themselves, he led me by the hand into one of the secluded rooms of the house and closed the door.

I was baffled but excited by the special treatment and kept looking at Wahid's familiar smile and eyes, which became more probing than usual, until I did not recognize him. How scary his face had become, as if it had curdled. His eyes turned glossy and his nostrils dragon-like, huffing and puffing as if he was trying to catch his breath. His mouth grew wet, and he started mumbling words I could not comprehend. That's when he reached out and started touching me before pulling me toward him and rubbing against me. Despite my confusion and the speed at which it happened, I knew this was something unholy. I knew this was not a game. This was not a benevolent touch of loving care. It was something creepy! But what was it?

A petrifying chill ran through my entire body. Physically, there was no pain, but why was my heart beating this fast? This went beyond having my feelings hurt. It was a frontal attack on my spirit. Wahid's actions were excruciating. How could a person who brought so much fun into our house be doing this? My confidence was shattered and would be all over again, whenever I dredged up this memory, no matter how many years had passed since the horrid incident. It was my first introduction to a different, non-physical pain that was more agonizing: the one that keeps piercing your heart and shadowing your psyche for the rest of your life. You can spend your lifetime trying to bury the memories of these few moments, but you will never succeed.

"You are a good girl, Huda," Wahid told me quietly. "This is our secret game. Don't tell Mama or anyone, or I will not love you." He threatened that if I betrayed him, he would be angry and never speak to me again. His words are still etched in my memory. I kept reciting them to myself so my tongue wouldn't slip. I feared saying them out loud to Mother. I did not want Wahid, my favorite person, to be angry with me.

Wahid did not stop after the first time. He continued until I was about seven. I want to think that he came to see his shameful behavior for what it was, though perhaps by that point, he had grown fearful I might tell Mother.

"Children are the living messages we send to a time we will not see," John F. Kennedy said. What was the perverted message Wahid sent by his serial pawing? He was aware he was a permanent part of my family. Perhaps he stopped because he did not want me to grow up and remember his disgraceful deeds. Perhaps he thought I might hate him, or I might just forget. I'm happy to say I cannot read into his mind.

Upon reflection, I do not hate Wahid. In fact, in my mind I forgive him. I pity his pathetic weakness, even though it was I who bore the shame and splintered trust he caused.

For the longest time, I even felt guilty for possibly having caused the incidents myself.

Wahid, I discovered, was not an exception. Uncle Maher (not his real name), his wife, Aunt Najwa, and their children were family friends with whom we celebrated Islamic festivals, shared weekends, and supported each other. We were that close. Often, our combined families would spend afternoons on one of the beautiful beaches of Kuwait. Because we were novices at swimming, the children were never allowed to venture into the deep.

Uncle Maher had other plans. "Huda, I will teach you how to swim," he said. "Would you like that?"

"Yes, uncle, yes," I enthusiastically replied as he scooped me away from the others and carried me out into the water. I was no older than seven.

Soon, he was instructing me in paddling my arms and kicking my legs while he was balancing my stomach on his forearms, until suddenly I felt his right hand slide to my pelvic area. He then sneaked his hand between my thighs and started touching me. That feeling of horrified helplessness I had experienced with Wahid instantly repeated itself. I recoiled.

"I don't want to swim, uncle," I said, my voice trembling as my entire body froze. "I want to go back."

"Not yet," he directed as he continued fondling me—only there was nothing fond about his violating me. I could hear him panting like an animal and could smell his breath on the back of my neck. Terror set in, but I could not break free because we were in deep water. Afraid of drowning, I had no choice but to hang on.

I don't know how long we werᴇ out there before he took me back to shore. I ran shivering to my mother and asked that she wrap me in a towel. I sat beside her the rest of the day as I tried to make sense of what had occurred. I knew what he had done was unsuitable but could not bring myself to talk about it. No one would believe me, anyway, and would insist I had imagined it. Certainly, Uncle Maher, a respected man of faith, could never be so wicked.

"No one will believe me," I kept telling myself, also assessing the problems it would generate between the two families.

I did not want to be responsible for the breakup of our great friendship.

Other men with similar bent plagued me throughout my childhood, all of them close male relatives. I used to pray to God to make me ugly so no man would look at me. How tragic is that? Young girls usually dream of being beautiful princesses, not ugly creatures. (Thank God my prayers were not answered.) As an adult, I found books on the subject of pedophilia, and a line from one of them, a memoir by an American named Dave Speller, titled *A Child Called "It,"* sticks out in my mind: "A child should be carefree playing in the sun, not living a nightmare in the darkness of the soul."

As a child, I lived the nightmare. I learned to conceal my pain with many a different mask, each one displaying an unyielding spirit combined with a passive positivity. I kept my secret locked in the dark side of my shadows, deep in the abyss of my psyche. Proud and smart, I wanted no one to find me fragile. Neither did I want anyone to see my wounds or need for protection. Feelings of dependency repulsed me. Those found vulnerable were defenseless against others exerting control over them.

I could take care of myself, and I did. Wahid kept up his visits, and while I treated him with the formal deference Mother taught us to show our elders, Wahid and I kept our distance. I did not want him to know I remembered. We saw less of him when he married, although we heard that the union was miserable and did not last. He became mentally ill, his wife left him, and he lived childless and alone, until one day he was crossing the street and hit by a speeding van. There were rumors it was a suicide.

Maher continued living in Kuwait, so interactions with him and his family ceased once we moved to Riyadh. As an older man, he suffered a stroke and remained paralyzed until his death many years later.

There was one lingering aspect to the experience with Maher. I developed a lifelong phobia of the deep and never learned to swim. I love the water but start to panic if I do not feel a floor beneath my feet.

When I built my current house a few years ago, the design called for a large swimming pool in the center of the U shaped back of the building.

I wanted a vista of water from every corner of the property.

But I also made sure that the pool had no deep end.

The sexual abuse I suffered as a child finally stopped when I was eleven years old, thanks to my own self-protective steps. I would push, scratch and bite any would-be predator, as fiercely as would a lioness. I may have been quiet and shy on the surface, but inside I was anything but defenseless. It wasn't only a physical defense. I fought back in my mind, in fact, perhaps overly so. I became thoroughly distrustful of the intentions of any man, believing his sole concern was satisfying his lustful desires. In many cases, that was true. Still, some men may have been honorable. The problem was, I did not engage long enough to find out.

I never told anyone—not Mother, or my siblings, or any friend— about these early incidents. (There is a certain sense of catharsis in opening up about them now.) Conceivably, keeping the stories inside me is why the abuse did not stop with Wahid. Girls of my generation had not been told to speak up about such acts. There was no awareness, no education, especially in our hemmed-in culture. The subject was strictly taboo. If somehow the topic did arise, it was greeted with silence, especially by the victims. The intention, I think, was to protect not only the abused, but also, depending on his status, the abuser.

The goal was to avoid embarrassment, disgrace and dishonor for anyone concerned. Such an attitude offers no solution. Sweeping the subject under the carpet only allows the abuse to lie dormant.

And, regrettably, it will continue to damage the innocence of young children until we take action by openly talking about the matter and dealing with it.

4. ROOTS

We remained in Kuwait until the summer of 1970, when Father decided to relocate us to Riyadh, where economic conditions were on the upswing. He was also bothered by the fact that all we had known for most of our lives was Kuwait. He was a proud Saudi.

I was saddened by leaving our joyful and colorful life in Kuwait. At the same time, I was excited by the adventure to a new place totally alien to our imagination and cultural upbringing. Neither Mother nor any of my siblings were prepared for the culture shock that hit us when we got there. Suddenly, we were confronted face-to-face with the fundamentalist culture of the tribal society. It was also the first time we were introduced to our father's family.

The stark realities of Riyadh hit us all smack in the face. Saudi Arabia in 1970 was barely on the brink of cashing in on its oil riches, while the country's social and economic structures had hardly shown any progress at all. Male power over women was absolute. Wives were chattel, girls were outlawed from mixing with boys, and schooling was stern and constrictive. Women, having no place outside the home, were forced to cover themselves head-to-toe any time they might be permitted to venture out in public. Even at home, women were rebuked for baring anything of themselves other than their faces, hands and feet to any man except their husband. Life was universally segregated; men and women never socialized together, unless they were immediate relatives.

These boundaries delivered a catastrophic blow to Mother. Besides losing her freedom to move about as she pleased, she had to abandon, practically overnight, a lifestyle to which she had been accustomed from birth. This new social straitjacket was to be her day-to-day existence for the rest of her life.

Father knew full well the challenges Riyadh would present. Nonetheless, he wanted his children to grasp our roots while we were still young and able to adjust. He had also noted our attachment to our Kuwaiti friends, speaking their dialect and identifying with their lifestyle. As for Mother's reaction, he knew it was her duty to obey his orders.

Considering the circumstances, Mother was resilient. As one example, the family's manner of dress had to be altered, drastically. No longer were women's short, sleeveless dresses tolerated, although we continued to wear them at home when no visitors were around. (When we first arrived in Saudi Arabia from Kuwait, the only long dresses Mother owned were her evening dresses.) The same went for women's trousers. For young girls, only ankle-length dresses with long sleeves were permissible. For boys, no more shorts. They, too, required ankle-length coverings.

As to where we lived, Father rented a villa in Malaz, a new section of Riyadh. We showed up a few weeks before the arrival of our belongings from Kuwait. While waiting to move into our own home, we stayed in the modest house of Father's widowed mother, my grandmother, Munira Al-Dughaither. (After marriage in the Arab world, women keep their family names instead of taking their husband's. Because my parents were related—Mother was Father's maternal cousin—Munira was not only Mother's mother-in-law, but also Mother's paternal aunt.)

This was the first time we had ever met Grandmother Munira, whom we called Ommi Munira, or Mama Munira. She was a kind soul, petite, soft spoken, and, like everyone else in the country, a devout Muslim. Ommi Munira was also a marvelous cook and would prepare, from grains, lamb, and vegetables, traditional dishes that we had never tasted before, such as marqouq, jereesh, and qursan (paper thin bread soaked in vegetable and lamb stew). Her earth-colored house was similarly traditional, with two bedrooms and a living room open to a small courtyard in the center of the residence. A small portion of the kitchen also extended into the courtyard for ventilation.

Because it was summer, with no air-conditioning, we returned to our familiar habit of sleeping on the rooftop. I was doubly delighted; first, to see that Riyadh's night skies were just as starry as those in Kuwait, and second, to reunite with my celestial friends. I must admit that, in a way, I never expected two vastly different countries to offer the same identical perspectives on the universe, and yet, finding Riyadh and Kuwait's skies similar provided a kind of comfort. How glad I was that my faithful companions were always there to watch over me, especially in this strange land.

Another newcomer to our world was Father's sister, Aunt Haila. Like Ommi Munira, she was sweet but strong. She was also very wise, very tall and very religious. Hers was a tough life, what with ten children at home and a husband constantly on the road. She visited every day during our stay with Ommi Munira, to make sure our needs were met and give Mother a hand. As I said before, we always seemed to have many parents.

Father had another sister who died young, along with five brothers still living in Riyadh. Because of his travels, Father had little in common with them. Besides, he was adept at putting a fence around himself and, by nature, kept his personal and business lives private. This did not mean our door was not open or that we did not meet a lot of cousins, because we did. Each one was as curious as the last when it came to our modern ways and manner. For one thing, except for their sisters, our male cousins had never been in the company of girls before and could hardly believe their ears when they heard we had not practiced traditional customs in our upbringing. They were intrigued by our free nature to sit around and socialize in mixed company without any concern for the traditional customs of segregation. You need to understand that in the 1970s the lifestyles and cultures of Kuwait and Riyadh were radically different.

To my cousins, we were like visitors from another planet.

To us, the entire experience was like traveling back in time, from the twentieth century to the Middle Ages.

Aunt Haila's eldest son, my cousin Ibrahim, and I became good friends. Even as a young man, Ibrahim, who is three years my senior, was a person of unaffected good character, high-minded and principled. I suppose it also didn't hurt that he was the proverbial "tall, dark and handsome." He had large, soft black eyes, lush black hair that was highlighted by his dark mustache, and a bright smile that always beamed with optimism. (I am pleased to say we are still good friends, and with his keen mind, he took up civil engineering.) If my life ever had its knight in shining armor, Ibrahim was the one. He, too, was an avid reader, except, instead of the long list of children's books I had come to know, Ibrahim's repertoire included adult fiction and nonfiction. His impressive personal library was second only to Father's.

During one of our nightly family gatherings—with so little television, we listened to radio as we joyfully filled our faces with cheese, jam, bread, boiled eggs and fruit—Ibrahim took notice of how detached I seemed from the others. To draw me out of myself, or perhaps merely keep me entertained, he began lending me his books. The first was Victor Hugo's *Les Misérables*. For a thirteen-year-old trapped in an insular environment, the dramatic ordeal of Jean Valjean was nothing short of eye-opening. Here was my introduction to true human suffering and the ongoing struggle between the heart and mind. Whatever Ibrahim's intention was, my literary indoctrination under his tutelage was a magic carpet that transported me into an entirely new world of fascinating civilizations, philosophies, politics and faiths.

Ibrahim's books left a permanent impression and served as a steppingstone to take on my father's formidable library of Kant,

Goethe, Dante, Nietzsche, Descartes, Camus, Sartre, Voltaire, Tolstoy, Dostoevsky, and others.

I read them all.

From the moment we stepped into Ommi Munira's house, it was essential Mother drape herself in a black cloak, called an abaya, whenever relatives or neighbors dropped by. To outfit the rest of us, given the limited number of clothing stores in Riyadh, Mother had to rush to the tailor's shop. Generally, these were run by Indian men. You would hand them the fabric along with your measurements and either a photo or drawing of the design pattern you want, then hope for the best. Later, Egyptian and Syrian seamstresses started working out of their homes, and that's where Mother took our business. Adapting to her new regime, Mother held to traditional social decorum but refused to cover her face in public and would not hide behind closed doors when my uncles and other male relatives came to visit.

For the first time in our lives, my fourteen- and eleven-year-old sisters, Ateka and Asma, and I also had to put on abayas. Mona, being only six, still had a few years left to enjoy the freedoms of childhood. The rest of us wore the abaya on our shoulders like a robe and then wrapped our heads with a black scarf to conceal our hair. It took time to get used to wearing the flowing garments without tripping over them, but we played our roles.

Befitting our backgrounds, we were now expected to behave like grown-up women, for, according to tradition, we were soon approaching the age of marriage.

Our exclusive new private school, Al Abna'a—meaning "the sons," although it was co-educational with two segregated wings, one for boys and a smaller one for girls—was operated by the Ministry of Defense for the offspring of its officers and staff. Father was able to enroll us because of his government connections from the early days of the camel caravans and his former position as Emir. Other prominent merchants and government officials were also able to place their children in Al Abna'a, which was the top-ranking academy in Riyadh in terms of education and discipline. But compared to our schools in Kuwait, it lacked the same pedagogical status and thriving infrastructure.

I had now entered the eighth grade, although I had already taken most of the subjects the year before in Kuwait. This allowed me to slack off and still receive full marks, but little of this really mattered. I was homesick for my friends, teachers and the energizing environment of my old school. Mostly, I missed gymnastics and music, but, here, sports were outlawed for girls and further condemned because they involved communal showers. To compound my frustration, we were taught that if we so much as listened to music, God would pour hot melted iron into our ears, and we would burn in hell. That did not stop there from being singing at weddings, just as there was music by popular local singers playing regularly on radio and TV—some of the many contradictions we were left to unravel on our own. Later in life, I compensated for my childhood restrictions by refining a taste for classical music and have fond memories of attending Mozart's *Marriage of Figaro* at the Vienna State Opera, Bizet's *Carmen* in London's Royal Albert Hall, and Puccini's *Madame Butterfly* at New York's Metropolitan Opera House.

Religious studies dominated our academic schedules, with endless lectures from men mainly chosen for their profession because they were blind from birth, a circumstance that rendered them unable to see us girls and transgress into sin. As a rule, they were middle-aged with long beards, big bellies and skinny legs, and they wore short thawbs, hanging garments placed over trousers, exposing a lot of shin above their sandals. Their appearance was less than pleasing to the eye, especially to girls whose hormones were kicking in. In fact, they were outright scary-looking. Then there were their lesson plans. On a daily basis, these men systematically set out to indoctrinate us with their own interpretation of Islamic teachings. Their goal was to minimize our potential as women, and there was to be no argument about that. As clerics, they had to be revered. Indeed, should one of us so much as question a teacher on any point, he was empowered to insult us.

Delivered somberly and presented as fact, lessons included "women who do not wear the hijab will burn in hell", "women who mix with strange men will burn in hell", and "women who do not rise to their subservient duties will burn in hell." A man has every right to whip his wife if she disobeys him. God created women with half the intellectual capacity of men, therefore we are not capable of making rational decisions by or for ourselves.

This was my first exposure to blatant discrimination against my gender delivered in an official tone as a matter of fact. The positive message of the holy texts was being manipulated to justify subjugation to men for our thoughts and our bodies. I couldn't believe my ears. Time and again, I would sit attentively in class and double-check that my mind was not playing tricks on me. I couldn't so much as gasp. The teacher may not have been able to see us, but he was able to hear us.

"Is he serious?" I asked, sotto voce, the girl sitting next to me.

"Oh, just ignore him," she whispered back, barely looking up from the mash note she was writing to her imaginary boyfriend.

Having a boyfriend, publicly or privately, was strictly against the rules of Islam, our society and our families. If a boy and girl were caught socializing, they would be prosecuted. To enforce this, police randomly stopped cars to check couples' identifications and relationships to one another. There were no places for boys and girls to gather and grow familiar. Because of the condemnation attached to liaisons, the only place to meet was at traffic stops. Imagine, if you will, car windows hastily rolled down so two people in separate vehicles could peek at each other. If they liked what they saw, they'd write down their phone numbers and toss the slip of paper into the other car. The only way to initiate and build a relationship was over lengthy telephone calls, and those could only be made in secret once everyone else in the house was asleep. Or some daring girls would recklessly disguise themselves in a thawb and shemagh and ride around with her beau without attracting the eyes of the police and mutawas. Sometimes, this led to marriage. Other times, it led to boredom and moving on.

Few in class gave ear to the teacher. Instead, girls would quietly chat among themselves, file their nails, read love poems, or leaf through fashion magazines—acting for all the world that these lessons had absolutely nothing to do with them. The truth was, they had everything to do with them. The girls were blind to the fact that the power lay beyond their control.

After another torturous day at school, I would go home in a state of shock and unload on my poor mother. She would listen patiently, heave a small sigh, then say, "Listen Huda, don't be a victim of life. Learn to adjust to it. You can't change people's minds or the rules of society. What you can do is weave your way around them in a clever way and live your life as you wish."

Wonderful words, but how does an adolescent process them? It was a long road Mother alluded to, one encumbered with seemingly insurmountable barriers. How many disguises could I possibly wear in my life? Was there no simple pill I could swallow so that I could suddenly find myself independent?

I did not fit in. The girls at school would square off together in cliques determined by their backgrounds and upbringing. There were the Hijazis (from the Western Province), the Najdis (from the central region), the officers' daughters, the merchants' daughters, the royals, the Palestinians, the Jordanians, and so forth. Occasionally, I would wander by and try to catch what they were talking about, only to envy how thoughtlessly they shrugged off the shackles being placed on all of us.

My own sisters, being outgoing and wildly popular, were equally as carefree. Others wanted to be part of their circle, and the bunch of them made a mockery of anything serious—and that included me. Rather than find myself further uncomfortable, or worse, the subject of their ridicule, I steered well clear of them.

I had a few casual acquaintances, but no one I could call a close friend. That is, until ninth grade, when I met Mashael, tall and slim, with beautiful almond-shaped light brown eyes and lush brown hair that dropped around her shoulders in gorgeous waves. We sat next to each other in class for two years. She did not suffer fools gladly—which left out the other girls—and could smell superficiality a kilometer away. She and I exchanged records and poetry books; wrote letters to one another; shared the work of such contemporary poets as Kamel El-Shennaawy, Nizar Kabbani, Ahmad Shawqi and Ibrahim Nagi; and copied lyrics of our favorite Arab singers, like Halim, Umm Kulthum, Fairuz and Najat. Knowing Mashael made my life bearable during this period, and though eventually our roads separated and then re-connected, only to separate again—today, she is a highly respected professor of geography—we still remain in contact, caring about each other and cheering on each other's accomplishments.

Thanks to my bonding with Mashael, school became as tolerable as it could be. Kuwait now seemed a long time ago, so, rather than turn outward, where I found the environment distasteful, I turned inward, aware that aside from universal moral codes, everything in life can become a personal choice.

True, I was not yet aware of what I wanted to be when I grew up, but I did know one thing: If ever I were to marry, it would be after I graduated from college, and it would be to the man of my choice.

How wrong I could be. My aspirations would evaporate in thin air very soon!

5. MARRIAGE AT FIFTEEN

Contrary to my first storybooks, in which love and romance ultimately led to a wedded happily-ever-after, daily life demonstrated that, as an institution, marriage was nothing but a conscription under which women were forced into hard labor. This was nothing I would tolerate at any age.

As I grew older, I started observing the relationship between husbands and wives mirroring the societal expectations projected by TV, films, Middle Eastern literature, religion, relatives, and my parents. The expectation that a woman was created solely to serve a man, bear and raise children, and run a household revolted and infuriated me. That was the expectation not only in the Arab world, but in most cultures around the world. I always felt there was something wrong with this picture.

I don't think the creator and designer of the universe intended for half of humanity to be subjugated and dominated by the other half. This is completely against the laws of nature. How can it be depicted in religious teaching? That a man has the right to beat a woman? Has the right to control and direct her life as a domestic slave? Every cell in my body rejected this dogma. What baffled me was that women accepted the situation as their fate and destiny.

My stance, iconoclastic as it was, would not meet with acceptance in any quarter, and I knew to keep my thoughts to myself. Women who did not devote themselves to domestic duties were found to be in some way deficient. Furthermore, single women beyond the age of marriage were the subject of abject pity. "Better to be in hell with a man than in paradise with my parents," went an old maxim that even girls my age would repeat. My mother's favorite, meanwhile, was, "A shadow of a man is better than the shadow of a wall." In other words, my own mother was telling me, better to be with a man, no matter how detestable he might be, than be alone.

Not that I was hard-hearted. As in the fairy tales, I, too, wanted to experience passion with a charming someone, provided he was of equal mind and spirit. I just never thought of marriage as a goal, as if it were a finishing line to be raced up to and crossed. Love, to me, was the end product of a relationship; marriage, only a byproduct. In my view, romance in marriage, if it existed at all, ended up being one-sided at best. Callous as that might sound, where love was concerned, I thought it wise never to fall victim to its heartache.

The teachings of the clerics at Al Abna'a only compounded my intransigence. Granted, throughout my youth (and with only slight revision today), women were wholly dependent upon men for their livelihood and protection. This division of powers was irrefutable: The man was to provide shelter, and the woman was to bear his children and acquiesce to his demands. If a disagreement arose, no recourse existed. Neither did laws against domestic abuse, even violence. What made the situation worse for women was the fact there was no escape, while the man could easily add another wife. Man was treated like God; not to be challenged, not to be disturbed, not to be neglected, not to be mistreated, and not to be disrespected – regardless of his character, behavior and moral standards. That was the practice that I witnessed in my little world. I found it scary!

I promised the little girl inside me that she would always be free and would never have to surrender control or allow anyone to treat her with less than honor, dignity and equality. It was a vow I would put to frequent pragmatic use as an adult; a vow that would color my future choices not only in relationships, but also in career decisions.

I viewed marriage as a realm I did not wish to enter.

Only, it seemed the universe decided to teach me a lesson in free will.

Arranged marriages were fairly commonplace in my world and looked upon as the only suitable way to marry off sons and daughters. In spite of Western misconceptions, these matches are anything but haphazard. Customary for centuries, especially among royal households—witness Prince Charles and Diana—arranged marriages took place worldwide until the eighteenth century. Even after that, the tradition carried on in many societies. Hoping to settle its various frontiers, especially the Pacific Northwest, America put its own spin on arranged marriages with mail-order brides.

In my circle, as well as throughout most of the Arab world, arrangements were meticulously handled by a professional matchmaker ("professional" meaning the person was paid, with fees ranging between $200 and $2,000, depending on the social status of the couple. Payment was due only if the match culminated in a marriage, with the cost being split between the bride and groom). In most instances, the matchmaker was a middle-aged woman with a firm knowledge of the community and every family's tribal backgrounds. Her skills preserved harmony and diffused any friction that might arise over conflicting lifestyles. She likewise took into account the personalities, physical appearances, habits and hobbies, and the finance resources of her clients.

In their way, matchmakers were the forerunner of today's online dating. Both are an expedient means to an end, with the same wavering degrees of success. The main difference is that in the end, in my culture, the decision about a proper mate is usually made by the parents of the bride-to-be, and Arab women, especially those in tribal and rural cultures, tend to marry younger than women in the West, usually between the age of sixteen and twenty-two. The religious belief is that men and women become eligible for marriage when they physically reach sexual maturity, although when that is determined is wholly subjective. I began menstruating at age twelve, which immediately sent me into a panic. "I'm dying," I cried to Mother, whose response was, "Congratulations, now you are a woman." She then fetched me some pads and gave me a rudimentary explanation of what was going on. Another difference in my society is that the union comes with a tacit understanding that the woman, once married, must accept her destiny, no matter how the marriage turns out.

To this day, divorce carries a heavy stigma, although the number of divorces in Saudi Arabia is steadily increasing. According to a recent count, thirty percent of all marriages (in the United States, the statistic stands at fifty percent) end with legal breakups.

But, in the 1970s, divorce was unthinkable.

From the age of fourteen, I had many suitors who asked my father for my hand in marriage. All of them were relatives. My father rejected their offers on the grounds that I was too young. He had already agreed to arranged marriages for my older stepsisters when they were seventeen and eighteen, although neither had laid eyes upon her future husband until after Father had agreed to their unions.

My unmarried status changed in the summer of 1973, when a proposal was presented by a gentleman named Ahmad, who came from a very good family in Qassim. Ahmad was twenty-seven years old and studying for his Master of Business Administration degree in Los Angeles—in the United States of America. Ahmad's search for a wife had begun when he tasked the women in his family to find a suitable young bride from his hometown, Buraida. The relatives spread the word and marched to their mission with zeal, sifting through school attendance records and asking their daughters and their daughters' friends. That is how my name cropped up, although I never found out who exactly had suggested me. Ahmad's widowed mother called my mother to test the waters before Ahmad officially approached my father. Mother consulted with Father, who was hesitant, given my age—I was still several months shy of my sixteenth birthday—but one of my parents, perhaps both, decided to put the question before me.

I was in my bedroom, reading as usual, when Mother entered, gently closed the door, and sat down next to me on my bed. "You are a lucky girl," she said.

"I am?" I responded, not knowing where this was going to lead. I had little clue that a formal marriage proposal was in the works, let alone that a candidate was about to land on our doorstep.

"Oh, yes," she said reassuringly, going on to describe this golden proposal from an outstanding suitor for marriage. Listening to her, I immediately shut down inside and could not follow. A dark cloud descended all around me and I began moaning inside, "Please don't do this," knowing full well that I was incapable of ever declining Mother's wishes.

She painted a glowing picture of how I would enjoy living in Los Angeles, a wonderful place we seemed to know so much about from movies, although I also detected an atypical nervousness in her, not that I could interpret any reason for it. Knowing Mother would never push me into harm's way, I replied in the affirmative. I would never say no to Mother. I always wanted to please her.

Without warning, I started to cry. Tears were rolling down my tender cheeks like streams of fire. I did not know why I was crying. Mother thought it was because I was scared about having to live so far away, about having to leave her. She offered an out. She said, "You do not have to say yes, if you don't want to."

I shook my head side to side, indicating the answer was no. As in, no, I am saying yes to the proposal. The tears flowed.

"Are you certain you mean it?" Mother asked. "You can turn down the proposal."

To this day, I don't know why I agreed to the marriage.

Everything moved so quickly. Ahmad and I met for the first time as soon as the deal was done. I thought he was good looking, but I felt no sparks, only fear. Not that I recall many details, because from that point on I was living in what felt like a perpetual trance. My body seemed to levitate off the ground, but I was not soaring. Strangely, Father never discussed the proposal with me, or any aspects of marriage. Although Mother was the one who presented the proposal, she never gave me "the talk" about sex, only the usual bromides on my having to be obedient, pretty, and clean. I couldn't even confide in my best friend Mashael, who was off on summer holiday with her family. I didn't write her about the impending wedding; in fact, throughout my lifelong friendship with Mashael, I don't think the topic of my marriage has ever come up.

The time from my bedroom conversation to my wedding day was only two months. Mother and my aunts saw to all of the plans, with no input from me. Two days before the reception, the religious ceremony was held with only the men present. I was not there.

Once the cleric delivered a speech about the sanctity of marriage, Ahmad formally asked Father for my hand, and Father formally accepted for me. The cleric read verses from the Quran, Father and Ahmad shook hands and signed the marriage contract, and this was followed by the signatures of witnessing members from both families, to attest that there no undue pressure on either Ahmad or me to enter into the union.

We were now officially married.

The celebratory reception for the men was held in my uncle's house across the street from ours, which was where the women threw their own festivities. Preparing for the women's party, I was in my parents' bedroom, wearing my wedding gown, my hair brushed and combed elaborately, and my face heavily made up. Looking in the mirror, I did not recognize myself. "This is not happening," I kept repeating, but my surroundings were boldly confirming the opposite. From the garden downstairs I heard the women ululating, singing to the music and clapping their hands, reminding me this was a wedding. And it was mine.

I felt like a sacrificial offering when Mother and my aunts burst in to escort me into the small crowd of other women. As if on automatic pilot, I sat on the designated bench as they formed a line and, one by one, kissed and congratulated me. At first, I was numb. Within ten minutes, the pain began inside. I felt it in my heart, and soon my lungs. I could barely breathe. "All right, you are not dying," I told myself. But all my dreams were. This was real. I was getting married. At age 15. Why? What happened to my dreams? What happened to my free will? What happened to my ideals and principles and beliefs?

I could no longer feign a smile and pretend any of this was tolerable. I had to leave the party. When I stood up, Mother grasped that something was wrong and hastily followed me back into the house, but then decided to leave me to myself. I tossed aside my bridal bouquet and dashed into my bedroom, weeping. Mother and my aunts chalked up my behavior to stage fright. The more traditional women were convinced someone had given me the evil eye.

I washed my face hoping to wash away this nightmare and wake up. I undid my hair, put on my pajamas, and went to sleep on the roof top. The women continued partying, giving no mind to me, just another uneasy young bride who eventually would come to her senses. Ahmad, meanwhile, was whooping it up with the men, unaware of what was going on with me. The revelry was expected to last until hours after midnight, and I somehow believed the entire nightmare would be over by the time I awakened in the morning. That was not to be. After a few hours, I felt Mother rousing me and saying, "Get dressed. Your husband is waiting for you."

Husband? That sounded surreal. "But I don't want to be married," I moaned so innocently. She ignored me and pulled me back into my bedroom, where she dressed me to start the rest of my life with a strange man.

The house was quiet, the guests long gone. Ahmad had been waiting silently downstairs to be led to my room, so the marriage could be consummated. The surreal had just become the real. There was nothing I could do. I could not blame anyone; I had agreed to the proposal.

If I followed my natural inclination and fled—only, where to?—people would think that my husband rejected me on our wedding night because I was not a virgin.

That would be the ultimate scandal and leave a permanent scar on my family.

I was forced to swallow my pride, which tasted like a scorching pile of ashes. My personal upheaval must be for a reason. "She was powerful not because she was not scared," the contemporary Canadian poet Atticus said, "but because she went on so strongly despite the fear." "God has a plan for me; this can't be my destiny," I assured myself as I suppressed the scorching pile rising up my throat.

On my wedding night, I sat on the bed in the enticing nightgown my mother had bought me, along with the satin lingerie underneath. Ahmad sat next to me, in the spot where Mother had first told me about him, and asked with a smile, "How are you?"

"Tired," I replied, staring the entire time at my feet and nervously fiddling with the ribbons of my nightgown. I could not look him in the eyes, gentle and beautiful as they were. He placed his fingers under my chin, lifted my face to his, and softly kissed my forehead, my eyes, my cheeks, and then, lightly, my lips. At this point, the groom typically unwraps the layers of garments covering his bride. I never looked up.

As he reached to unlace my silk ribbons, I pulled away and declared, "No. I want to sleep."

"Okay," he said. "Don't worry. We will sleep." He then added, "Can I just hold you?

I did not reply. He came closer, embraced me tenderly, and whispered in my ear, "I love you."

I felt sorry for him, yet I was incapable of a response. As he undressed himself, I crawled under the sheets and, still wearing the nightgown and lingerie, pulled the covers over my head. He turned off the lights and crawled into bed next to me. Nothing happened.

The following day, Ahmad and I boarded the plane to Beirut and then Madrid for our honeymoon. We explored the mountains, the beaches, the rivers, but my mind was elsewhere. I watched the other couples holding hands, laughing together, gazing into each other eyes, but all I felt with Ahmad was torment—clearly his, and certainly mine. Our nights during the honeymoon were not much different than our wedding night. He saw me trying to hide my discomfort, but he said nothing. The poor, dear fellow. He could not understand why I agreed to marry him only to reject him.

But he was patient and believed it was the separation from my family that was making me homesick and so unhappy.

We proceeded to Los Angeles, where we lived in a fairly nice apartment off-campus while Ahmad studied for his MBA at the University of Southern California. Nothing was familiar to me: not the land, not the people, not the person I was living with. What I did find striking about this new environment was how men and women naturally blended together and freely expressed their opinions—women, especially. What's more, as I learned from television, women were fighting for equal rights, seeking to eradicate discrimination against our sex and promote self-determination. Amazingly, to me, the Arab women I met in Los Angeles acted like women's liberation did not concern them, as they continued to defend male supremacy over women, whom they themselves saw as weaker creatures.

I enrolled in the local public high school, hoping to continue my education. I was now in the eleventh grade, and Ahmad would drop me off and pick me up when he could; otherwise, I took the public bus, another new experience. At the beginning, it was difficult to adjust to school, and I never really fit in. I enrolled in a class to improve my spotty knowledge of English, but the other students considered me an unwelcome intruder.

The oil embargo that lasted from October 1973 until March 1974 made things worse. There were long lines at gas stations and shortages of fuel, with prices skyrocketing and the Saudis being blamed. At school, I was scapegoated by the students, bullied, threatened and called names I had never heard before and did not understand. But I did not complain, not to Ahmad, not to anyone.

I cried in private, knowing that I was on my own and needed to build strength and resilience, as Mother would have in such a situation. I wanted to be just like Mother. And yet, more.

I told myself this would only last a year.

Then, Ahmad would complete his studies and we would go home.

The year passed. We returned to Riyadh in the summer of 1974 to live in Ahmad's family home with his mother, brother, his wife and their children. There was no privacy at all, and I had to share the bathroom with the children. Being a traditional household, the wives would take turns cooking and washing. Because I was studying at school at that time, I was not required to cook but assigned to do the dishes. When I didn't have my nose in the books or the dinner plates, I kept my distance, isolating myself in the bedroom I shared with Ahmad.

I coasted through the days, oblivious to the world, watching my friends and sisters enjoying themselves. It was not a healthy situation. I repressed my resentment, rage and melancholy inside my tender body and buried my emotions in my bones, until one day my body gave up in protest and I fell sick – really sick, with a high fever, falling in and out of consciousness for days. I refused help, despite my family and Ahmad's insistence that I be taken to the hospital. I knew what was wrong with me, and I assumed all the blame. To put it plainly, this was not the life that was aligned with my soul's desire. So, I gave up on life.

Ahmad, being concerned and kindhearted, moved me to my parents' house, so my mother and sisters could look after me. After some time, I recovered and regained my strength. At that point, when Ahmad came to check on me, he asked if I felt ready to go back home with him. I told him no, not now, not ever. And that was it. I never went back to him.

For Ahmad, my reaction wasn't exactly a surprise, but he took the news badly, I'm afraid. His worst fear had come true. He had shown such patience, hoping that, somehow, I might change, and we would make our marriage work. But it was never meant to be.

The protocol was simple: Ahmad met with a cleric from the justice department and said he wanted to divorce his wife. The cleric issued the necessary document. I was not involved beyond being casually informed later by Mother that I was officially divorced. Otherwise, there was nothing to work out. In terms of financial compensation, our system calls for divorced partners to receive only whatever material assets he or she had brought to the marriage. There is no division of goods or money, unless they are in the names of both parties. If there are children, our religion dictates that full custody be awarded the father when the youngsters reach age seven, unless the father waives such a right. In these cases, the mother can keep the children, which happens frequently when the husband marries again and starts a new family.

Ahmad, I was happy to hear, re-married a few years after we broke up, and, I believe, had four children. Putting his degree to good use, he became a highly respected and successful businessman. Our paths never crossed again.

Life for me essentially picked up where it had left off. I don't think Father was shocked by my divorce; the only sense I felt was that both of my parents were panged with guilt for what had taken place. This was especially true of Mother. While my paternal aunts and uncles deemed it customary for girls to marry so young, my maternal side of the family, residing as they did in enlightened Iraq and Kuwait, thought it wrong and gave Mother a particularly hard time about her not having stopped the marriage. Mother herself did not marry Father until she was twenty-five.

Then there were the relatives who stood convinced that someone had given me the evil eye and I was possessed. By and large, however, I think we all pretended that nothing had ever happened.

The subject of my marriage never crossed our lips again.

At the time of our breakup, I saw the attempt at marriage as a profound experiment that offered no right or wrong conclusions, simply a lesson under fire about my true nature. That is, my free spirit could never be caged. That is how the Creator designed my life to be. I applaud those who find fulfillment in marrying and having children. But I am not one of them, despite going on to have four more engagements in my lifetime, each one confirming what I had learned from my first: that I could count upon my inner voice to speak my truth, no matter the consequences.

So, there I was, divorced at the age of seventeen. I was now branded damaged goods.

And yet, I breathed a heavy sigh of relief. There would be no suitors for me in the immediate future.

"I am not what happened to me, I am what I choose to become," according to Carl Jung.

I could now get on with my life.

6. LIFE THROUGH LITERATURE

Propelled by an economic expansion caused by the surging global demand for oil, Father's vehicular tool and equipment business flourished, just like most everything else in the country. With his strong connections to the National Guard, Father established lucrative long-term contracts as a supplier. Only soon his daily presence was no longer necessary in the day-to-day running of his operation. Simultaneously, the cloistered atmosphere of Riyadh was beginning to suffocate him, especially after his many years of traveling the world. His solution, in 1974, was assigning a manager to the business and relocating himself to a sprawling villa with a magnificent garden in an affluent neighborhood of Cairo, where he staffed his house with a driver, cook and housekeeper.

Every three or four months, he would return to Riyadh for about two weeks, not necessarily to see us—his brief stays did little or nothing to cement any kind of relationship between us and him—but to handle paperwork and refresh his government connections. We visited him in Cairo during some of our school breaks and holidays, but most of the time, especially in summer, we preferred to go with our friends to Europe, particularly to Paris, Genève and London. Mother understood how the lack of scope in Riyadh was dulling our senses, which is why she granted us our freedom alone with our friends. We would stay in service flats or hotels together, but what I remember about my travels as an eighteen- and nineteen-year-old was the thrill of taking in the majesty and beauty of the cities I saw and just how strongly they made me feel. They reminded me of the incredible possibilities and potentialities out there to live my life as an independent free woman.

"I want that" became my mantra.

At the time of my return from the U.S. and the breakup with Ahmad, the religious establishment controlled the Riyadh Board of Education, and its officials refused to accept my certificate of studies from Los Angeles on the grounds that my classes there did not include Islamic studies. This forced me to repeat eleventh grade, even though I was more than eligible for twelfth. I was not in a position to argue. And that is when I met my best friend, Amani. She was someone I badly needed in my sphere after my forlorn experience of the previous two years. See how the universe works!

Amani was Jordanian and, in personality, a near mirror image of me: quiet, self-disciplined and naturally curious. We both excelled at math and science, loved literature and poetry, and idealized and obeyed our mothers. We were inseparable. When graduation came, both of us were uncertain about choosing our major fields of study for university. For women, the only available roads were medicine, business, and humanities. Having witnessed the opportunities open to women in the West, I did not want to attend the University of Riyadh. I wanted a school in the U.K. or the U.S. and brought up the matter for family discussion. Sending word from Cairo, Father would not hear of it.

Amani's father had his opinions, too. He was fine about her going to university, but when she told him she was interested in studying business, he replied that would be "useless for a woman." The same applied to what he considered any serious studies. "Girls should not worry their pretty heads with subjects like science or business," he said. "A college education will not help you run your household or be a good wife and mother." He suggested an English literature major, "so at least you will learn English."

Taking her father at his word, Amani pleaded with me to join her as an English literature major, at the University of Riyadh.

It did not take much convincing.

I was not about to lose hold of my best friend.

And that is how I ended up with an English literature degree.

To its credit, the University of Riyadh, created in 1957 and renamed King Saud University in 1982, two years after I graduated (when males and females were still taught separately), became one of the top universities in the country and ranked third in the Arab world in 2018.

My studies of literature helped me acquire the art of reflection, as I scrutinized the complex characters of Jane Eyre, Anna Karenina, Elizabeth Bennet in *Pride and Prejudice*, Beatrice in *Much Ado about Nothing*, Jo March in *Little Women*, and even Edmund Dante in *The Count of Monte Cristo*, Heathcliff in *Wuthering Heights*, Hamlet, King Lear—it didn't matter what gender the protagonist was, if she or he were rich or poor, queen or warrior. What mattered was the connection I made. Some of them I would not meet until after my university studies, but my classes not only opened my mind to a new world of literature, but also how to approach a story analytically, satisfying two of my favorite pastimes: exploring new horizons and problem solving. Reading became more of an exciting adventure than a mere hobby to pass the time. The characters I studied were not superheroes, except, perhaps, those in mythology. But my heroes did not need supernatural powers. Fictional as they may have been, they were fierce and fearless, complex and creative, and unapologetically independent, for better or for worse. I wanted to touch their joy and happiness, their suffering and sorrow, their pain and anger, their lust and jealousy, and the love and passion in their hearts. I allowed their emotions to seep into my bones and the deepest cells of my body.

I lived their stories in my mind and dived into their psyche with my heart and all my senses. I could smell their seasons, taste their emotions, hear their thoughts, touch their skin, and picture their dreams.

I found joy in their realism and imagined myself in some hidden corner of their unfolding dramas, or else completely assuming their identities, dealing with their obsessions, helping disentangle their dilemmas, all the while sharpening my own critical abilities through what they endured or enjoyed. This was my real education, along with my lessons in Eastern and Western philosophy, although those were cloaked in darkest secrecy. They took place alone in my father's library, because the university prohibited the study of the subject. Islamic teachings were handled through videos beamed in from the men's section of the university; we could see the clerics, but they could not see us.

In retrospect, the University of Riyadh was the right choice for me, even though I personally had not made the decision to go there. While this might not have been the school's intention, I was afforded ample time to discover myself and indulge in the subjects that fired my passions. My four years provided a solid foundation upon which I could deal with the eventual challenges I would face on my career path.

I don't think this was an accident, because I do not believe in coincidence. I am sure it was part of a divine design.

"God," said Albert Einstein, "does not play dice with the universe."

Without question, the greatest lesson I learned during my time in school was that speaking my truth contributed more to my sense of inner peace than all the fame and wealth in the world. But this is a lesson I learned independently. In class, we were discouraged from speaking up and expressing our thoughts, because that contradicted the insistence that we uniformly conform.

Whatever worthwhile motivations I absorbed came from my readings and exposure to the world of philosophy and literature. Still, my university courses did underscore how I could clarify and express my thoughts. By valuing linguistics, I learned their potential for complexity and elegance, as well as their persuasive and manipulative power. Literature broadened my imagination and let me see the world through metaphors, symbols and actions.

If I may paraphrase Mark William Roche, academician and author of *Why Choose the Liberal Arts?*, by nurturing my critical skills, literature showed me how to succeed in any complex and demanding situation. Literature also steered me toward acquiring new knowledge, shedding old beliefs in favor of seeking more compelling evidence, and finding fresher and more relevant concepts. Literature trained me to evaluate different perspectives, tolerate conflicting opinions, and accept defeat graciously. Literature liberated me from prejudice, intolerance and old doctrines. In studying drama and criticism, I uncovered ways to be shrewd and observe events with an inquisitive eye, apply reason to evidence, and cultivate the art of debate.

Today, many of the abilities I picked up at university are considered soft skills, critical for success in the business world and taught in popular five-day professional seminars, which give the unrealistic impression that miracles can happen, especially among older, more experienced groups. Like riding a bike, it is much simpler to gain the required skills at age five than it is at age thirty. I am convinced that technical knowledge alone will not help anyone with aspirations to become a leader. Neither will it assist you in leaving a lasting legacy. We were all given hearts. It is imperative that we exercise them.

Time and again, I have seen top leaders in my field, those with flashy engineering degrees, dismiss the humanities as an impractical, useless commodity. How arrogant and shortsighted. Leaders who lack a capacity for intellectual generosity have only one thing to offer the world: egotism. How can clear-eyed decisions be made when a mind is blunted by insecurity, fear, and distrust of that which it cannot fathom?

"The decline of literature indicates the decline of a nation," Goethe warned. And the British logician Bertrand Russell said, "There will still be things that machines cannot do. They will not produce great art or great literature or great philosophy; they will not be able to discover the secret springs of happiness in the human heart; they will know nothing of love and friendship."

How right they were.

And Amani? She only got as far as dipping her toes into the great well of literature. During our second year of college, her parents married her off in an arranged marriage. She never so much as laid eyes on the man, a fellow Jordanian, until her engagement. Dutifully, she followed her parents' orders. When I asked if this was what she really wanted, she replied, almost robotically, "My parents know what's in my best interest."

Amani married and left the Kingdom with her husband, who worked in Morocco. She and I then lost contact for nearly forty years. (There were no mobile phones or social media for most of that period.) We reunited in Amman, Jordan, in August 2018. The meeting was awkward. I studied her face, trying to find the familiar sparkle in her eyes and old buoyancy in her voice. I only could detect a shadow of what had once existed. She told me her marriage was far from tranquil, among other disappointments, but she took comfort in the accomplishments of her three beautiful daughters.

Her departure from school left me shattered. Leaving our reunion in 2018, I felt that same sense of loss. Only, this time, it was steeped in melancholy. She had been my lifeline when I returned from Los Angeles. Once she was plucked from my side, I felt exposed to the harsh solitary confinement of my little world. I looked to my sisters Ateka and Asma for someone to talk to, but they were occupied with their large circle of friends. They were lighthearted and laidback. I know now they were only taking advantage of their carefree youths, but that didn't ease my situation at the time. My sister Mona was still too young to hear me out on exploring the depth of the human soul. As for Mashael, she had just married a cousin and was adapting to her new life.

So, I found solace in my books.

And then I started writing.

I began publishing essays in the university newspaper, mainly about my internal struggles with life challenges, moral values, freedom, suppression of women, universal love, and righteousness. Eventually, these attracted the attention of the editors of the widely circulated national *Riyadh Newspaper*, who approached me with an eye to publishing my pieces. I agreed on the audacious condition that my articles be printed exactly as written, devoid of any changes and editing. They reluctantly agreed.

Echoing what I had gleaned in class, my essays were chockful of metaphors and symbolism. I believe the editors either chose to overlook or did not fully comprehend the subtle messages of my articles—which held a light to just how unjust the social environment was for women. Surely, if the editors had paid close attention, they would have exerted a heavy blue pencil, unless they secretly agreed with me, which was unlikely.

The essays continued until I went to work for Aramco, which hurtled me into a brand new life and a whole new language: Business English.

Sadly, the elegant Arabic expressions I had developed from the poets I had studied my entire life diminished and lost their sparkle as English leisurely but deliberately creeped into and wholly consumed my lingo and intellect.

As a result, my Arabic language skills evaporated drop by drop, day by day, driven by neglect and abandonment. In a way, I couldn't help but feel I was abandoning my past.

7. LIGHT

It was in the autumn of 1979. I was still in university. I had an out-of-body experience. My world—and my belief system—were never to be the same.

Mother and I were at the tailor atelier for what was another routine dress fitting. In those days, very few decent boutiques could be found in Riyadh. The only practical option was to have clothing handmade by one of the many tailors who could be found on nearly every street corner. Ours was Hiyam, a talented Egyptian seamstress known to the city's elite. Her private atelier resided within a small villa that was outfitted with spacious fitting rooms, each with a neat little pile of fashion magazines—although, flipping through any of them, all you would find were photos of models in the latest couture blackened out by the heavy ink of government censors.

Inside one of the fitting rooms, I was standing on a pedestal in front of a three-sided mirror, assessing my twenty-one-year-old body, while Hiyam and her assistants took my measurements for an upcoming social event, to which I would wear a long dress.

Hiyam was regaling Mother and me with hilarious gossip about her most finicky clients when, all of a sudden, a dark cloud enshrouded me and sapped the soul out of my body. The last thing I remember was Mother screaming and Hiyam shouting, "Oh God, she is falling."

At that moment, everything went completely quiet. No chatter, no laughter, no movement of any kind. When I looked down, I saw

63

Mother's face contorting from fright, Hiyam crying, and the two assistants frenetically running in circles, clasping their heads and hastily reciting versus from the Quran. I had no idea what the commotion was about—until I saw my body lying supine on the sofa like a piece of lumber. Was I dead? I felt fully alive. I looked up and instantly became aware that I had left my body and was now floating peacefully into an unfamiliar dimension. The funny thing was, I was not the slightest bit afraid. In fact, I was ecstatic.

As I still vividly recall, I began drifting like a feather upwards toward a luminous white light, surrounded by stillness and overcome by an exalted happiness. I felt I was touched by the hands of God—breathing God, allowing God to fill all of me. I dissolved in the light and became one with it. No matter how much I try, how often, or the effort I put into it, I do not think I can fully describe the sensation of this divine experience.

My ethereal visit continued until I heard a distressed voice shout out my name from what sounded like a great distance, as if from another world. I gazed down and saw my mother calling for me to wake up, to please come back. I wanted to tell her not to worry, I was in good hands.

Much as I desired to continue my ascent, the luminous white light gently released me back to my mother.

It was not time.

I awoke to find Mother clutching me to her chest, while Hiyam and her assistants massaged my hands and feet. When they saw I had regained consciousness, they began reciting prayers of gratitude to God for bringing me back. I kept telling them I was fine until, finally, their fears dissipated. I did not tell any of them what had transpired in the moments before. I did not tell anyone afterward. I felt privileged to experience the Divine on so intimate a level, a fact I wanted to keep to myself. I was afraid that by sharing what had happened, those moments might lose their magic, or, just as bad, they might be trivialized as a freak incident. I also knew no one would believe me, and, if I did reveal what had happened, those around me would start trying to repress my spiritual potentiality and yearning.

To this day, I don't believe that the incident in Hiyam's atelier was a freak incident. Everything happens for a reason, and what I experienced altered my perspective on reality profoundly. I believe I was taken to this special place so I could see that there is more to the universe than that which we only perceive on the surface. The world is not our sole reality. Another dimension is linked to our creation, one with a formidable meaning that I have yet to fully uncover. I have spent long years attempting to analyze its implication and causation.

In recent years, I was pleased to discover that an out-of-body experience, or OBE, is not that uncommon. It's just that people who have one don't always talk about it. In fact, one in ten people have an OBE one or more times in their lives. A spontaneous OBE, as opposed to one that is induced, sometimes leads to an intense existential shift in a person's view of the world, as was my case. Further analyzing what happened to me, I see that transformation was not immediate. It was slow and gradual, and it took years before I grasped its nature. It was as though it was waiting for my intellectual, emotional and spiritual maturity to evolve before revealing its true essence.

I have concluded that all of us live in two different spheres, the inner world and the outer one. My struggle has been in reconciling the two. The Indian yogi Gopi Krishna (1903-1984), in his book *Kundalini: The Evolutionary Energy in Man*, said in describing his transformative awakening, "When I look within, I am lifted beyond the confines of time and space, in tune with a majestic, all conscious existence, which mocks at fear and laughs at death." He calls the experience "absolutely removed from everything in this world." And when he looks outside himself, he says, "I am what I was, an ordinary mortal in no way different from the millions who inhabit the earth, a common man, pressed by necessity and driven by circumstances, a little chastened and humbled that is all."

Over the years, I have spent a great deal of time in ongoing "conversations with the finest minds"—to borrow from Descartes—as I explored the wisdom and insights of the great Eastern and Western philosophers and scholars. I asked them, not unreasonably, to guide me throughout my life's journey of self-discovery. Invariably, I found that all of them, including Islamic scholars, advocated one common philosophy: Find yourself and you will be able to live in harmony within *and* with the world around you. It was Prophet Muhammad (PBUH) who said (unverified), "Whosoever knows himself, knows his Lord." The remark, intuitive and simple as it sounds, is, in reality, the most complicated test of our existence.

It takes years of deliberation, courage, and perseverance to reach a divine state of Being. It is not something you reach merely by schooling yourself and delving into esoteric literature and ancient scripture. Knowledge will help, just as it will provide you with the proper tools. But you have to do the work alone. You must embark upon your life's journey with an intuitive heart and inquisitive mind as your faithful companions.

Throughout my youth, I could find no assurance or gratification in the spiritual and cultural teachings I had received from the religious extremists in my world; my mind was too restless and hungry for knowledge to accept on face value what was being taught. Those lessons also lacked convincing explanations for my existence or for the intricately complex universe of which we are but a part. Furthermore, because I believed our religion fundamentally sought to address personal and spiritual development, I was disturbed by the glaring paradox in our conventional social systems, especially those that attempted to influence my perception of reality, let alone manipulate my mind to adopt specific tenets about our current world. We were trained to adhere to restricted views to prevent us from making any attempts to distinguish ourselves from the psychology of the masses. Societies do not freely acknowledge individual freewill. Socrates called popular beliefs "the monsters under the bed," because they were only useful for frightening children. Regrettably, in my world, popular beliefs were used to frighten an entire population.

For centuries, religious establishments in all corners of the world have employed social and cultural standards to strip people, especially women, of their sense of their own uniqueness and potentiality. There is one place for a man and a lower one for a woman. Their coaching denigrates and denies the fact that you are perfectly capable of walking a straight line to enlightenment entirely on your own. They don't want you to discover your inner supernatural powers—because if you did, it would bring an end to their powers.

The teachings of fanatical clerics in my world terrorized the crowd with fear of annihilation should they not surrender their intellectual curiosity and rational faculty. It suppressed freewill and reason and did not invite investigative pursuit of the truth. It was as if God was telling us to be stupid. How absurd is that? Rational speculation and inquiry about the fundamental doctrines of our beliefs were to be rejected, coercing people to refrain from questioning religious matters, and branding anyone who contradicted such teachings an infidel - as if reminiscent of the twelfth-century inquisitorial courts of the Catholic Church. Disputing and challenging their rationale was considered blasphemy. Those who dared reject their lies and myths found "whips were raised to strike them . . . and the sword was drenched with their blood," to borrow from the tenth-century Arab philosopher Abu Al-Ala Al-Ma'arri, as he described the practices of religious extremists throughout time. Their ruling system was in clear violation of the teaching of the Holy Quran, which clearly states, "There is no compulsion in religion" (2:256).

In my childhood, I was forced into a chilling submission to irrational, conformist teachings I could not comprehend until my spiritual experience awakened resentment and repulsion against the rigid system that obscured the compassionate, peaceful, and tolerant messages of Islamic texts and replaced them with propagandized and prejudiced thinking. Instead of achieving harmony, serenity and equanimity associated with spirituality, we find fear, bigotry and violence dominating people's hearts and minds. Although we may pride ourselves in our religious richness, our souls continue to suffer spiritual poverty.

Nations cannot progress and prosper without moderation, tolerance, and an appreciation of independent thinking. These were the principal impetuses and stimuli for the intellectual and cultural accomplishments of the Islamic Golden Age from the eighth to the fourteenth century—a period of prosperity and affluence in culture, economics, politics, and all sciences and knowledge. It witnessed the greatest creations of the Islamic intellectual civilization in Baghdad, Egypt, the Levant region, Andalusia and Persia, where its rise was buttressed by free dialogue, criticism, and the scientific method in debate and experiment, not by surrendering and acquiescing to the sayings of strict jurists, following ancient traditions, and memorizing and teaching ancient texts as is the case today. That era was a fertile testing ground for an impressive number of Islamic scholars in a variety of disciplines, what with the likes of Al-Farabi, Ibn Sina (Avicenna), Al-Razi, Ibn Rushd (Averroes), Fatima Al-Fihriyya, Ibn Khaldoun, Ibn Al-Haytham, Al-khawarzmi, Al-Ma'arri, Ibn Alnafi, and numerous others. Their tremendous presence was not an exception but the norm of that time, when religious tolerance, independence of thought, and intellectual pursuit of veracity were the dominant attitude. "The seeker after the truth is not one who studies the writings of the ancients and, following his natural disposition, puts his trust in them, but rather the one who suspects his faith in them and questions what he gathers from them, the one who submits to argument and demonstration, and not to the saying of a human being whose nature is fraught with all kinds of imperfection and deficiency," said Ibn Al-Haytham, an Arab scientist and philosopher (965-1040) of that Islamic Golden Age.

Like everyone else, I was not immune from the extremist doctrine that was downloaded into my young mind by parents, teachers and zealous clerics. But my experience helped me realize that if we accept these rules, they become our values, our convictions, and our dogmas—in a word, our biases. We never question them, because we have been taught that they will lead us to our salvation. The result is we start living life according to other people's ideas of how life should be lived. We conform completely—and in the process, lose our true identity and find ourselves in a wasteland that bypasses the magic of life. This "bankruptcy of the soul" is what editor Diane K. Osbon examines in her *Reflections on the Art of Living*, on the teachings of scholar Joseph Campbell. The book says that "doing what someone else wants us to do is slave morality and a path to disease and disintegration of the spirit and body."

I am not disputing the universal moral codes and ethical disciplines. No rational and sensible person would. Principled codes, such as non-violence, not stealing, honesty, justice, compassion, generosity, integrity, humility, civility, and so forth, are the rules of decency for any society. The alternative is chaos and violence. No one with an intuitive moral compass disagrees about the necessity to practice these canons. Such commandments transcend creed, nations, age, race and time. They are the common thread of all religions and faiths, be it Islam, Judaism, Christianity, Buddhism, Hinduism, Taoism, Confucianism, even agnosticism and atheism, or any other ism. These codes govern human behavior and relations and don't restrict individual freewill and intellectual exclusivity.

That is why public behavior, when it impinges on the well-being of society, becomes everybody's business.

But other than that, you don't owe anybody anything.

How you live your life and choose your path for self-discovery should be your own private business.

For me, spirituality became a deeply personal journey, an open invitation to explore the meaning of life, free from rigid doctrine or any particular ideology that monopolized sacred exegesis. I have forever craved rationality and truth, having failed to find credible answers from many an otherwise intelligent individual who offered only ludicrous notions that even the simplest of minds could see through, "simply because it formed an article of his faith to which he must hold at any cost, even if that cost included the sacrifice of reason and truth," to quote Gopi Krishna once more. Conversely, "the irrationality of those who attempted to squeeze the universe within the narrow compass of reason was no less deplorable." He finds such people "ignorant about the nature of their own consciousness," and reminds us, "The unknown entity that inhabits human bodies is still enveloped in mystery, and the rational faculty, one of its inseparable possessions, is no less an enigma than the owner itself."

Following the will of the masses may get you success in terms of worldly materials, but it will never allow you to discover the real treasures that lie inside. My experience inspired me to pursue investigative learning and rely on my intellect and intuition to seek the truth about our reality, just as the Holy Quran has inspired us to do, and to better ourselves through acquiring knowledge.

I take comfort in the fact that thousands of people in my world support religious moderation and tolerance, even if they don't speak up about it. Fortunately, the situation has changed with the recent social and economic reforms introduced by the government. Moreover, Crown Prince Mohamed bin Salman, in an April 2021 interview, stated that we cannot transform the country and prosper with extremist thinking. He said, "Extremism is not permissible . . . [A]nyone who adopts an extremist approach, even if he is not a terrorist, is a criminal. . . [W]hen we commit ourselves to following a certain school or scholar, this means we are deifying human beings." Alluding to the fact that Islam has graced us with independence of will and independence of thought, he denounced the slavish imitation of ancient practices that were based on circumstances and mindsets particular to their epoch. These are the messages that should be propagated in our religious teachings, not xenophobia and bigotry. Suddenly, most of the puritanical scholars came out supporting and agreeing with the message of the crown prince and changed their attitudes overnight. Some of them publicly apologized to the masses for their prejudice and extremism in the past. And, as simple as that, they abandoned decades of their absurd fatwas and teachings. Indeed, when leaders speak, people listen.

Many of us agonized in silence over the criminalization of our moderate attitude for decades, and finally it has been appreciated and reflected in our social, educational and jurisprudence systems.

Of course, it will take years to fix the deep-rooted damage caused by extremists and fanatics.

But the day is done that they monopolized the truth.

I am sharing this experience with you, dear reader, because it had a profound effect on shaping my personality and intellect.

It helped me realize that everything in life happens for a reason, even bad things offer us wisdom, and I am not alone; the whole universe lives inside me. All I needed was to reach out and touch it. I felt blessed and protected; I could completely surrender and let life unfold through me.

"If light is in your heart," the thirteenth-century Sufi mystic Rumi said, "you will find your way home."

8. SOLITUDE

My graduation was a big deal for Mother. My father, true to form, was nowhere to be seen. He was occupied in Cairo, tending to his worldly pleasures. Mother, however, was not only present, but living on cloud nine; one of her children—the very first—had earned a college degree. This was a rare accomplishment where women were concerned. To honor the occasion, Mother presented me with a twenty-four-carat gold pendant on a gold chain. I cherish her precious gift to this day, even though I rarely wear it. Instead, I hold it in my hand and remember Mother as she was on that special day. It is as if we are together again.

The modest commencement ceremony—the first official one for women at the University of Riyadh, as I recall—was held in an indoor sport stadium on loan from the men's university. Modest might even be overstating the case. There was no stage or platform. (Such niceties were reserved for the men's graduation, where government representatives officiated and, as with our school years, males were kept at a far distance.) Of the few attendees in the huge stadium, we students were divided into sections based on our academic disciplines. When our individual departments were called, we walked one by one to shake hands with the dean and members of the faculty, collect our certificates, and then make our way into the world. No music, no speeches, no photographs (cameras were not allowed, so none of us dressed up for the occasion). I put on a smile for Mother's benefit, but I couldn't say I was jumping for joy, despite the jolly mood surrounding me. All I could hear was high-pitched chattering about how my sister graduates were going to find the right husband and make the short, quick leap from parental restraint to spousal control. Not so much as a word about career or autonomy. Not a peep about aspirations.

Indeed, many of these girls were engaged to be wed in ceremonies planned for shortly after graduation. In a moment of weakness, I asked myself, why can't I be like them? But that quickly passed.

The bigger question I asked myself was, "Now, what?" The summer after graduation was tough on my psyche. The only things I knew were that I did not want to be married and I did not want to be a teacher. An idea to pursue graduate studies in America was quickly shot down by Father, although he was not entirely to blame. My idealistic plan was further crushed by the political turmoil in the aftermath of the Iranian revolution and subsequent siege of Mecca.

At home, I watched my sisters indulge in their active social lives as their many friends came and went all night long. At first, I envied them and attempted to join in. That effort was short-lived. The moment they detected my awkwardness, I was subjected to their ridicule.

What I realized was, it is possible to change your life by changing your thoughts, but it is almost impossible to change your nature by changing your life.

Face it, I thought, I was an introvert, a hermit whose soul thrived in isolation and vibrated with the sound of silence.

And I was fine with that.

Solitude is a cold, cruel creature. If you wrestle and fight it, it will split you into a thousand pieces and jab you with despair. Resent it, and it will twist your peace of mind and ravage your sanity. So, I did not contest it. When solitude came knocking, I surrendered and befriended it. Little by little we grew intimate, and solitude made me feel cozy and comfortable in its cosmic space. In one fell swoop, I discovered that the silent universe could become audible in the soothing quietude of my inner world. The Bengali poet Rabindranath Tagore described this mystical connection in his poem, *Stray Birds*, when he wrote: "Listen, my heart, to the whispers of the world with which it makes love to you."

Solitude infused me with fortitude and strength, patience and self-discipline. The expression, putting one's head on straight? Solitude did the deed. Solitude became my new best friend, a guide to inspire me with words of wisdom. I never felt lonely. Solitude was like a lover that I longed for whenever I was with other people. I couldn't wait to race to my room and nestle in its waiting arms. "Great men are like eagles, and build their nest in some lofty solitude," the nineteenth-century German philosopher Arthur Schopenhauer deemed. Besides, I was never alone. Not truly. Rumi would often be at my ear, whispering, "Don't feel lonely. The entire universe is inside you."

Solitude rewarded me with motivation for my writing and lucidity for my thoughts. It became my safety net where I could hide from the hustle-bustle of life in our house. As Jane Austen's Emma said, I felt "blessed with so many resources within myself, the world was not necessary to me. I could do very well without it."

And so, I resisted group activities and large gatherings in order to protect myself from the influence of popular beliefs. I cherished my seclusion—and my books. Days were spent immersing myself in the words of the world's great philosophers. I learned about the internal intelligence and unlimited power women have to change and conquer their lives. So many glorious historical examples exist in which women prevailed over repressive systems and dared to stand up for their emancipation: Simone de Beauvoir, Emmeline Pankhurst, Theodora of Byzantine, Christine de Pisan, Mary Wollstonecraft, Louisa May Alcott, Elizabeth Blackwell, Charlotte Brontë, and such powerful rulers and warriors as Zenobia, Artemisia, Boudicca, to name only a few.

But I could not understand why then, in our modern time and in many parts of the world, women were still being marginalized and abused?

How did women descend from such a sacred place in ancient civilizations to their place today, as domestic slaves of the social contract?

Autumn arrived and there I was, a university graduate still cooped up in my own room, reading, writing, and reflecting. Initially, the room, which was the largest, belonged to Asma and me—until Asma decided I was boring and moved in with Ateka, the eldest sister. I was not insulted; I was in fact relieved to have my space and privacy. And as an added bonus, I ended up with the biggest bedroom in the house. Having my own quarters, I stayed up all night putting words to paper, not going to sleep until four or five in the morning, waking up at noon before repeating this unremarkable cycle, like an addict. Mother, despite my claims that I was happy with my own company, tried to break my habit, but that was in vain. She would invite over friends to shatter my confinement. When that didn't work, she urged my sisters to spend time with me—a situation we all hated. Going out was not an option. Riyadh offered nothing in the way of social life that appealed to me.

My turnaround began on a cool November day that same year. Oddly, Mother was not in the kitchen when I went down for my tea and toast; usually at this hour, when the city was preparing to close down for lunch and siesta, she would be cooking our midday meal. In this instance, I was alone in the house. My sisters were at school and my brothers, as usual, away. As I waited for the kettle to sing, I opened the window to check the weather (as if it really mattered in my case). The air was fresh and crisp, and a cool breeze caressed my face with promises of a wonderful day. I felt good. I couldn't explain why I was so upbeat, unless it was the weather. I finished my toast and took my cup of tea upstairs to my bedroom, back to my books.

I don't remember how much time passed before Mother came bursting into my room flashing a beaming smile. She was holding a copy of the Riyadh Newspaper in one hand and a green folder in the other. Sitting down next to me on the sofa and catching her breath, she handed me the paper and pointed to an ad on a folded page. It was placed by an oil company, Aramco, to announce job opportunities for recent college graduates, both men and women, regardless of their field of study. There was a promise of lucrative remuneration, training and development, housing, free medical care, and other long-term benefits.

"Why are you bringing me this?" I asked with a little bit of dread.

Mother had decided it was time I faced my demons. "This is a perfect opportunity for you to get out of here and build a future for yourself," she said. "Fill out this application. I've already made copies of all the necessary documents." That's what was in the green folder, along with brochures about the company.

"How did you get these?" I asked, feeling my morning happiness dissipate, replaced by apprehension.

"I saw the ad in the paper this morning, called the number and got more information, then raced to the employment office on Takhasusy Street for the application form," she said. "The representatives were happy to see me. They said the company is eager to hire Saudis and offer them a bright future. Now, hurry and fill out the application, so I can take it back before they close for the day."

Mother was so excited that you would have thought she was the one applying. Frankly, my apprehension had already turned to indifference. I wasn't sure I wanted to break away from my placid life with my books, a roof over my head, and Mother taking care of me. Besides, I thought, I could always make a modest living from my writings.

"But the job is in the Eastern Province," I whined in my best defeatist voice. "Where would I live? I don't want to live with my aunts and uncles."

"Don't worry," said Mother. "I have already checked. You will be accommodated in the company's residential compound. It has everything—a supermarket, post office, restaurant, dry cleaners, sports facilities, even a cinema. And it is fortunate your aunts and uncles are back in the Eastern Province. They will take care of you any time you need them."

I could not think of any further excuses to postpone the inevitable. Mother had already checked all the boxes. Still, I could try.

"This is just too sudden. I want to think about it. Why rush into this now?" I protested. She could sense my reluctance—and would not have it.

"This is your future calling. Go out and make something of yourself. Opportunities like this don't come knocking on your door every day. At least give it a try."

Then came her most powerful weapon.

"Do it for my sake." She pleaded.

I obliged. As usual.

Not a single scintilla of hope entered my mind as I began filling out the job application. To make matters even more dispiriting, the form required my father's consent and signature, or that of a legal male guardian. As demanded by laws that only recently have been rescinded, a woman, regardless of her age, could not finalize any important matter in her life without a male stamp of approval. She was not able to purchase property, open a bank account, study, work, travel, or pursue several other opportunities on her own. The signatory was usually her husband, or, if she was unmarried, her father. If the father was deceased or mentally incapacitated, the responsibility fell to an uncle, brother, son, or, if necessary, a distant male relative. If absolutely no next of male kin existed, the court would assign a male representative from the justice department.

As I filled in the blanks, Father was in Cairo, and I had no idea how he would react to this pipedream of Mother's. I asked her.

"Don't worry," she said. "I will take care of him. I will be your guardian."

That took my breath away. I could not think of anyone better, or more courageous. I completed the form and, without giving it a second thought, Mother signed for Father, indicating his consent. Just like that. I bow to her.

A few days later, I received a call to schedule, as soon as possible, an in-person interview with Aramco in Dhahran, a good four hundred kilometers, or two hundred fifty miles, from Riyadh. The calendar was quickly approaching Christmas and New Year's, so we agreed to meet after the holidays. Without delay, Mother determined I needed a new wardrobe appropriate for my new professional environment. I tried telling her to wait until I got the job, but she was certain I'd land on my feet right away. We bought a new wardrobe.

To boost my confidence further, and because none of my brothers, Fahad, Muntaser or Mazen, was in Riyadh at the time, Mother arranged for the son of her elder brother Abdulaziz, my cousin Essam, to accompany me to the Eastern Province. Although a Saudi woman could not travel by herself to another country, she was permitted to go alone within the Kingdom, but Mother thought I needed the company. Essam was a couple of years younger than I, but we were close, and he had a great sense of humor. Having him around did a lot to assuage my anxiety, especially on the flight as we reminisced about our good times together in Kuwait. He also kept trying to convince me that this was the right move for me.

When we arrived in Khobar, one of the three major towns in the Eastern Province (the others being Dammam and Dhahran), we stayed with Aunt Naima and Uncle Abdul Majid and had a cousin reunion with their five children. I stayed there only one night before I moved into Steinke Hall, the guesthouse at Aramco. The time spent with them reminded me of my happy, earlier life in Kuwait and what it meant to have a family. The rigid life in Riyadh had stripped this sense of warmth and support from our lives. We did not have a close family at home. My brothers were no longer there; Muntaser had moved to Jeddah in 1973, to become a pilot with the Saudi airline Saudia, and Mazen was studying business administration in the U.K. Father lived in Egypt. My sisters clung to their friends all the time. I hid in my room, reading.

And my mother was all alone.

I had no clue what Aramco was about. The company kept a low profile and never publicized its activities. Very few people outside the Eastern Province were familiar even with the company name. It's not as if I could have Googled it back then, so I was in no way prepared for the sense of wide-eyed wonderment that overcame me when an employment representative named Mohammad, a lively fellow in his early 30s—and dressed in Western clothes (not a cowboy costume, but casual office attire)—drove me inside the expansive office complex.

Mohammad and I arrived early for my first appointment, so we cruised around the grounds. Not including the offices, the residential portion was approximately sixty square kilometers (nearly forty square miles), with a population close to ten thousand—a city unto itself, with its own governing rules independent of local and national rules and traditions. A double fence surrounded the property to keep out the preying eyes of those who dwelled in a starkly contrasting underdeveloped world. A small phalanx of sentries stood watch at the front gate to inspect all who entered. Once I was inside, I understood why: Outsiders would disapprove of those inside the camp not living in accordance with local laws and traditions.

The Aramco compound resembled a Midwestern American town, with split-level and ranch-style homes, red roofs and two-car garages built around small parks or the golf course. Time magazine once described it as "a typical American suburb with cookie-cutter houses, softball fields, and Christmas trees in December." The pavement was wide. Women walked around in short dresses and trousers, uncovered, riding bicycles and driving cars. There was not a hijab in sight; not a single sign, that I could see, of any local customs. The Saudis who worked there also dressed and acted like Westerners. Everything seemed transplanted: the houses, the schools, the restaurants, the supermarkets, the swimming pools, the cricket field, the Greyhound buses, the cinema Mother had mentioned, even the people milling about, all minding his or her own business.

"Well …well," I thought, "I could not go to America—so America came to me."

9. DAWN

Saudi Aramco was founded on May 29, 1933, when the Saudi Arabian government, offsetting a bid from the Iraq Petroleum Company, granted the Standard Oil Company of California (later renamed Chevron, after U.S. government antitrust action) the right to explore for oil in the Kingdom. Drilling began two years later, with the first discovery made in 1938. In 1944, the company uncovered the world's largest oil field, Ghawar Field, in Saudi Arabia's Eastern Province. It measures two hundred eighty by thirty kilometers, or one hundred seventy-four by nineteen miles. By then, Standard Oil owned thirty percent of the operation. Starting in 1936—when reserves had yet to be found—the Texas Oil Company (Texaco) and Exxon (formerly Standard Oil of New Jersey) had each purchased their own thirty-percent stake, and Mobil (originally Standard Oil of New York) the other ten percent. These four oil majors partnered to manage the company's assets and operations. In 1944, with the Ghawar Field discovery, the company's name became the Arabian-American Oil Co., or Aramco.

In 1973, the Saudi government assumed twenty-five-percent ownership of Aramco, expanding its holding to sixty percent the following year. In 1980, the Saudi government officially assumed total ownership, but requested that the consortium of U.S. oil majors continue to manage and operate the company's assets until 1988, when full operating control would be transferred to the Saudis. It was at this juncture that the name of the company was changed to Saudi Aramco.

In the early 1970s, the company began hiring and training professional Saudi nationals in large number with the goal of gradually replacing American and other foreign labor. A certified Saudization strategy was formalized in the 1980s in preparation for a full takeover of the company. Among the hurdles to be tackled in the transition was the fact that local Saudi education did not meet company requirements. The solution was to award scholarships to qualified Saudi high school graduates for the study of engineering and other disciples in the United States.

Simultaneously, recruitment efforts were intensified throughout the Kingdom for college graduates, no matter their gender, no matter their field of academic endeavor, as long as it carried a bachelor's degree.

That's where I came in.

As planned, the government took the reins of Aramco in November 1988 and appointed as its CEO His Excellency Ali Al-Naimi, who had served as the company's president for the previous four years. He was the first Saudi to rise to such a position. Previous to that, he had served the company as a geologist, having first arrived at Aramco as a twelve-year-old junior clerk, in 1947. In 1996, he was appointed Minister of Petroleum and Mineral Resources, an office he held until his retirement, in 2016. Although company management was now wholly controlled by the government, Saudi Aramco continued to enjoy full autonomy in running its operations, an indication of how thoroughly the government trusted the company's leadership.

My first two job interviews—I was scheduled for three—took place in an intimidating ten-story glass-and-steel tower packed with serious-looking people buzzing about like bees, each with a discernably vital mission on his or her mind. There was no way, I thought, that I would fit in. Every floor had a central hub, around which were work-cubicles surrounded by private offices whose vast picture windows overlooked other office buildings. Beyond them were dramatic views of Dhahran, which means "rising" or "emerging" in Arabic, so named because of its location on a hundred-meter-high (about three hundred thirty feet) lime mountain rising above the town below. Out the windows to the south was the leafy green residential compound with its red-tiled roofs; to the north, a contrasting vista of deserts and rocky hills above the small town of Khobar, on the coast of the Arabian Gulf. Flanking the tower to the east and west were other office buildings. The architectural design, both inside and out, made me feel like a tiny mouse trapped in a complicated laboratory maze. I wanted to go home.

Two interviewers ran each session. They all were all-American, all-business and, as best I could detect, all but interested in meeting me. Even without their cool detachment, I felt completely out of my element. Mother, in an effort to ensure I left a good impression, had prepared my interview wardrobe—a beige dress suit with jacket, along with brown shoes with French heels and matching handbag. She used to say that "when you are on the stage, everything comes under scrutiny." But I was not psychologically and mentally prepared for the job interview. Mohammad sat in on the sessions, and his presence only made me more nervous, because there I was, failing before someone I knew. As a defense mechanism, my innate shyness shut down my communication skills, not that I knew what to say in the first place.

As they continued to fire questions at me, I turned a deaf ear and said to myself, "Why would they take me? What do I have to offer? Why would they even like me?" The only answer that came to my mind were words from Henry David Thoreau: "What a man thinks of himself, that is what determines, or rather indicates, his fate."

Further exacerbating the situation, I failed to ask the interviewers a single question in return. When I did manage to squeak out something, my voice was shaky and barely audible, out of fear the American men would laugh at my English.

I never felt so humiliated in my life.

"If you are not serious about getting a job in this company, please don't waste my time," Mohammad blurted as he was driving me back to my room. "Otherwise, you better show some enthusiasm and interest." He wanted to know what had happened to the smart, cheerful young lady he had met when he first brought me onto the compound.

"I was nervous," I said apologetically, too embarrassed to admit that I was also frightened. "This was my first job interview, ever, and I didn't know what to expect. And those 'people' . . . they were condescending and conceited. That wasn't an interview. That was an interrogation."

Mohammad shot me a look, and his scornful gaze quickly turned into one of sympathy. He made light about what had just happened, then advised me on how to handle the third interview, which was set for the next day, but I had already convinced myself that if that didn't work out, which it probably wouldn't, I would be heading straight back to my mother in Riyadh. I told this to Mohammad.

The new day brought a new me. Overnight, I somehow developed a healthy dose of confidence, convincing myself that I had already been through the worst of it. Mohammad collected me from Steineke Hall for my appointment at the Medical Services Organization to meet with its Director of Operations, Adnan Jum'ah. The department operated the company's hospital and clinics. Adnan was soft spoken, calm and kind. Being Saudi, Adnan was accustomed to women not speaking up in front of unfamiliar men, let alone a young woman having her first encounter with a completely new (to her), alien and diverse corporate environment. Rather than scrutinize me the instant I walked through the door, as had been the case with yesterday's inquisitors, he smiled and started talking casually about what life was like at Aramco. None of the trepidation that doomed me before impeded my behavior this time.

We chatted pleasantly about my background, the work environment, and what the future might hold. Just as I was realizing that this was going well and wondering if my two failed attempts yesterday might cancel out this one successful dialogue, Adnan addressed me with a question.

"When can you start?"

The query caught me completely off-guard. "Hopefully . . . soon," I stammered. "I just need to sort out some things in Riyadh. I can be back in a couple of months."

"A couple of months?" he repeated.

He then asked if I could come back sooner.

Mother packed my suitcases with new clothes and shoes and securely wrapped my favorite cookies along with other provisions. I tossed in a few of my favorite books, along with my journals and notebooks. I said I'd wait for Mother or one of my cousins to visit and bring the rest of my library, having figured—wrongly, as it turned out, what with the pile of guidebooks and manuals soon put before me—that I would have plenty of time to read for pleasure in the evenings after work.

I was also taking on another burden. And I felt that Mother shared my concerns, although she skillfully concealed her feelings so as not to exacerbate my anxiety. My departure from my mother's nest was seen as a radical defiance of the traditional social standard. Single people did not live away from their parents. Period. Not men, certainly not women. Not moral women, anyway. They left only to start their own family. And often they would marry and remain in their parents' home with their own family and children. No individualization. No independence. Separation from the flock was considered a wicked notion by traditional norms. Most adults become addicted to dependency. And that is no wonder as we spend the first two or three decades of our life dependent on our parents to provide for us and our teachers to educate us. And then we marry, and our spouses and children become our safety net. Carl Jung commented on this situation saying that "at a certain point in life, society asks this dependent little creature to become a responsible initiator of action, one who does not turn for help to Daddy or Mommy but is Daddy or Mommy."

Our psychological development is influenced by years of dependency that make responsibility an unfamiliar beast everyone wants to dodge. Some people become psychologically unbalanced, lost between dependency and responsibility; unable to function on their own, especially when removed from their familiar environment and comfort zone. I have seen many people panic with fear and anxiety when thrown into an unfamiliar place or forced to be on their own. They become incapable of thinking and making rational decisions about their situation.

It has been long established by experts in the field that "human evolution does not happen intellectually but psychologically." And if you don't have the environment to nurture this psychological development and integration, then you will be stuck in a world of inflated egos and neurotics. And there were so many of them in my world.

My defense for moving on my own, away from my family, was that I was living in the Aramco gated community with security and protection. Though not even that, I was to learn, could protect me from sick-minded men who would harass me in the workplace. Aramco single women living in the company compound were, in those days, considered loose and immoral by the local community. I am happy to say that this unjust and cruel attitude has changed in recent years to that of respect and admiration for independent women, and their critical role in supporting the social and economic development and prosperity of our nation is finally recognized.

Mother teared up as we hugged and exchanged our goodbyes. She was concerned for my safety, sad for the separation, and hopeful for my future. She promised to visit soon to check on my accommodations and she did. She continued to do that every few weeks or so, always bringing another load of domestic supplies and food.

At first, I shared a small house with two Armenian/Lebanese women, each with our own private room, on a tiny street off King's

Road, where the cinema, dining hall, recreation hall, and pool were all within walking distance. My house mates Rosie and Maro were neonatal nurses at the hospital. They were sweet, beautiful souls searching for a decent life away from their troubled history and the injustice they faced in their home country. We connected right away and became good friends, enjoying the limited time we had together before they migrated in the mid-1980s to the U.S., where they settled and built their families. A few months later, I moved into my own three-hundred-square-foot studio apartment, practically right on the golf course, then, two years later, into a four-hundred-fifty-square-foot one-bedroom apartment in a brand new building and again on King's Road, the main drag.

Whenever Mother showed up, she would take notes on what I needed, then come back with carton boxes carefully packed with teacups, trays, plates, towels, bedsheets, tablecloths, pajamas, dusters, kitchen utensils, sponges, bathroom loofas, doormats. I used to imagine Mother back in Riyadh, buying out all the housing-goods supply stores.

Mother's generosity didn't stop with me. Once she met my friends, she brought them gifts, too. Yes, despite my lifelong introverted nature, after a few months at Aramco I had befriended countless young men and women of my generation. Besides Saudis, I got to know and like those from elsewhere in the Middle East, as well as the U.K., America, Germany, India, Pakistan, the Philippines, Australia and New Zealand. All told, there were eighty different nationalities in the company, which made for a fun new education. It was a true melting pot of cultures and civilizations.

I must confess that I would have been lost without my friends, particularly whenever Mother would announce she was coming to visit. They would turn up right beforehand and help me scrub and put my apartment in order.

Mother couldn't get over how neat and tidy I'd become since leaving home.

Mohammad was once again at my side, this time to guide me through the orientation process. My first official day was April 13, 1981, sure enough, about two months after I'd met Adnan Jum'ah. My first placement was as a patient representative in the Aramco hospital, which the American oil company shareholders had established in the 1930s to remedy the lack of available medical care. In the beginning, physicians, support staff and technicians had to be imported, while state-of-the-art upgrades to the facility were added over time. The more than six hundred patient beds and six primary and specialty clinics were exclusively for the use of company employees and their dependents, who numbered four hundred thousand. As a patient rep, it was my role to make sure that every patient's voice was heard, and appropriate care provided.

The majority of Saudi women on the hospital staff were assigned to Adnan's department as other patient reps or as social workers or on his administrative staff. During my initial probationary period, Adnan assigned Samira, who was about two years older than I was, to be my mentor. I learned under fire by following her on morning rounds with patients, then spent afternoons filling out reports for review by our supervisor.

The ten or so other young Saudi women at the Medical Services Center had all been hired within a few months of each other, and most had come from the Eastern Province. I was the only one from Riyadh, while another came from Jeddah. They gave various reasons for applying to work for Aramco; some wanted to support their families and themselves, others simply wanted to pass the time and find a husband, and others wanted to build a career for themselves.

Of the friends I made, Nafisa Koheji became the closest. She was a beautiful woman, inside and out. She had lush black hair, dark thick eyebrows, big hazel eyes with long, thick lashes, a small nose, full lips and a well-defined jaw. She was five years older than I, and was divorced, with a handsome nine-year-old son, Yasir. Nafisa lifted my spirit and opened my heart to the goodness in people. She and I became best friends from the moment we met. Unlike most people, she was never judgmental and, as far as I was concerned, was always a pillar of support.

She used to say that "it is not our business to judge other people for we are not acquainted with their circumstances. We should leave that to God. He is the only judge in this universe." We were as close as siblings and, in fact, I had more in common with Nafisa than I did with any of my sisters.

Nafisa came from a very large and prominent family spread out between Saudi Arabia and Bahrain. We ended up sharing practically all our time together, and though we lived in separate apartments, we shared domestic chores and running errands together, too. She was a wonderful cook, so our arrangement was that I would do the dishes—and often babysit Yasir—and she would prepare one of her specialties, including kabsa (rice mixed with lamb, practically a national dish), maqluba (an upside-down dish of rice topped with eggplants, tomatoes, potatoes and chicken), lasagna, fried local fish and shrimp, and homemade carrot cake.

One of the many employee benefits was a five-week vacation, and I planned to make something special out of it. This was the first time I was free in my life to do whatever I wanted, and Nafisa and I painstakingly planned our first holiday together over the generous time we were allotted. TWA stood for Trans World Airlines, and we took the American carrier (may it rest in peace) at its word. In order, our itinerary covered Italy, Spain, New York, Los Angeles, Hawaii, Hong Kong and Singapore. Every destination offered its own great discoveries, whether it was the spectacular art and architecture of Italy, the Islamic and cultural history of Spain, or the overwhelming energy and steel canyons of New York. We had fun with the eternal youthfulness of Los Angeles, felt rejuvenated by the harmonious natural landscape of Hawaii, appreciated the fusion of East and West in the streets and shops of Hong Kong, and admired Singapore's discipline and racial harmony.

We were so energized and had such a good time that Nafisa and I became frequent travel partners for many years afterward. When Yasir turned twelve, Nafisa sought the best and most unrestricted education possible for him, in a cultured and tolerant place, and enrolled him in a boarding school in Switzerland. That meant that she and I started spending time seeing him there before we would move on to the museums, theaters and ancient corners of Austria and Italy.

Travel became an important part of my education, entertainment, and psychological development. I was thrilled to escape the homogenized culture in which I had been raised, to satiate my curiosity and sense of wonder. Experiencing different cultures builds your emotional resilience and intellectual hospitality. It offers a different lens through which you view the world. When people limit their experience to one culture, they become incapable of embracing new perspectives with intellectual tolerance. People's psychology becomes similar and their belief systems identical, absent of the variety that makes life so vibrant and enjoyable.

I traveled the world and ventured into new territories, curious about what made life with all its glory and mystery tick in different cultures and civilizations. I found that, regardless of color, taste, scent and scenery, and despite differences of religion, language and custom, people fundamentally shared the same dreams, moral codes and aspirations. People wanted to be safe and happy. In the distant past, people used to find happiness in the simplest things, reflecting peace of mind. And that is what I witnessed in my childhood. Bibi Lulu used to say "happiness is being content. Those who keep looking at the other side of the fence, die in despair." She repeatedly told me, "Don't give permission to others to determine your happiness. Only you hold the key." Wise words! But, sadly, the culture of consumerism has metastasized all over the world, hypnotizing people into believing that happiness comes with the accumulation of stuff.

My travel education showed me how the spiritual wisdom of past civilizations has been obscured by shallow political and social creeds. Worthwhile ancient knowledge has been beaten into the ground by a global popular culture propagated by social and mass media and promoted by corporate elites dominating the thought-scape. Their seductive, subliminal messages are dedicated to convincing the masses that happiness and well-being depend on conspicuous consumption and garish displays of status. The result is a lust for the same look, behavior and attitude of those idealized by the social media—especially, I find, in the big cities. Tragically, people all over the world have replaced values of the past with a monolithic lifestyle that embraces a uniform taste when it comes to fashion, food, music, playthings, speech and outlooks.

In some cases, but clearly not enough, we have concern for the environment and the welfare of others, but, by and large, what we have is a global culture increasingly dominated by consumerism and greed.

My mother and sisters loved Nafisa, too. Mother was particularly relieved that I had finally found a trustworthy companion after all my years of self-imposed isolation. In turn, I was also embraced by Nafisa's sisters, nieces and nephews and treated as another member of their family.

Nafisa and I served as each other's confidantes, sharing every little secret and providing mutual support whenever trying times arose. We celebrated good times, too. We shared the same moral principles and never took issue with each other when our spiritual philosophies drifted in separate directions. She became more devout in her religious practice. I, on the other hand, became more skeptical. That did not stop us from greatly enjoying each other's company. For thirty-five years, I relied on Nafisa for a welcome dose of optimism and was convinced our friendship would last for many more years to come. But this was not to be. In 2015, she was in Istanbul being treated for cancer when she contracted meningitis and fell into coma. Within months, she passed peacefully in her sleep.

"The tender friendships one gives up, on parting, leave their bite on the heart," Antoine de Saint-Exupery said, "but also a curious feeling of a treasure somewhere buried."

The void her death left in my life will never be filled, although I do take solace and tremendous joy spending time with Yasir and his four charming children.

Their good spirits carry on the legacy of Nafisa's kind nature, grace and goodness.

10. IN CONTROL

It took no time at all to learn the critical techniques of the job—much of it was writing reports conveying the patients' experience to management and translating the patients' Arabic to the English-speaking doctors—and I was sorry to find the everyday routine quickly grew tiresome. Worse, I saw little chance to build any fundamental skills that would support my career growth.

Granted, no one had informed me about the nature of the job when I signed to come aboard, but I would be doing Aramco and myself no favors with my flagging enthusiasm. I deduced that going back to Adnan and asking for another placement would not be a wise career move fresh out of the starting gate. It was also not in my makeup—not yet anyway—to speak up for myself.

Besides, there was a severe shortage of patient reps in the hospital.

So, I decided to honor our agreement for the time being.

One advantage of starting new was the opportunity to make a first impression on key people in the organization. This could end up being positive or negative, but that was a risk I was willing to take, especially in exchange for an opportunity to show my credibility and build my reputation. I began to explore the avenues at my disposal.

Aramco offered a three-year Professional Development Program for recent college graduates as a way of accelerating professional growth by training them for their target jobs. Over the course of the program, the PDPs, as the participants were called, were assigned different functions for four to six months each before moving on to the next task. I desperately wanted this training but did not want to spend three years doing it. So, I decided to self-instruct.

Step One was to sign up for a women's assertiveness training course, a series of group sessions held in a makeshift classroom every day, two hours a day, for two weeks. Our leader was Moneera Man'a, a social worker at the hospital. We had to be discreet, because emboldening women was not condoned in our world at this time. The dozen or so of us in the program shared an ongoing conversation in which I talked about my weak social skills and how my urge to speak my truth was stymied by a fear of repercussion. (I left my personal life and family out of this, concentrating only on work relations.) I said that I often behaved against my nature simply to please my colleagues and superiors, pretending to approve of actions that were tedious or wrong. By attending these meetings, I hoped to shed myself of my shyness and dispel lingering doubts about my self-worth and, instead, learn to speak up with confidence and challenge ideas that didn't make sense to me. The time I spent with the other women and Moneera provided welcome relief, as if someone came knocking on the door and woke up my inner self. My major takeaway was that assertive behavior requires three elements: a shift in thinking, a healthy dose of courage and self-confidence.

I could now actively change my reality.

One topic not discussed in the seminar was sexual harassment in the workplace. The very term dared not be uttered, because men were immune from criticism. A woman faced condemnation should she even acknowledge the existence of harassment and would be told it was her just desserts for venturing outside her home into a mixed working environment.

Farid (not his real name) was a senior physician in his mid-fifties and held in high regard by management and his colleagues. When the two of us were introduced shortly after I arrived at Aramco, he invited me to come to him with any question or issue that might arise. Only I never had to come to him. He came after me.

He began making his presence known by popping up as I made my rounds, then showing up in the lounge at my breaktimes and employee gatherings. I knew something was off kilter but tried to convince myself it was my imagination. Nonetheless, I kept my distance and remained professional, even at staff celebrations.

Given Farid's position at the hospital, when he asked me to come to his office to discuss business matters, I was forced to oblige. The business matters, it turned out, were purely invented. He would instruct his receptionist not to disturb us, close the door to his office, then sit next to me before scooting closer and pretending to peek at my notes— so close I could inhale his tobacco breath. One day, he wrapped his arm around my shoulder to lean in for a kiss. I could not shout or scream— that would create a scene, which was unheard of—so I pushed him away and stormed out of his office. He knew I would not talk.

Farid was relentless, smiling and greeting me effusively whenever our paths crossed and expecting me to do the same in return, which I did not. I avoided any chance of our being alone together and, if he asked me to see him in his office, I would bring a colleague and insist the door be left open.

Had I spoken up I would have been punished for accusing a man of his standing. I had to weigh the consequences. Only his side would be considered, then taken as the final word. It would tarnish my reputation and cast a shadow over my professional life, possibly my entire career. Anxiety, disgust and anger overtook me. Here was my wounded childhood thrust before me all over again, except this time I refused to let anyone rob me of my power and self-esteem. "No one can make you feel inferior without your permission," Eleanor Roosevelt said.

I carried on, somehow aware that, given where I intended to go, there would be other Farids along the way. How right I was.

After a while, Farid lost interest and stopped harassing me.

It seemed he had found another victim.

After a few months on the job, I decided to take control of my training. I scheduled a meeting with Adnan Jum'ah, in which I told him I wanted to hasten my training in preparation for becoming a fully contributing member of the organization. My plan, spelled out in a written proposal, covered every important patient-care function, from admissions to nursing, medical technology, central supply, housekeeping, meal preparation, medical records, surgery—everything. My training would let me see firsthand how the components connected and prevent some minor glitch from mushrooming into a major problem. I divided my proposed training into a few weeks in each individual division. In all, this would take twelve months. My plan was solid. I had done my homework and was pragmatic with my approach, despite still being relatively new to the job place. Adnan was impressed. He approved my plan with no hesitation.

What I learned in coming to him was that it is perfectly acceptable to deviate from the standard model, provided you deliver the intended results in the end. Standards are meant to establish discipline, consistency and quality, except sometimes some people and some things do not fit within the standard box. I saw this in school, I saw this with my family, and now I was seeing it in my job.

An alternative plan can easily be as effective as a conventional one, or even better.

As Mother liked to say, "There is more than one way to slice the cake."

The twelve months passed quickly, and in the summer of 1982, I began to work directly in addressing patients' concerns. Initially, there was some animosity between the patient reps and the medical staff, out of dread that we might expose their deficiencies. Fortunately, once it was evident this was not the case, I was able to gain their approval as a trustworthy ally.

The speed and proficiency by which I did my training impressed the powers-that-be and placed me squarely on their radar screens. My name started being brought up in staff meetings, another good sign. What those in charge did not know was that I was already finding my job less than challenging and wanted more. Apparently, someone heard my prayers. Management decided I was ready to take on more responsibilities and promoted me to Medical Training Coordinator, in charge of organizing and monitoring the progress of medical students and then providing status reports to the students' sponsors. My promotion was definitely exceptional because the policy did not allow for promotions to be granted to fresh college graduates before they completed three years of service.

My new boss was Dr. Hasan Johari, a gentleman with a heart of gold but also a serious stickler for details, which, to my surprised delight, further honed my skills. He also allowed me full autonomy to make any necessary improvements in the medical training processes. I was assigned a large office—with its own private restroom. I loved my new status and finally felt I had landed in my comfort zone.

Within a few months I exhausted every aspect of the job and began to contemplate the next step. It finally struck me: I wanted to be part of the planning and budgeting functions of the entire medical organization. I had the ambition. What I needed was a plan.

In the back of my mind, I was aware that Aramco offered scholarships for high-performing employees to pursue bachelor and advanced degrees at reputable universities abroad. My new goal was to earn a master's degree in business administration in America. I met all the criteria and consulted with Dr. Johari, who proved extremely helpful with the paperwork. I optimistically submitted the application to the career development department and eagerly awaited word.

I was rejected, a victim of timing.

"Women are no longer eligible for the company scholarship program," was the reason.

The severe rules put in place for women were just beginning.

The geopolitical turmoil that erupted in the late 1970s dramatically redefined the social landscape of the region. The Iranian revolution and the siege of the Grand Mosque in Mecca triggered a backlash to the modest progress that had evolved slowly during the 1970 oil rush, ringing in a new era of conservatism and the dominance of the religious establishment. Women were the primary victims. As a result, our educations, careers, social status and livelihoods suffered for decades to come.

In the past, the government's relationship with Aramco kept the two entities at a safe distance from one another. For the company to continue the privilege of its independence within Saudi Arabia, it became necessary that it observe social laws and customs, particularly those involving women. Religious authorities had already put Aramco on notice, having condemned the Western-style practices in what they called the "corrupt" workplace, one that "contaminated" the minds of young women by filling them with foreign ideology. Yet, try as they might, the zealots were unsuccessful in changing company policy. Aramco was a red line no one was allowed to cross without the consent of the country's highest powers.

Nevertheless, the company was sensitive not to provoke and give the religious establishment an excuse to meddle, so Aramco's attitude toward women needed to reflect the general mood. Painful restrictive measures were instituted to fend off criticism. Consequently, recruitment for women was suspended in the mid-1980s, except for a few positions in Medical Services. Promotions and job assignments in core areas nearly ground to a halt. Housing for Saudi women in the company's residential compounds was also suspended; single females already living there were ordered to relocate to a building under monitored 24/7 security. Apartments there were a tight four hundred fifty square feet. Those of us not adhering to the edict would have to find their own place to live outside the gates—which, for a single woman, was an impossibility.

To its credit, Aramco did not segregate the sexes in the workplace, although new dress codes were imposed on women, calling for modesty and propriety. Hijabs and cloaks were never required. Looking back, I see that the pushbacks put forth by Aramco were admirable, considering what it was up against.

As it was happening, though, we female employees did not see it as such.

Naïve and foolish, we complained about the unfair treatment, unmindful that the measures were necessary to protect our employment.

I was not deterred by the rejection letter from Career Development. My recourse would be to go after my MBA on my own, using my personal savings. My entire life I had never been a spender, and now that I was making money, I could still hear Mother's voice advising me when I was only nine, "A shiny penny will become useful on a dark day, and I guarantee the day will come when you need money for something important." As if Mother's words weren't enough, I also learned from Confucius, "He who will not economize will have to agonize."

With regards to my job, two options were on the table: resign, or secure a two-year leave of absence. If I quit, there was the strong possibility of not being re-hired because of the employment restrictions on women. The last thing I wanted was to get a degree and then return to Riyadh with the prospect of no job. But, again, I was willing to take that risk.

"If you are serious about getting an MBA, better do it while you are still young, before time dampens your enthusiasm," Dr. Johari said, being his usual encouraging self. He warned that my intentions would not be easily accomplished without the safety of a support system.

I dug into the company's voluminous Industrial Relations manual to see if any guidelines might be of help, or at least provide a way to detach myself partially from the corporation while I studied. The IR manual—we now call Industrial Relations by a more encompassing term, Human Resources—was divided into several large green binders that were guarded like sacred scriptures within the administrators' office. A lengthy form to explain my reason for the inquiry had to be submitted before I would be granted—or denied—access. (Today, such information can generally, and freely, be found on employee-services websites.) Should there be a green light, a personal advisor had to sit and watch me as I went through the binders.

It turned out, Dr. Johari had his own copy of the manual in his office, and he allowed me the luxury of sidestepping any watchful guard and leafing through the pages there. I found a policy that provided leave of absence without pay to employees for a limited period of time. We also found another policy that reimbursed ninety percent of educational expenses for employees studying on their own time, to be paid after the successful completion of their programs.

I could not have been more thrilled.

By now it was the fall of 1983, which gave me a full year to save up before the start of the next academic year. I estimated the costs and calculated what I needed. I did not want to go to Father for help, knowing he would not let me live in the U.S. on my own. When the time came, I would simply tell him I was going. Luckily, during this period, women could travel without a guardian's permission. (Eventually, such restrictions were imposed.) Mother, I knew, would understand, although she would worry about my being so far away. I told her of my plan only after I had secured all company and university approvals.

The approval process was long and tedious. Finally, the personnel department said yes, but it came with a caveat: I had to successfully complete the first year of school before the company would approve a second year of leave. I applied to American University and George Washington University, both in Washington, D.C., and New York University, in Manhattan, and was accepted by the first, but they, too, spelled out a caveat: Because my undergraduate grade point average at the University of Riyadh had only been an above-average 2.8, I would have to maintain a first-semester grade point average at AU of at least 3.0.

I did not disclose this stipulation to anyone, as I did not want anyone to question my capability and jeopardize my MBA, which, combined with my degree in English literature, would perfectly join the quantitative and qualitative intelligence of the left and right halves of my brain.

I completed all the required paperwork, packed my bags, and was ready for the next stage of my adventure. It proved to be the best investment I ever made with an incredible perpetual rate of return. The MBA, I was convinced, was going to be my passport to the corporate world.

11. AMERICAN STUDIES

Serine and I met in 1983, when she worked in the finance organization and I was gearing up to study in America. Astute and pragmatic—today, she heads her own private wealth-management firm in London—Serine had been brought up in Washington, D.C., where her father, Ibrahim Al-Sowayel, served as Saudi ambassador to the United States from 1964 to 1975. Her elder sister Naila was the bureau chief of the Saudi Press Agency, also in the American capital. After her time in the States, Serine returned to Saudi Arabia and while at Aramco, she, too, planned to pursue her MBA in America, at Columbia University in New York City. She was also due to start the same time as I, September 1984.

We set off for our American studies together and temporarily stayed at her family's home in D.C. I couldn't have asked for a better introduction to America; their house was continually packed with dignitaries and fascinating people, and Serine's family treated me as one of their own. It was her mother, whom I called Aunt Ibtisam (she looked like Elizabeth Taylor and was, in her own way, just as dazzling), who found me a one-bedroom apartment in an elegant building on Massachusetts Avenue, behind the lushly verdant Glover Park. Its rent, $900 per month, was a bit steep for my budget, but the neighborhood was beautiful and secure, and you couldn't beat the proximity to school.

No sooner had I moved in than very welcome guests arrived on my doorstep, Nafisa and Yasir. Nafisa wanted to see I was properly settled.

We did the historic sights of the capital for our own benefit, but mostly for Yasir's, and when the two of them departed back to Saudi Arabia and Serine took off for New York, it hit me that I was now alone in a place so alien and remote.

I was homesick.

Loneliness differs from solitude. Solitude had long been my constant companion; I had sought it out on my own and tamed it. Solitude is something that you seek; it does not seek you. Loneliness is another beast altogether. It can attack even if you are surrounded by the most wonderful people on earth, which, with Serine's family so close, I was. I learned that I had the ability to make friends and put that into practice. But loneliness does not ask permission before sweeping in and shattering your sense and sensibility. I did not realize its potency in manipulating one's perspective. Suddenly, you are not yourself and life around you begins to take shape from a perspective that is not your own.

"Loneliness fosters that which is original, daringly and bewilderingly beautiful, poetic," Thomas Mann wrote in *Death in Venice*. "But loneliness also fosters that which is perverse, incongruous, absurd, forbidden."

For the first time in my life, I was haunted by loneliness and homesickness. I was surprised at myself. I was also fascinated by the experience in spite of its agony. I wanted to chew on it, taste it, and then spit it out. It was not pleasant. I wanted to give up and return home. But something inside told me to hold on. That little voice inside came to the rescue again guiding me with sympathetic insight.

Thank God.

American University was multinational with a student body that resembled the United Nations. Nevertheless, some aspects of the school were highly provincial. Some white American students were not happy to be in class with Africans, Arabs and Latinos, even if these people were Americans. They nicknamed the cafeteria "TWA," to stand for Third World Assembly, because so many diverse students congregated there. Sometimes, these bigots would make offensive remarks when we passed by, but we learned to ignore and avoid getting into arguments with them.

This prejudice extended beyond the student body. One course I took in the first semester was accounting, my introduction to the subject. The teacher, let's call him Professor Brooks, was outright belligerent and unapproachable. This being my first go-round with accounting, I had many questions. He was not receptive to them. Worse, from the day I walked into his classroom and introduced myself, he was sarcastic bordering on hostile, spitting out cruel insinuations intended to belittle me. "If you make a little effort, you will find the answers in your textbook," he would snap, or, "I will not reward this culture of laziness. Do the work yourself." He thought I was illiterate and lazy?

I do not suffer from a persecution complex and got along very well with my other professors, so I really didn't know why Professor Brooks targeted me for such animus—until it struck me: He was bothered by my background. Well, I further deduced, that was his problem; I was not going to let him deny me my right to succeed.

I applied extra effort: first to arrive in class, assignments completed on time, quizzes passed with the highest marks. I was convinced I did equally well on the final exam, and at worst expected an A-minus on the final, which would determine the class grade. My grades for my other two courses, Marketing Management and Organizational Theory, were both A's. How wonderful it will be, I thought, to pull down a 4.0 GPA my first semester. How impressed my managers, friends and family back home will be.

Professor Brooks shocked me. He gave me a C on the final. This was beyond belief. Two students from class whom I had tutored both got Bs. I was enraged. My friends encouraged me to speak up.

I made an appointment with Professor Brooks and maintained my composure when we met in his office, suggesting there must have been a mistake in the grading system. I also let him know that those I had tutored scored better than I. He posited that there had been no mistake, I simply messed up and a C was what I deserved. Not only did I disagree, but I refused to leave his office until I received a satisfying resolution. I requested that the final be reexamined and reassessed. He finally understood that I was ready to escalate the issue unless it was solved equitably. He agreed to review my paper and told me to return in a couple of days.

When that took place, he said, unapologetically, that he had overlooked a couple of points and he had changed my grade to B-minus. I knew I deserved better and asked if he would allow a formal review of my paper, but he refused. I did not want to quarrel. I knew he could agitate other professors against me by labeling me a troublemaker.

It turned out that I was not alone in being disgruntled. Professor Brooks had a reputation among foreign students, especially those who dared challenge him. Those who did found themselves slandered by him in a whisper campaign to other instructors. As Socrates said, "When the debate is lost, slander becomes the tool of the loser."

I did not wish to be distracted by dirty politics.

I was satisfied that, in retracting his original position, Brooks had exposed himself for the bigot he was.

The experience of mixed company, although my first in a classroom, was not all that unique for me. After all, at Aramco I trained and worked in a mixed environment with men, and at home in Riyadh we frequently socialized with our male cousins. Being in mixed company at AU seemed as natural as life itself, reflecting a wholeness and unity in its duality. I can admit that, like most young women my age, I was a bit vain in enjoying the attention men paid me in class, although most knew the cultural parameters and exercised caution not to offend me with their flirting because of my background, being an Arab and Saudi.

My decision to take only three courses in the first semester was so I could accustom myself to my new surroundings. The classes took place in the late afternoons or early evenings, Mondays, Tuesdays and Wednesdays. Daytimes were spent studying either in my apartment or the library. Evenings were devoted to discovering America with my dinner in front of the television set. So many channels! News shows, talk shows, shows about people's dysfunctional lives, or sensational investigative shows about murders, kidnappings, and robberies. Anytime the subject matter got to be too much—these shows could be grisly—I would flip the channel to my favorite program, *The Tonight Show Starring Johnny Carson*. It was glamorous, entertaining and witty. The people who bantered with the show's handsome host seemed so accomplished and yet relaxed and fun to be with. It confirmed my conviction that life should not be taken seriously, and it is okay to laugh at ourselves every now and then.

Fall was about to turn into winter, and I found myself with plenty of free time every Thursday to Sunday. Wanting to sidestep the rowdy student social scene and having exhausted most of D.C.'s major sights with Nafisa and Yasir, I elected to spend my long weekends with Serine in New York. This was my first exposure to the great metropolis. If my introduction to American television was eye-popping, that was nothing compared to my reaction to New York.

Manhattan is this overwhelming combination of noise, crowds, dirt and stink. And yet, it draws you in. It is edgy. It is pulsating. It is *alive*. Suddenly, its energy will seep into your veins, without waiting for permission, and fill you with vigor and vitality. To enjoy New York, one needs to be grounded and unfazed by the madness and ruggedness of its mood, for you can easily be swallowed by its craziness and roughness. You learn to shrug off the madness and keep your cool. And then, enjoy it.

Serine, whose apartment was centrally located on Fifty-Seventh Street between Third and Lexington Avenues, was already an expert on city life. She knew what to do and how to navigate practically every street between Harlem uptown and the Financial District downtown. I fell in love with New York because Serine taught me how to respect it. Besides, I wasn't living in New York. I was only there for a few days at a time.

For the next few months, I routinely spent four days a week in New York. Immediately after my final class on Wednesdays, I would take the eight p.m. air shuttle from National Airport, only a fifteen-minute drive from my apartment, and land at New York's LaGuardia at nine, then stay until Monday morning. I took along my books and spent the daylight hours studying while Serine was at Columbia. Evenings, we might walk, go out to dinner, or hit a movie near Bloomingdale's department store, or take in a jazz or comedy club in Greenwich Village. Just watching people was entertaining—and educational. I don't think I ever walked so fast in my life, trying to match the speed of New Yorkers. Serine said that acting like the natives was the best way to avoid any lurking menaces. She taught me to be streetwise and stay safe, not that we ever had any trouble.

But all good things must come to an end. After months of shuttling between D.C. and New York, I knew it was time to acquaint myself with the people and my surroundings around school. Besides, once I had started tutoring, I needed to be available for weekend sessions in case the students needed me. All in all, I thought staying put was the stable thing to do.

To my minor disappointment, I found my MBA classes were not as thought-provoking as I had wished for. My high school proficiency in math and quantitative classes were more than adequate prerequisites for my studies at AU, and I was able to grasp the financial models and macro- and microeconomic principles easily. This meant that the time I saved on my assignments could be spent expanding my horizons beyond the classroom, and suddenly I had a social calendar. Friends and I spent a lot of time in Georgetown, shopping, eating, dancing, walking around, even people watching.

Any nights out uncharacteristically culminated in my tending not to hit the books until the last minute, but, to my credit, I would then address the texts with laser focus.

Unnerving as that could be, it helped me discover how well I maneuvered time, paced myself, and filled in the gaps in my schedule.

Second semester, I studied hard and managed to stay at the top of all my classes—so much so that my Managerial Statistics instructor, Professor Green, waved the final exam, saying I knew the curriculum so well that any test would be meaningless. With that, he gave me an A for his course. I also aced my three other classes: Managerial Economics, Business-Government Relations, and Financial Management, landing me on the Dean's List. I heaved a great sigh of relief knowing that I had kept my part of the deal with Aramco. Approval surely would be granted for my second year of leave.

AU's MBA program included six credit hours for field experience, which I would undertake over the summer break. I chose to return to Dhahran and work on my project at Aramco; this way, I'd earn the credits and generate money to help handle my school expenses. My topic was employees' productivity, with a focus on how to improve the performance of those who had recently graduated from college. My AU professor approved the subject, and I was good to go.

The first thing I did when I got back was show my first-year grade report to Dr. Johari, who took pride in my accomplishment. I also couldn't help but tell him about Professor Brooks, and Dr. Johari expressed his disappointment but wisely advised that life is full of such people, and we must never allow them to put us off balance. My leave of absence for the second year was approved without issue. I discussed my field assignment with Dr. Johari, who offered me office space and agreed to sign my weekly progress reports, which I then forwarded to my professor. My research in Dhahran—which I interspersed with visits to Riyadh every few weeks to see the family—was based on interviews, focus groups and surveys, and underscored the importance of ongoing guidance for inexperienced new recruits. Among my major findings was that giving them feedback about their work would allow them to assess their own strengths, and that showing them appreciation and trust would build their confidence and open the door for creativity and self-expression. Most importantly, training should be based on each individual's capacity for, and speed of, learning.

I got an A for the course.

Year Two at AU brought a different living arrangement. Friends I had made the first year, Yamila Rodriguez from Puerto Rico and Lamya Arrayedh from Bahrain, and I decided to move in together after finding a two-bedroom apartment in my same Massachusetts Avenue building. Lamya was a very smart woman with an undergraduate math degree from McGill University in Canada. She later earned her PhD and became a professor in her own right at Bahrain University. Yamila was a very cultured woman and an avid reader. She understood politics, history, culture and the arts. Later, in her forties, she decided to go back to school and study Law. She is now practicing law in Puerto Rico and is a partner in one of its big firms.

Our new apartment contained a spacious living room bathed in natural sunlight all day long, and two balconies overlooking Glover Park. The monthly lease was $1,200, half of which I decided to pay so I could have my own private bedroom and bathroom. (It was a good deal, as it was better to pay $600 than the $900 I was paying, and have good company.) Yamila and Lamya shared the other master bedroom and split the other half of the rent.

My room had a spectacular view of the park with its abundant shades of green. During the fall, the leaves turned to magnificent hues of orange, purple, yellow and red, and I would get lost in the sight of them. They would sparkle in a joyful dance with the breeze, playing hide and seek in the mist, under the sun. It was poetry for the heart and a feast for the eyes. I would sit in my room and stare at the trees until they swallowed me inside their world as I lost sense of my own world. I discovered the charm and allure of autumn in Washington, in that apartment, Avalon Point, on 1400 Massachusetts Ave.

Washington truly had its own unique beauty, with nature everywhere: brooks, rivers, and heavy foliage and trees that peeked at you from behind stately white monuments and buildings. No steel canyons like New York, but it was a good walking city like New York. Yamila, Lamya and I played, partied, and met interesting people from all over the world. We did libraries and we did nightclubs, museums and restaurants, city parks and ethnic neighborhoods. Two or three times during the week, Yamila and Lamya prepared basic menus, and pals would drop by to study, socialize, and eat, even if the emphasis was not always on studying. Weekends we would spend the day in Alexandria or Annapolis with a group of friends or explore the surrounding areas of Virginia and Maryland.

Over Christmas break, Yamila invited me to join her family in Puerto Rico. I was slightly embarrassed that I did not speak any Spanish after spending so much time with Yamila (Lamya, on the other hand, who headed to Montreal with friends for the holiday break, had picked up Spanish very quickly), but language barrier or not, Yamila's parents could not have been sweeter—or more festive. Every evening brought a feast of local food and drink either at home, their friends' houses, or at one of their favorite hangouts. Yamila drove me all around and we took in secluded beaches, fishing villages and the natural reserves. Puerto Rico is magical, with a stunning, shimmering azure sea. And the people are fun loving and know how to enjoy life. Music and dance are their life support system. People dance and sing in the streets freely and spontaneously, and greet you joyfully with unreserved friendliness and laughter. I don't remember how many days I spent on the Island, but my memories of the short time I was there remain fresh with fondness, often evoking yearning for the sound of joy and the scent of the salty humid sea breeze.

It was the perfect antidote to the snowy Washington winter that followed.

By this point, with my degree in sight, I had the confidence that I would graduate with ease. Confidence, like a business degree, was something I had ardently sought. Now I had both.

Shortly before graduation, I learned that my beloved grandmother Bibi had died. She was in her eighties and had lived life on her own terms, unfortunately within the limits women of her generation had to endure. She taught me to be independent and never to compromise my values and beliefs or surrender my power. I miss her to this day.

In August 1986, I picked up my diploma, packed up my things, and headed back to Saudi Arabia. I returned home with the joy of achievement muffled under a heavy heart, searching for Bibi's scent and warmth in the corners of my memories.

On my desk at home sits a black-and-white photo of her posing with her sister, my great aunt, Habayyb, and Mother, the three women who are the source of my inspiration and strength.

12. POTENTIAL

In the end, Aramco never reimbursed my educational expenses because, I was told, I did not seek the career development department's pre-approval for my field of study, a fact of which I was ignorant at the time. I had only received a green light from the personnel department. Hence, my two years at American University came entirely out of my own pocket.

Let me say, it was worth every penny.

It wasn't simply the matter of the degree itself, which, as time bore out, did prove to be the passport to success I had imagined it would be, even if it took the company longer than expected—some twenty years—to acknowledge my worth. It had to do with the satisfaction of *achieving* the degree, which validated my intellectual capacity as a woman, especially given the way I had been raised. My MBA experience strengthened my self-confidence, honed my social skills, and built within me a tolerance of different opinions—along with an ability to change my own mind when presented with the facts. Contrary to the preconceptions in my world, there was nothing lacking in my mental construct, certainly not genetically. In fact, there was nothing that could prevent me from surpassing men professionally. I had outperformed the male students at AU. All it took was willpower.

The degree also helped me put into practice business vernacular and financial concepts and hold knowledgeable conversations with business leaders. I now understood financial market dynamics, supply-and-demand forces, and their impact on our business, allowing me to think strategically and gain a competitive advantage over others.

I also loved America during my time there—its authenticity, ingenuity, democratic system, freedom of expression and ease of human relations. I loved how women had a voice and stood up for their rights, being ardent, outspoken and resolute. I learned to be strong-minded just like them. In simple terms, the timid quiet girl morphed into a badass woman!

America in those days had a good heart and soul, a caring nation that was not wholly consumed by power, racism and sectarianism. At least, that's how I found it, and why I returned many times and for many years after my studies there.

Today, when I think of America, I think of this expression by Descartes: "The greatest minds are capable of the greatest vices as well as of the greatest virtues."

And there was another side benefit from my degree.

A few months before his death, Father expressed his pride in my intellect, independence and willpower, and also his regret for not paying more attention to my education and potential.

That was the first time I had ever heard him apologize.

Upon returning to Aramco, I was assigned to the medical planning department, precisely where I had hoped to be before departing for my MBA. My situation, however, was not what I had hoped; management did not find my advanced degree to be an attribute, even though it traditionally was with the male graduates who returned with the same credential. Degree in hand, they were immediately promoted and allowed to assume greater responsibilities. In contrast, I was told I had to make up the two years' on-the-job experience I had missed. I could offer no rebuttal beyond expressing my willingness to remain patient.

Naturally, I was disappointed, but never was I bitter or resentful; there was no room for negativity. The company was merely reflecting the global corporate attitudes I had come to expect, that women had to put forth twice the effort that men did in order to get noticed. Also, it was not as if I could seek employment elsewhere. Frankly, there was no elsewhere—not with any decent jobs, at least. Fortunately, I was convinced that I'd make up the two years' experience in no time at all.

My new responsibilities placed me as part of a team effort involved with accountability and business reports that I then forwarded to executive management for approval. Overall, I enjoyed the effort, we worked well as a team, and I did not mind the long hours and weekends. In my desire to avoid the conventional, I was never one to fulfill my tasks exactly as spelled out. Yes, I would follow instructions, but would add unexpected enhancements. My instructions to myself were to tweak it here, polish it there, insert more supporting data, simplify the analysis, double-check the accuracy, and give it professional panache.

"We are what we repeatedly do. Excellence, then, is not an act, but a habit," according to the historian Will Durant. (The quote is frequently, but wrongly, attributed to Aristotle—see what I mean about injecting an enhancement?)

For many years, I was the only professional Saudi woman in the planning function. The director was Saeed Naji, who was demanding but fair— and not above challenging me so he could take my true measure, even though I did not report directly to him. He ended up being both a teacher and a big brother. He assigned challenging projects with tight deadlines and did not accept my work until he deemed it of superior quality in terms of language, logic, analysis and findings. Intellectual debates with him were educational and fun. We would discuss lessons from history, human-behavior theories, education, science, and a wide range of subjects, and our conversations would spill over and bring in others when we met by chance at the cafeteria for lunch. He wisely told me that two topics to avoid bringing up, because he never did, were religion and politics. "No one wins," he would say. "People become too emotional, and friends turn into enemies." Between ourselves, he generally won our debates for coming up with the most rational conclusions. But I won, too, by always learning something new.

My direct boss was someone I'll call Jackson (not his real name), from the American South. Few in our division felt comfortable around him, and I was no exception. He was insecure, deceitful, and openly antagonistic toward the Indians, Pakistanis and Filipinos on my team, despite their hard work and loyalty. He referred to them—and, therefore, to me—as "the brown people," and felt no compunction to disguise his prejudice against anything that is not white. Working for him was hideous and not pleasant at all. But at least it tested my endurance and professionalism. He once told me, a Saudi national, that Saudi nationals should not be allowed to live inside the company compound and mingle with Westerners. He regarded us as dirty, uncultured Bedouins with limited brains, and was never shy about saying that out loud.

"They turn this place into a ghetto," he told me about working at Aramco. "This is not what we signed up for." He bandied about the word "savages" and was convinced we would trash his neighborhood.

The U.S. oil majors involved with Aramco early on designed the residential compound and its amenities like cold water fountains, recreation centers, commissaries and dining halls for the exclusive use of Western employees. Saudis and other Asian labor were housed outside the camp perimeters in shacks roofed in corrugated tin and lacking basic hygiene and sanitary conditions. Before he died, King Abdulaziz ordered the Americans to clean up the camp and build real dormitories. The new structure was more permanent than tents and shacks but was no bigger than chicken coops stacked one atop another in a series of blocks. That changed with the Saudi government takeover in the mid-1970s.

Many Western employees, especially those hired when the company was owned by the U.S. majors, had been "company people" for thirty years or more. Some of them, either because of fear, lack of interest, or simply arrogance, never set foot beyond the compound, except to go to the airport for their annual leave. Their biases ran so deep that they were not even curious to see how anybody else lived on the other side of the double fence. Just to be fair and clear, there were also those cultured and tolerant expatriates who socialized with the locals, visited our homes, ate our food, listened to our music, respected our tradition and learned our language. Every society and nation has two kinds of people: the narrow-minded provincial fanatics, and the broad-minded tolerant friendly ones. Jackson represented the former kind.

Jackson's remarks about my own people were shocking. How dare he utter those offensive racist words before me? The only excuse I could think of was that he shared a misleading expatriate opinion I had heard before, that somehow I was not an "authentic Saudi," but a converted liberal Westerner.

I could not remain silent. "We have the right to live anywhere we want in our country," I told Jackson. "If expatriates don't like our rules and way of life, they always have the choice to leave. There are planes departing Dhahran everyday by the way!"

He was taken aback. But it did not teach him a lesson. If anything, he became even more snake-like. He took to keeping a close watch on me, looking for the slightest slip-up. That I could tolerate, unpleasant as it was. What I could not tolerate was him stealing my ideas and presenting my reports to management as his own.

When I finally reached breaking point, I barged into Naji's office and exposed Jackson's game of deception. To my surprise, Naji was well aware of the misdeeds. Apparently, I was not the first to raise concerns about the tiny tyrant.

Not long after, Jackson was dismissed, replaced by a Saudi.

Evidently, Naji had been plotting to swap out some of his expatriate division heads in favor of native-born executives, in accordance with the company's Saudization strategy. A Saudi Arab Management Committee (SAMCOM) was established in the early 1980s to monitor the expansion of the Saudi workforce and the systematic process for prudently replacing foreigners in leadership positions. Obviously, most expatriates felt threatened and were not happy realizing that they could lose their job sooner rather than later. Their insecurity colored their actions, and some could not hide their contempt for Saudis, calling us "lazy ignorant Bedouins" and using every opportunity to degrade and marginalize us.

My new boss, Mohammad, turned out to be a skillfully tactful and broad-minded breath of fresh air. His background was financial, as evidenced by his brilliance with numbers. He assigned me the studies of major capital projects usually handled by senior employees, which provided me a precious opportunity to present before the executive director of the medical management committee. With my new acquired business acumen, I designed my first-ever statistical model to forecast the medical population thirty years in the future. The findings emphasized that the current facilities had to be expanded physically in order to house new equipment. Unfortunately, the oil glut in the 1980s caused a collapse of oil prices to fall below $10 per barrel, which slashed Aramco and our nation's revenue. The medical project was shelved until our financial picture improved in the early 1990s, only, by then, I had moved out of the department and was no longer involved in the study.

Not that I always did the right thing. Sometimes I would look for short cuts to circumvent the system and complete my work expeditiously. Naturally, this did not always impress my bosses; and a few times I was reprimanded and warned. I remember, for example, one time when computers had just entered the workplace, two were assigned to our division. Using them was not an easy process, requiring a sign-up sheet and an hour maximum at the computer due to the long waiting list. Rather than deal with these annoyances, I purchased my own laptop, which quickly turned me into the envy of my colleagues.

But that is not what bothered Naji. He walked into my office and told me I was violating confidentiality and information-protection policies. He instructed me to erase all company information on the laptop and return it home immediately or the consequences would be severe.

For security reasons, we were not allowed to do company work on non-company machines.

I closed my laptop and kept it at home. I had two choices to finish my statistical models, either wait to use one of the two company computers, or work outside working hours when the machines became available for me to use freely—and that is what I did. From that point, it became a habit to start my day early and finish after the regular working hours—and that habit continued until the day I retired from the company.

One morning, I walked into my office and found something on my desk I never expected: a handwritten romantic poem. At first, I smiled, only to become flushed with anger. How dare anyone do such an inappropriate thing in the workplace. And who would be so foolish to do this? From the overabundance of male employees around, I had no idea. The workforce did socialize in the workplace. That is natural when you spend more than eight hours in a confined space with other people. Sometimes it becomes necessary to strengthen collaboration and teamwork. And in some instances, people, both men and women, flirt and behave in an unprofessional manner. It happens everywhere.

As for my own comportment, anyone who tried to flirt with me at work quickly got the message I would not condone such behavior. Yet, the love notes—which grew increasingly suggestive—continued to come. Who thought I would go along with this? What sort of image was I projecting? Was I inappropriate in some way? Too friendly? Someone, obviously, was after me, and the prospect was unsettling. I grew suspicious of any man who cast a look in my direction or crossed my path.

Before I fell into the old familiar well of self-doubt, I decided to uncover the offender—and deal with him. I did so by playing Sherlock Holmes. I staked out my office—which had a large window overlooking the street and parking lot—to see who was entering. I would drive onto the lot early in the morning and park behind some shrubbery, then wait in my car. (Yes, though banned from driving in Saudi Arabia, women had the privilege of taking to the wheel inside the company compound.) First, I saw that his car was the only one there at six a.m., before the official start of the workday at seven. Then, through the window, I saw him inside my office by my desk. I recognized him immediately.

The notes had developed into quite a stack, which I brought into his office and waved in his face. "How would you feel if I showed this filth to Mr. Naji?" I asked.

Stunned, he pleaded, "No, no, no. I am sorry. I had good intentions." He did not deny he was behind the notes. In fact, he blurted out that he was in love and wanted to marry me.

"Then, why act like a coward and go sneaking around?" I asked, angrily. "Besides, aren't you already married?"

"Well," he sheepishly replied. "Yes, I am."

"Is there something wrong with your wife?"

"No," he said. "She is healthy and fine."

"Then why do you want to marry me and break her heart?"

"Our religion allows it," he stated.

I heaved a heavy sigh. "Are you saying our religion allows you to break your wife's heart?"

Early Islam had reasoned that polygamy would support, care and protect women left widowed or orphaned when their husbands and fathers were killed in battles fought by the prophet and his followers as they spread the faith. It was legalized for a reason and that reason is no longer relevant, with many Islamic scholars indicating that polygamy was not intended to be practiced in modern times. Some countries, like Turkey and Tunisia, banned polygamy for degrading women and destroying their lives. Other Islamic countries have restricted the practice, allowing it only with the consent of the first wife, and only if she is unable to take care of her family and execute her marital duties. Rather than divorce her and inflict more hardship, the husband would keep her as an act of compassion (until death do them apart) and marry another. Today, polygamy is more prevalent in Saudi Arabia than any other Islamic country. It has nothing to do with the original intent of Islam, and everything to do with narcissism, lust and chauvinism.

As for my office Romeo, he proclaimed, "It is with God's blessing that I am entitled to four wives. Don't you know your religion? Do you wish to challenge God's judgment?"

I just wished for the conversation to end. "You are a pathetic and foolish man," I said. "I feel sorry for your wife for having to put up with your sick ego."

I let him know that if he ever crossed the professional line again, the consequences would not be pretty.

He didn't.

I received my second promotion five years after my first, and two years after my return from the U.S. But I was not jumping with joy; the delay had dissipated my excitement when the promotion was not awarded after securing my advanced degree similar to my colleagues. I was more gratified with the trust and respect that my work was commanding. By now, I was handling the majority of planning work for the organization. This wasn't as dry as it may sound, as my role involved developing a five-year business plan and economic analyses for capital expenditures, as well as generating forecasting models for our services and assessing their implications for the capacity of our facilities. The findings ended up in reports that I submitted to the members of executive management for their review and approval.

My big break came in 1989. Abdallah Jum'ah, then the senior vice president of Industrial Relations, asked for my transfer to his staff.

Apparently, he had heard good reviews about me and wanted to offer me broader exposure to the company's operation. He was also looking for talented Saudi planners to be part of his otherwise all-expatriate team.

My aspiration to become a major player in the company's core business was finally realized. I did not plan this move. I did not compete for it. I did not demand it. I did not fight for it.

I just worked hard, learned from every duty I carried out—and carried on.

As I stepped into the industrial world, I instantly knew that I was stepping into treacherous currents and my voyage was going to be slow and rugged.

13. WAR

Healthcare tends to be gender neutral. At least half of its workforce is generally female, and gender issues, should they arise, are likely to be subtle and less toxic than they can be in other fields, particularly the oil industry. There, institutional prejudice reigns unabated and unapologetic. Compounded with cultural and societal pressure, male prejudice—not only from Saudis working for Aramco, but also from among expatriates, some of whom came from conservative backgrounds—fueled a deeply entrenched conviction that women were unfit to be leaders. In the first fifty years of the company's long history, there had been only one Saudi female manager with a petroleum-engineering background. Her name was Naela Mousli, and she was promoted to manager in the mid-1980s. By the early 1990s, she had resigned rather than continually face the constant barrage of blatant discrimination.

This was the new, politically fraught world I was about to enter, but I was not concerned. All I needed was courage. "It is easy to stand in the crowd," Mahatma Gandhi said, "but it takes courage to stand alone."

True, I had every reason to be apprehensive. My eight years in the medical organization had isolated me from the principal activities and players in the oil business. I didn't know them, and they certainly didn't know me. My job transfer removed me from my experienced role in healthcare services and placed me in the vulnerable position of novice, where the odds were stacked against me. There were not many other professional Saudi women around to bond with and learn from. Then, there were the questions of the oil business's functioning system, about which I knew nothing.

How was it structured? How did its processes work?

Starting from scratch, it was essential that I cultivate a support system to navigate my way.

The wise thing any rookie could do was listen, observe and learn.

I may have been starting with a clean slate, I decided, but I would have to get my hands dirty.

Industrial Relations was a major function of Aramco, covering five support-services organizations: Medical Services, Community Services, Public Affairs, Employee Relations (later called Human Resources), and Safety & Industrial Security. My training called for spending time in all areas (except Medical of course) to familiarize myself with their particulars. I approached my training with enthusiasm and passion and strived to absorb every piece of information that might help me execute my new job successfully. The transfer to Industrial Relations left me highly optimistic that good things were coming my way.

Besides the improved corporate position, I was eligible for a beautiful new home in the company compound. After so many years of confining women to substandard living quarters, management realized we were perfectly capable of taking care of ourselves and allowed us to apply, just like the male employees, for decent accommodation.

Aramco's housing policy was operated on a points system based on job level and years of service. Using these points, workers could bid on new houses when they became available every month, with rents determined by the size of the space and their amenities. Basic rental furniture was available from the company warehouse, although most expatriates, especially the Americans, preferred to import their own from back home. The company covered all shipping charges to and from their countries.

I was thrilled at the prospect of moving from my tiny apartment to a sizeable twelve-hundred-square-foot, two-bedroom house with a small garden. My first order was to convert the second bedroom into a cozy study where, at last, I was able to display my books and my memorabilia from years of travel. The house itself sat in a quiet cul-de-sac in the Kenwood neighborhood, approximately seven minutes' drive from my office. The location, on Third Street, one of the major pathways, couldn't have been more ideal, with one of the camp's three recreation centers—each with a swimming pool, sports facility, track field and snack bar—right nearby.

I did not want my old belongings contaminating my new home, having projected that this bright new domicile represented a bright new future. I also do not like clutter. So, other than my clothing and the kitchen utensils Mother had bought me, the only items I ended up bringing were my books and my Nakamichi stereo system. Another truth to tell: I love buying furniture. Call it a very expensive personal passion. To furnish my current home, inside and out, I spent an entire week in 2014 at Furnitureland South in Jamestown, North Carolina, reputedly the world's largest furniture store. I stuck with American designers and devoted twelve hours a day to picking and choosing. I had the time of my life.

One of the main problems with shopping outside of the compound was its inconvenience. All Saudi Arabian stores, supermarkets and other businesses dealing with the public are forced to close their doors for thirty to forty minutes four times a day for prayers: noon, afternoon, sunset and evening. If shopkeepers don't kick out customers and close their doors, they risk losing their businesses. Shopping, for the customer, then becomes a race against the clock, and this was long before the welcome advent of online retail.

In setting up my new house, I chose one store for all my purchases, Habitat—the only decent furniture store at the time. It took a few weeks, but I ended up extremely proud of the final look of the place. Pardon my self-indulgence in describing the purchases, but as I said, furnishings are an obsession with me. My living room had matching sofas and armchairs upholstered in cream-colored satin damask, a large mahogany coffee table, and two glass-top brass side tables. The damask draperies were pistachio-colored with an inner layer of sheer white voile; my first dining table came with four chairs that were also cream-colored, and the master bedroom contained my first king-sized bed, with a magnificently carved cream-colored upholstered headboard. I wanted a light look for a relaxing sense of tranquility after a long, hectic day at the office. The living room had two large sliding windows: one, to the right, overlooking the front porch, and the other, to the left, opening to the back garden. Light filtered inside day and night. As much as I adored my new place, the house really had a number one fan in Mother, who brought me exquisite handmade embroidered tablecloths from Syria, Egyptian cotton bedding from Cairo, flowing gowns to lounge in from Kuwait, and the necessary basics: towels, placemats, and pots and pans for the new kitchen.

This, then, became my sanctuary after work, where the pace kept increasing. To keep up, I instituted Mother's plan for organizing, setting aside specific times for work, play, eating, exercising, sleeping, and so forth. I exercised for ninety minutes after work each day, usually at six in the evening. My workout regime—done with a friend, but mostly alone, which afforded me time to reflect on my day—varied from day to day and included yoga, aerobic classes, brisk walks around the golf course (five to six miles), strength machines at the gym or on the treadmill, which was strategically placed in my large bedroom in front of the TV. Then I showered, had something light like a mixed salad, eggs, or a cheese and turkey sandwich, watched the news or a movie, or listened to classical music and read, before collapsing in my grand bed at around ten p.m.

Grocery shopping took place after work once a week on Wednesdays, before the weekend. (Our weekends were Thursday and Friday before being switched in 2013 to Friday and Saturday.) Week nights I tended to stay in, but come the weekend I was constantly surrounded by a few close friends. They would come over and we usually ended up in the kitchen, putting its expansive space to good use. Having learned from Nafisa, I became a good cook, with my specialties being baked chicken with vegetables, moussaka, and all sorts of pasta dishes, such as spaghetti with meatballs, penne arrabbiata, fettuccini alfredo, and lasagna. Besides cooking, we also listened and danced to music and immersed ourselves in conversation about a variety of topics, mostly about the various personalities at work. We also had stories to share about travel (as single Saudi women living independently for the first time, we used every break to see new places), current affairs, our families, our childhoods, movies and TV shows, as well as any and all gender discrimination we were experiencing.

Once or twice a month, during weekends, my regular group of friends and I would head to Bahrain to shop in its upscale malls, dine in one of its many international restaurants, and get massages at the Ritz Carlton spa. To get there, we would hire one of the company's private taxis, or a male colleague would drive us over King Fahad causeway linking the Eastern Province of Saudi to Bahrain. Since the twenty-five-kilometer (fifteen-mile) causeway had opened over sea and reclaimed lands in November 1986, Bahrain had become a popular weekend destination for locals and expatriate employees in the Eastern Province as well as other parts of the kingdom. Its restaurants, stores, hotels, beaches and nightclubs provided breathing space, especially for expatriates who could enjoy a glass of wine with their meals without rigid Saudi restrictions.

Other times we would spend the day swimming and barbecuing at the company's private beach—not worrying about being prosecuted for being uncovered and in mixed company.

Aramco was more than its own municipality. It was a giant protector. It was like a mother embracing and caring for its children, so they could execute their duties effectively, without being preoccupied by the routine household issues. Among the benefits it dispensed, the company provided domestic helpers from India or Sri Lanka who were available for eight dollars an hour to assist us with house chores and errands. My hardworking helper, Ramoo, from Sri Lanka, and sometimes his brother Raja, cleaned my house three times a week, and they were my right arm. Later, as I moved to bigger houses and my workload and travel increased, Ramoo was at my side six times a week, four hours a day. Besides cleaning and running errands, he did my grocery shopping, stocked my fridge, and served my dinner guests. With his earnings, Ramoo was able to send his son, Dinesh, to the U.K. for his education and, today, Dr. Dinesh Ramoo is an associate professor at Thompson Rivers University in British Columbia, Canada. Ramoo and I were together until 2014 when, at the age of seventy-three, he thought it was time to retire. Disappointed as I was, I then sponsored his younger brother, Chandra, from Sri Lanka to work with me fulltime, and he is with me to this day.

To acclimate to my new job with Jum'ah, I was guided by two Americans and one Brit —Scott Stanaland, the head of the Industrial Relations planning staff (reporting directly to Jum'ah), and senior consultants Charles Haeussler and Barrie Doughty (reporting to Scott). They brought me under their wing, and I took so quickly to their mentoring that my orientation was finished in record time.

I suspect I was the first professional Saudi woman with whom they had ever dealt, and there was some apprehension. Stereotypically, to outsiders, Arabian women are a mystery: exotic, enigmatic, unapproachable and untouchable. Too many old movies, I suspect. One thing for sure, Scott, Charles and Barrie were puzzled. Here I was, a Saudi woman who dressed, talked and acted like a Westerner. For the initial few weeks, their interactions were stiff and awkward. They were adjusting as best they could. For me, the funny thing was, I would follow them casually as a shadow and pester them with my unending questions to learn from their experience and knowledge.

Over time, our relationship evolved into one of warm ease and trust. Scott, who taught me the company's planning function, was a Texas good ol' boy, and his gregariousness spilled over from the workplace to his home. Besides introducing me to people in our business group and partner departments, he and his lovely wife, Audrey, invited me to social gatherings in their home, so I could meet future colleagues and augment my budding support system. (One thing Scott couldn't teach me was his great passion for golf, as I could find no sensible reason to spend hours of my precious weekend in the excruciating heat and humidity all for the sake of a little ball.)

Charles, the Capital Expenditure specialist, mostly kept to himself, though he and his wife Judy were there for Scott and Audrey's get-together. (Charles retired from Saudi Aramco in 1998, and, in 2018, became part of a board of advisors to then American President Donald Trump.) In stark contrast, Barrie was a model of British reserve, with the stiffest upper lip you would ever want to see. But later, when I got to know him better, I came to realize that his reserve was just a pretense to discourage people from getting too familiar with him. It was also an attempt to hide his sensitive and compassionate nature, which other men usually disparage as a feminine quality. A gentleman, he lacked only one thing: tact. Still, he put his bluntness to eloquent use. Whenever I might start to overelaborate about something, he would cut me short and blurt out, "Brevity is the wise man's language. Keep it simple and get to the point."

Weekends, Barrie and I frequently hung out and talked for long hours while we washed our cars, worked in the garden, or cooked with other friends. I am grateful for the knowledge and experiences I gained from Barrie, which traveled beyond the corporate walls to the playgrounds of world cultures. Our conversation often revolved around art, music, history, philosophy, and even culinary delights as we sat side by side on our rooftops and watched fighter jets thundering their way to Iraq.

The airbase stood adjacent to our residential compound, and the bombers would rocket above us day and night.

This terrifying display of might and right was known as Operation Desert Storm.

Suddenly, the streets of Dhahran were swamped by U.S. military personnel, HMVs and artillery. The Americans and allied forces—altogether, seven hundred thousand troops—established bases in the Eastern Province to defend the Saudi borders, drive Iraq out of Kuwait, and protect the oil fields, which constituted twenty-five percent of the world's proven oil reserves. Within Saudi Aramco, we opened our homes to the troops, offering them a social break, entertainment, and food, although it came as a shock to Saudi civilians and our all-male Army personnel to see female soldiers working and cohabitating with their male counterparts, not only as equals, but also, in some cases, as superiors.

Cultural clashes often cropped up among the multinational troops. Saudi Air Force men spoke up in defiance when told to train with American women officers who had authority over them. Our government also had to bend some of its own rules. These included permitting Army women to drive their jeeps and be seen in their uniforms, uncovered. This triggered protests from Saudi women who demanded the same privileges. On November 6, 1990, forty-seven Saudi women took to the streets in bold defiance of the Kingdom's laws. "For half an hour, they drove their cars in a convoy around the capital city of Riyadh until they were stopped by police," America's National Public Radio reported.

I did not know any of the women who participated, but I do remember that the general public reaction was mixed. The majority of people did not support what the protestors did, thinking the timing of their demonstration was wrong given it was wartime and the country was in the midst of protecting the safety and well-being of its citizens. Personally, I felt sorry for the women because of the harsh backlash inflicted upon them and their families afterwards. All the women, and their husbands, were prohibited from traveling abroad for a year, and those women with government jobs were fired. "And," NPR noted, "from hundreds of mosque pulpits, they were denounced by name as immoral women out to destroy Saudi society."

As a peaceful warrior myself, I am never one for confrontation and violence. I believe there is always an orderly way to resolve problems. You can petition your grievance or engage in a civilized dialogue.

It may take time to see the results, but eventually the will of the people prevails.

To quote an Arabic proverb, "Constant hammering crumbles iron."

It took nearly three decades, but on September 26, 2017, women got their wish: King Salman issued a statement allowing Saudi women to drive, effective the following June 24, making mine the last country in the world to finally grant that right.

The Gulf War also brought something else new: American satellite news channels such as CNN and other broadcast networks entered our world, becoming the lone sources of information in the region. Their coverage, wholly supportive of the United States' actions, influenced our attitudes and convinced us to accept any position taken by the American government. This was but a small part of the turmoil brewing around us.

Iraq's invasion of Kuwait was wrong, and Kuwait needed to be liberated. The Saudi people were grateful for U.S. protection, but at the same time we were deeply agonized by the killing of innocent men, women and children whom the warlords dismissed as "collateral damage."

"Peace is the virtue of civilization," said Victor Hugo. "War is its crime."

In the aftermath of battle, tensions metastasized in the region, inducing fear in the local and international communities. Fear is a contagious dark force that can rob you of your mental faculties and leave you prey to exploitation by evil agendas. Allow fear to propagate and people begin accepting any desperate measure they think will make them feel safe. They will follow you like sheep because of fear and evil.

Crafty politicians and religious extremists play this card all too well. That's how they get their power!

Over the decade that followed the Gulf War, the fears, perpetuated by falsehoods about Iraq possessing weapons of mass destruction, escalated into the 2003 Iraqi War. Many peaceful alternatives had been available. Instead, a regrettable unjustified confrontation was launched to topple the Iraqi regime in a declared attempt to "spread peace" in the region. More than one hundred thousand civilian lives were claimed. No weapons of mass destruction were found.

The little peace that was spread turned out to be fragile and short-lived. The majority of us naïvely hoped the war would eradicate evil from the region. Instead, it obliterated the cultural riches and legendary heritage of Iraq and transformed the country into a veritable breeding ground for extremism, terrorism, death and disease. Today, thirty years after Operation Desert Storm, the region still continues to be ravaged by political factions, greed and poverty.

I know I'm not the first to say this, but the opinion bears repeating. Nothing good can ever come out of war. Nothing noble, moral, or honorable can justify the killing of one innocent soul, let alone hundreds of thousands.

"Mankind must put an end to war before war puts an end to mankind," John F. Kennedy said.

During Operation Desert Storm, my office work assignments were temporarily interrupted so I could help evacuate women, children and non-essential foreign workers out of Dhahran and back to their home countries. Expatriates, particularly Americans, were terrified by media reports that Saddam Hussein was coming to slaughter them and their families and/or release chemical weapons.

Among our first contingency procedures were establishing a rumor-control center and holding CEO town hall meetings where employees could obtain reliable information about the state of affairs. Gasmasks were issued, if only to give people a sense of security, along with instructions in how they could prepare for the worst inside their homes. Windows were sealed, kitchens were stocked with food and water, and suitcases with necessities were packed and ready. Amid the curfews and blaring sirens, we in Industrial Relations had to supervise logistics, priority lists, waiting lists, children's schooling, housing, food, medical care, and security. Our main mission was to provide assurance to the families that their safety was our paramount concern.

By the time Iraqis began firing Scud missiles at Saudi Arabia nearly six months after the invasion, most of the foreign women and children in Saudi Aramco had been evacuated. I saw them leave for their planes, with the tension visible on every face. As the war progressed, missiles targeting our facilities were intercepted by Patriot missiles, which resulted in falling debris inside and outside the camp. We counted our blessings not to have been struck. And no one was hurt in our compounds.

Being only three hundred fifty kilometers (fewer than two hundred twenty miles) from the conflict, we were not without worries but we did not leave or abandon our duties, especially Saudi employees. My family in Riyadh feared for my safety and wanted me to come home, but my colleagues and I thought it our duty to stay and support the company's ongoing operations, which never closed down. On the contrary, we had to augment production to compensate for the shortage of crude brought about by the oil embargo placed on Iraq and occupied Kuwait. Suddenly, 4.8 million barrels per day disappeared from global markets and oil prices more than doubled, from $16 to upwards of $35 a barrel. We were able to increase production from 5.4 million barrels per day to 8.5 million in only a matter of months and keep the global energy supply in balance while we also provided fuel to the armed forces.

The dramatic rise in production mandated that essential employees make themselves available around the clock. This did not prevent expatriate employees from leaving, but those who did needed to understand that they would be permanently replaced. American employees balked at this and took their complaints to the U.S. media, saying that Saudi Aramco was blackmailing them. In response, Saudi Aramco explained to war reporters that people were free to evacuate but their jobs could not be placed on hold with the urgent demands placed on us. As it was, the majority of essential personnel stayed and helped us meet our obligations. But the labor skirmish was just one more forfeiture to war.

Once the evacuations had taken place, the setting turned palpably grim. Suddenly, there were no children playing in the fields or laughing in our streets, and our stress levels kept most of us awake at night. Yet, we stuck together.

After work, a group of us would meet for a light meal and watch the news until we could take no more of it.

The situation united us as never before.

The war ended on February 28, 1991, but not before the Iraqis had pumped Kuwaiti oil into the Arabian Gulf, creating a massive environmental disaster that threatened both marine and human life. A major source of our drinking water came from the adjacent seawater desalination plants. More than four hundred fifty personnel from international oil-spill teams worked for several months in order to recover and clean up the spill.

The experience took its toll on nearly everyone, but there were lessons learned and people to be admired. Thanks to Saudi Aramco's crisis management plan, the evacuation procedure and, later, the influx of thousands of employees returning to work from around the world went seamlessly and humanely.

Working under these circumstances proved an endurance test in resilience and equanimity. I saw how our leaders got the upper hand on the emergency by plowing through layers of management and traditional hierarchies.

Without delay, they prioritized supplies and operations, defused fears with humor, and kept their staff engaged and informed by giving them the occasional reality check to keep them on course, creating a spirit of camaraderie, and effectively dealing with malcontents.

I was truly overwhelmed with marvel and esteem for the leaders of the company who created and managed a multifaceted structure that operated as reliably and smoothly as a Swiss watch. They were big men to me; they were giants. That inspired me to learn everything I could about our support functions and how they fit in the big scheme of the oil business.

Experiences like these, thank God, don't come every day. But when you are forced to go through them, you better keep every cell of your body attentive, or you will lose a precious opportunity to learn and ascertain your priorities.

As for me, I remained alert, and I watched and took mental notes.

My parents on their wedding
day, April 14, 1953.

Enjoying their honeymoon in
Beirut, Lebanon, 1953.

My Father, the
Emir of the
Neutral Zone,
1955.

Father (right),
with J. Paul Getty,
circa 1957.

Me, six months old,
1958.

In kindergarten, 1961 (I'm the self-conscious one on the right).

The overachiever; my first award, for being top in class, age seven.

Me (right) with brothers and sisters - circa 1966 Syria.

With mother,
1990.

Our nonagenarian
father with my
sisters and me; from
left, Mona, me,
Father, Ateka and
Asma.

Sheikha Althakafi,
me and her
children. From
left—Yousef, Sara
and Dana.

At the launch of
the Sirius Star
crude oil tanker
in South Korea,
2008.

Art Show Award
with CEO Khalid
Falih, 2009.

Operation review
in Abqaiq training
facility, 2009.

Management safety
review, Ras Tanura,
Saudi Arabia, 2010.

With HE Ali Naimi (left) and Khalid Falih (right) celebrating the college sponsorship program for women, 2011.

Receiving a recognition award from Kuwait's head of the Council of Ministers, 2012.

With former CEO Abdallah Jum'ah (left) and current CEO Amin Nasser (right).

With HE Dr. Ibrahim Assaf, Saudi Arabia's former Minister of Finance.

'Lady of Aramco' - On the cover of *Arabian Business*, November 2015.

Dhahran compound.

Ras Tanura compound.

At the Global
Competitiveness
Forum in Riyadh,
2016.

With my friend
Nafisa Koheji
in Zermat,
Swizerland, 1987.

Girls Scouts in
Dhahran, 2017.

14. ATTITUDE

Saudi Aramco was not only a producer and refiner of oil, but a vast, vertically integrated company with global interests in shipping, aviation, transportation, distribution, marketing and sales, real estate, education, health care, security, even media production, publishing magazines and owning and operating TV and radio stations. As a self-contained entity, its services and amenities supported local communities by building schools, roads, homes, parks, and power stations. All this I learned over my three years with Industrial Relations planning, and it came as a pleasant discovery.

What I was not prepared for was the unnerving shift that abruptly shook Aramco in the late 1980s, when the company was forced to adapt to the newly empowered ultraconservative movement in my country. In contrast to the caring, collegial atmosphere that greeted me at the time of my hiring, the office mood, even socially, turned cold and stern. When I first joined the company, most of the Saudi men who worked in the company treated us Saudi women like sisters, supporting and protecting us. Even those industrial workers at the plants, the kitchens, the commissary and the security posts were warm, kind and pleasant. The old cooks in the cafeteria and dining hall, and the coffee stations attendants would greet us with genuine smiles, and serve us our favorite food with open hearts.

These comfortable relations between men and women—casual downtime breaks and laughter in the corridors—quickly evaporated.

Seemingly overnight, people began avoiding eye contact and whispering their greetings under their breaths, if at all. Those responsible for this change were some men who worked in engineering, technical, and finance jobs and had aligned with outside religious enforcers. They were easy to spot, with their long beards and short thawbs—an entirely new look as far as Aramco's corridors were concerned.

The influence of these men went far beyond what they wore. These new arrivals took to harassing Saudi women and pestering management to impose stricter dress codes and segregate the sexes at work. To stem the ceaseless persecution, some women voluntarily donned head scarves and ankle-length coverings. Others went as far as cloaking themselves head-to-toe, as if they had never exercised the freedom to dress otherwise.

Only a few non-conventional women, I among them, stood their ground, unfazed by the prospect of a backlash. "Our attitudes determine whether we experience peace or fear, freedom or limitation, and to a large extent whether we are well or sick," American author and physician Gerald Jampolsky said.

I was resolute in remaining at peace, free, and healthy.

But the tide of conservative Islam that had swept the Kingdom had now flooded through the Aramco gates.

Once targeted, women at Aramco became the biggest losers. Mingling with men and learning of the latest goings-on in the field became impossible. Developmental opportunities and promotions were decelerated. Management made every conceivable effort to make women not only inconspicuous but invisible, because the last thing Aramco wanted was instability in the workplace. Women's aspirations and issues of gender inequality were no longer on the table. Behaving more like politicians than leaders, company managers first and foremost wanted to protect Aramco's longstanding autonomy. However, the invasion—there was no other word—by religious conservatives had the opposite effect.

It wasn't only enervating, it had the potential to be destructive, especially to the technical side of the business. Everyone was well aware that if the zealots were allowed to impose their restrictions, Western workers would walk out, taking their critical technical knowledge with them. Saudi workers were not yet ready to fill the roles carried out by expatriates, even though the company was recruiting and training Saudi men in large numbers. Building the necessary experience would take time.

At this point, at Scott Stanaland's suggestion, I was acquainting myself with functions considered the backbone of any planning job—the company's capital budgeting and policies and procedures within the Facilities Planning department. Some of the people I met in Facilities Planning, namely Ben Benson, John Mag and George Krigsman, were incredibly supportive and intrigued by my relentless enthusiasm and vigor. They kept pushing me and giving me bigger assignments to test my intellectual capabilities and resilience. And I loved it. Sometimes we would work until ten p.m. with full energy and without a hint of fatigue. The hours were long and exhausting, but none of us on the team, comprised almost entirely of expatriate men, complained. In fact, the work had been invigorating us. They pushed me to present to executive management and allowed me to attend management committees to observe our leaders in action. They were tough and firm. And I liked it. And they liked that I liked it. That toughened me up and helped me learn how to deter, with poise, the harassment and provocation that I would soon encounter.

Being the only professional woman in Facilities Planning, and a non-traditional Saudi woman with no hints of conventional attachments, I was the subject of all manner of threats and abuse from the tight group of traditional Saudi men within the engineering organization. Unsigned nasty notes were left on my desk, and offensive phone calls frequently disturbed my peace at home. (This was before caller ID.) The voices would order me to renounce my blasphemous lifestyle, or they would come to my house and have me arrested by the Mutawa—the special police force charged with enforcing the strict Shari'a religious law, and about as fearsome a group as one would never hope to encounter.

The Mutawa acted like a vice squad on steroids and were emboldened to carry out their own punishments. Three or four of them at a time, escorted by two policemen, would patrol the streets and, under the guise of "forbidding wrong," see that the Islamic dress code, prayer attendance, closure of shops at prayer time, and other restrictions were carried out. They ganged up on women whose faces were uncovered; stopped young men with long hair, took out the shears, and cut their locks; broke into private homes at will on suspicion of illicit behavior; and arrested people deemed not to be behaving properly. The Mutawa held so tightly to their religious beliefs that they caused the fiery deaths of fifteen schoolgirls whom they prevented from leaving their blazing classroom because the children were not covered in scarves and robes and accompanied by a male guardian.

Their power to arrest did not hold much sway in the office, although that did not stop fanatics from stomping into my office and, convinced I was an evil influence on society, reprimanding me for my liberal expressions. There were the usual warnings about my burning in hell if I didn't cloak myself, hide out at home, and repent.

At times it was almost amusing to debate with fundamentalists on why women should be submissive. Their response invariably boiled down to the tired, old rhetoric I'd heard in school. When I'd question their stance, particularly why I should hide and stay covered at home to protect men from having impure thoughts, their only response was a loud cry of "Nonsense." They had no backup argument to support their dogma.

Then again, how could they support such illogic? For instance, if men act like animals, not controlling their sexual instincts when they see women, why should this be a woman's problem? Those men are the ones with a problem and should be caged at home for they are danger to society! As for denying women positions of leadership, isn't history full of glorious female rulers who brought prosperity to their people? Meanwhile, last time I checked, most dictators and tyrants were men, and what they brought to their people was suffering and catastrophe. As a matter of fact, they also brought it to themselves.

"We can easily forgive a child who is afraid of the dark; the real tragedy in life is when men are afraid of the light," Plato said. Not that I bothered to quote him to these men. Why fan the flames?

The intimidation infiltrated every corner of the office, from the cafeteria to the conference room, which the fundamentalists would not enter if I were there. Or they would leave immediately were I to walk in. They also refused to ride in the elevator if I, or any woman, was inside. Rather than make eye contact—forget about shaking hands—they would gaze at the wall or the floor or ceiling instead. And should a woman be in their presence, they would shield their faces and whisper a prayer to protect them from temptation.

I learned not be defeated by their narcissistic insularity. If anything, I felt sorry for them with their insecurities about women, especially when it came to our emancipation. But what did they have against women? What drove their obsession with suppression? "Once made equal to man, woman becomes his superior," Socrates said. Was that what these men feared?!

Today, if such harassment took place, the offenders would be immediately terminated and punished, not only by the company but also by the local authority. They would be fined and jailed. The country and its people no longer tolerate bigotry and indecent behavior in the workplace.

Complaining to management would have been fruitless. Besides, I knew the drill. I would end up the one being punished and would be forever chained to non-challenging, conventional jobs designed to stunt my development. The damage these men were causing was already evident throughout the company.

Women were denied access to many organizations and positions. Recruitment of women was suspended.

This would remain the standard operating procedure until midway through the first decade of the new millennium.

Scott and I agreed that I should remain in Finance but only briefly, given my already-strong acumen in fiscal principles. The emphasis, once again, would be on meeting key people. The stint lasted two months. Next, Scott suggested Community Services—responsible for office services, residential and recreation services, food services, and amenities and services connected to the municipality business—because it was a part of Industrial Relations. I approached with hesitation because it would remove me from the stimulating environment in the core business.

As it turned out, it proved advantageous, with my eighteen months there, starting in 1991, a crucial channel to my future with the company. That it was so beneficial was thanks almost entirely to the organization's general manager, Ahmad Nassar, who pretty much became my life coach for the next twenty years. Call it the meeting of two non-conformists.

Progressive, witty and broad-minded, Ahmad was also handsome, tall, and fit as a fiddle from playing soccer. He was also the best dressed man in the company. Always concerned about the welfare of his coworkers, Ahmad appreciated my enthusiasm and no-nonsense approach, which he helped nurture. He also recognized my weaknesses and shortcomings, which he helped correct.

His watchwords were, "Capabilities alone will not make a leader. You have to be willing to put up the time, take risks, overcome obstacles and give it all you got. And never give up believing in yourself."

This prompted me to keep repeating in my head, "I am willing and able, willing and able, willing and able."

My assignment to a supervisory position in Community Services for housing policy and administration brought out resistance not only from men, both nationals and expatriates, but also from women, a type of discrimination that was new to me and an issue it would take me several years to analyze and cope with. But the daily bias was among the least of my issues. Being that this was my first supervisory role, I felt out of my element. At heart, I am someone who enjoys working on my own, who finds no joy in being bogged down by others or their issues. To state it plainly, I am not a people person. How could I be, after spending my teenage years in total isolation from the world around me?

Compounding my discomfort, the immediate world around me kept growing darker. When it came to the art of management, which the new job demanded, I had no experience whatsoever. Here I was, having to handle, manage and motivate people. But how? And what about gaining their loyalty while getting the best out of them? Not a clue. I wanted to create a spirit of camaraderie and be firm with troublemakers, but the courses I attended and the books I read did not truly prepare me for real-life situations involving leadership and organizational behavior.

But then a lightbulb went on in my head. I remembered balancing myself on the gymnastics beam when I was in school in Kuwait. I acted intuitively with confidence and without pretense.

It's amazing what determination can do.

Housing policy and administration function had me working with a small group of Saudis and expatriates, with the aim of improving outdated processes and simplifying procedures. In addition to my ignorance of the functions, I lacked any allies. The well-entrenched staff perceived me as an aggressive young Saudi imposed on them by management. That I was the first female supervisor worked as a double whammy. Shortly after I joined the team, an American named Judy requested a transfer out of my unit. She never told me why. I learned later that she found it demeaning to work for a Saudi woman. "We came from America to train these lazy locals how to be productive," she confided to one of her colleagues, who passed word on to me, not that Judy, whom I discovered was an all-round agitator, had asked her to. "I won't accept being bossed around by an inexperienced Saudi, especially a woman," was Judy's sentiment.

The staff went out of its way not to assist. Documents and files that I did not quite understand piled up on my desk, waiting for my signature. When I asked for clarification, all I got were dribs and drabs of information. In meetings, no one would actively participate, preferring to withhold information instead. Frustrated as I was, I still managed to keep my cool. Invariably, no matter what I needed, everybody came up with creative excuses not to come near my office, except for one.

Barbara was a middle-aged and seasoned professional. Like Scott, she was from Texas. (Aramco also had a lot of expats from Oklahoma, Missouri, Arizona—wherever there was an oil industry.) Barbara was also the longest serving employee in the group and very well liked. Best of all, she was not threatened by my presence. On the contrary, she was excited to see that, finally, a local woman had landed in a chief position, and she was eager to support me.

Barbara became my informal advisor. "They are good people, Huda," she said of the staff. "They are keeping their distance because they don't know what to expect from you. Have a friendly conversation with them. Ask them about their families, their children. Take in their concerns. They will come around. Just give it time."

Sensible as that sounded, I simply did not have the time—my mission in the department was due to end soon. Neither did I wish to give the impression that I was vulnerable. Acting on another of Barbara's suggestions, I called a staff meeting to hold an open conversation regarding any concerns. I ordered refreshments and cake, then stood back and listened. Among their chief complaints was that the status quo was working just fine, and what wasn't broken didn't need fixing. Clearly, there was an uneasiness about their having to learn something new, and outright fear that they would fail at it. They saw me as a transient intruder who would wreak havoc on their business and then disappear and leave them to deal with the messy aftermath.

"Whenever you're in conflict with someone, there is one factor that can make the difference between damaging your relationship and deepening it," said the nineteenth-century American philosopher William James. "That factor is attitude."

When it was my turn to talk, I told them how much I appreciated them, even the ones whom I knew resented my presence, and that I was there to lend support so they could excel at their jobs. I let them know that they were the chief asset of the unit, and my success rested on their success, therefore providing us with a common goal.

As a follow-up, I instituted an open-door policy and was generous with my time. Things improved significantly as a result. People worked collectively, smoothly and cheerfully. It is easy to gain willing commitment if you know which buttons to push. In my case, I behaved like a mother—yes, a bit like my own mother—never belittling or patronizing, but nurturing, concerned for the well-being of the others.

After a few weeks, Judy canceled her request for a transfer.

Scott and Ahmad never heard a peep from me about the dissonance in my unit, lest they question my ability to handle conflict or develop a negative impression about the staff. I had handled the conflict, and that was that. After all, I had dealt with the insecurities, inadequacies and anxieties of the challenging personalities in my literature books. The same could be applied to flesh-and-blood personalities. The nature of most people, I found, is fundamentally good. It is the social and cultural environment with which we interact that brings out the best or worst in us.

My stint in Engineering, Finance, and Community Services was complete, and I returned to the IR planning staff having learned a great deal about myself when it came to capabilities, limitations and potential. I discovered how easily bothered I could be by friction in the workplace. And I realized that the coherence and harmony that I always longed for in my daily life can, at times, be an unrealistic fantasy. But I also learned to fortify my inner strength by dismissing thoughts and situations that might foster negativity. I had no place for pessimism. Let it get the better of you, especially in the workplace, and you'll find your sleep impeded, your enthusiasm dampened, and your general mood darkened. If I am unable to resolve an issue, then I must resolve my reaction to it, protect my peace, and move on.

I also discovered that I possess an infinite supply of patience, coupled with heavy doses of compassion and tolerance, qualities that used to frighten me and make me feel fragile. They certainly are not appreciated in the oil industry's raw environment of which I was now a part. I resolved to toughen up. I started emulating the masculine leadership style around me, focusing more on tasks and achievements and less on interpersonal relations.

Unfortunately, that did not work out too well, as it unsettled my internal equilibrium. I became cold and competitive, alienating colleagues, including my supporters. It also helped fuel my detractors. Luckily, I soon realized that I had to be true to myself—and, more importantly, there was nothing wrong with feminine qualities of leadership: soft without being weak; sensible without being overprotective, assertive yet showing humanity.

Later in my career, when I enlisted a visiting professor at the University of Reading in England, Nick Holley, a distinguished executive coach for global organizations—and a leading voice in Human Resources—he told me that what we consider "feminine" qualities were critical for impactful leadership and they should be embraced, not repressed.

Nick understood my predicament and helped me confront my reservations about myself. He also understood my company's mores and personalities, and suggested ways of dealing with conflicts and adversity. "The world," he said, "is full of solutions looking for problems."

Although I enjoyed the challenge of managing people and triggering behavioral transformations in them, I was relieved when my assignment was over.

I further came to the conclusion that I didn't ever want to be in charge of people as a manager again.

15. RESILIENCE

My next assignment was in Employee Relations Policy & Planning, a mysterious black hole within the universe of the company, one that followed heavily guarded practices disclosed to only a privileged few. Each of its staff members was given a private office with a window overlooking the rocky hills to the north, as if to underscore the division's detachment from the rest of Aramco's daily operations. Responsible for policies and regulations relating to all facets of the employment contract from hire to retire—as spelled out in twelve densely worded Industrial Relations manuals—ERP&P was the legislative arm of Human Resources. Even the entrance to the department was imposing, through an internal corridor lined with steel cabinets overstuffed with files containing every last bit of contextual knowledge and historical company records dating back to the 1930s. I was denied access to these cabinets without permission, as I was considered an outside guest.

With its vast scope, ERP&P was divided into four divisions, each overseen by an American or British expatriate holding the title of Corporate Advisor. Working directly with corporate management, the CEO and the board of directors, these corporate advisors wielded tremendous influence in their purviews of pay and promotion policies, pension and medical plans, employee schedules, personnel contracts, leave, and any other rules and regulations pertaining to work.

I was assigned to the compensation division, which was made up of one Saudi professional, a few expatriates, and no professional women whatsoever before my appointment. The major reason I was accepted was because I was a staff member of the senior vice president's office—in other words, it was an offer they could not refuse. Even so, as an introvert, the sequestered assignment seemed custom-tailored to fit me, especially given its access to a professional, as opposed to managerial, track. Its chief appeal, however, was that it placed me right in the middle of the action. It required an intellectually strategic approach substantiated by quantitative evidence; its programs delivered a fundamental and long-lasting impact on productivity and the company's bottom line; it was critical to the company's mission (and yet did not require a science or engineering degree); and it served as an open window to international labor markets and global trends. Equally importantly, it provided exposure to high-level corporate management, which was pivotal to my career progress.

When I wrote Scott to request a permanent transfer to ERP&P, he was disappointed because he was grooming me to be a senior planner on his staff. Still, not wishing to stand in my way, he acceded. Less pliable was the vice president of Employee Relations, whom we shall call Salim. Not pleased by my transfer to his organization in the first place, Salim only bent because my assignment was suggested by his boss.

Salim did not appreciate women in the workplace, although at that point I was so low in the corporate ladder that I foresaw very little opportunity for us to interact. The job ladder within the department, in fact, had six rungs, starting at the bottom with four layers of analysts, then a specialist, then a consultant. I began as senior analyst, which was the highest level in that category.

To advance to the specialist position required special certification by the American Compensation Association, granted only after you've passed seven arduous exams whose two-day prep courses were exclusively offered in the U.S.

I was excited by the possibility.

David (not his real name) was the corporate advisor of the compensation division and my boss. My initial duties were to assist Dieter, the only consultant in the division and the head of European and Far Eastern compensation programs. Dieter was a German American, very sharp-minded and very precise. He taught me how to present a winning argument, how to compose a compelling letter, and how to focus analysis to reach a perfectly logical conclusion. I shadowed Dieter everywhere, trying to predict his moves and read his thoughts in meetings. He was preparing to retire soon and wanted me to be able to function independently once he was gone. I could not have asked for a more valuable teacher or experience.

Aramco's compensation plan was based on home country orientation, meaning that employees were paid a salary competitive to what they would have received in their native lands, plus a cost-of-living allowance to cover the costs of a foreign work location. To sweeten the deal, we used a Foreign Service Premium incentive program to entice people to leave their home countries and come work for us in Saudi Arabia. This was further augmented by free healthcare for the employee and his family; free education through high school for children; five weeks annual paid vacation; free ground transportation through a bus service; free recreation and sports facilities; subsidized food in the company dining hall and snack bars; and subsidized rent for company housing, with all utilities free. On top of that, employees who chose to live in the local community were provided with a housing allowance to assist with rental charges. In terms of the pay envelope, there were annual salary increases, saving plans, pension plans, incentive plans, and other job specific payments to cover the irregular work environment. The remuneration programs would also adhere to labor laws and tax regulations in the home and host countries, although, as a side benefit, there are no income taxes in Saudi Arabia. The pay package being what it was explained why most employees remained with the company until retirement.

As for the wives of expatriate employees at Aramco, to keep them busy and entertained, some worked in clerical or teaching jobs, while others volunteered at the hospital and in the schools or joined one of the more than sixty various special-interest groups the company offered, ranging from photography and natural history to environmental protection. Some ran their own private businesses, such as nurseries or catering, while others, with small children, were stay-at-home moms. For the majority of them, life was never dull.

An essential part of the ERP&P's job was having to make frequent trips to various parts of the world to secure our close ties with the U.S. majors (Exxon, Chevron, Mobil and Texaco), European companies like BP and Royal Dutch Shell, and any other organizations with whom we maintained interests. As part of this process, Dieter planned his annual salary survey in Europe, this time with me accompanying him as both an associate and a trainee. Our plan was to meet with oil companies in the U.K. and the Netherlands, and I could not have been more eager. It was to be my first business trip. I got my paperwork in order and obtained the necessary visas. I bought a new wardrobe for the trip to make a good impression on the heavy hitters we were set to meet. I also read up on the Netherlands, as this would be my first trip there. I gave it my usual scholarly effort.

As Dieter and I were reviewing our itinerary in his office, my boss David walked in and asked me to see him in his office. He looked displeased. I soon found out why. "I'm sorry, Huda," David said, "but Mr. Salim rejected your travel order. You will not be traveling with Dieter."

"Why?" I asked with all the composure I could muster, given I had just had the breath knocked out of me. Salim, David told me, thought it immoral for women to travel overseas without a legal guardian. Furthermore, Salim reprimanded David and my manager, Ali, for initiating the travel request on my behalf in the first place. He told them I should be grateful to be working for the company, especially because I was taking a job away from a man. Salim also said I could leave if I didn't like his travel ban.

I had no recourse. Dieter was disappointed, but his hands were tied. He continued to mentor and keep me abreast of developments during his business travel, while David and Ali tried their best to console me, but that offered no relief. My thought was, I would confront Salim, and then take my concerns to the senior vice president. Both Scott and David predicted I would lose the challenge. Salim had tradition and religion behind him. I had only impudence and no clout whatsoever.

David continued to extend his sympathy and promised change would come, perhaps in only a couple of years.

"Salim will retire," he said. "Then it will be fine."

He suggested I use this time to prefect my skills.

I raided the file cabinets for historical records of labor laws and our remuneration policies. I examined the disparity in employment benefits between male and female workers—and found that the gap was seismic. Women were ineligible for home loans, housing allowances, children's medical coverage, company scholarships, and company housing if they were married, because, under the guardianship system, the man was considered head of the household and responsible for providing these benefits. The company, therefore, considered providing these policies to female employees as double-dipping.

I copiously took notes and kept conspicuously quiet. I realized it was not wise to rock the Titanic while Salim was her captain, as he was now on the lookout for any opportunity to cast me overboard. Likewise, any attempt by me to highlight the gross inequities in our system would result in my demotion to an inconsequential position, which, in turn, would torpedo any hope of seeding changes from the inside.

As time progressed, so did I. My circle of colleagues widened, *The Economist* magazine became my best friend, and my professional network grew more durable, both in and out of the department. Nevertheless, I wished there were other professional women with whom I could share my stories and try out my ideas. Nafisa and I maintained our connection, but our worlds were by now so diverse that reaching out to her no longer seemed the ideal solution. Then one literally landed on my doorstep.

"Hello, Huda. Do you remember me?" It turned out I did. Sheikha Althakafi, with whom I had briefly become acquainted while we were both studying at American University; her master's degree was in Public Administration. Sheikha walked into my office with her dazzling smile that made her eyes dance with joy and her face shine with optimism. Sheikha was a compassionate and kindhearted woman. She extended herself beyond the call of duty to help and support her friends, family and community, and anyone in need. We called her Mother Teresa for her authenticity and generosity. She was altruistic and gallant, never acting out of a personal agenda or self-interest. She was smart, inquisitive and had unlimited drive to improve the status of the social structure, particularly in areas related to women's empowerment and development. She addressed these issues directly, by writing articles calling for social reforms, organizing seminars to discuss women's rights, and working with women's charities to improve the lot of widows, orphans and those in need.

We immediately started catching up. She was married to Ali Bugaighis, a Libyan-American with equal authenticity and graciousness. The two had recently joined the company and moved into the compound in Dhahran with their three children, Yusuf, Dana and Sara. Ali was a mechanical engineer, and Sheikha was hired into Medical Services planning, which did not match her interests but was the best she could get with the suspension of hiring women in the industrial sector already in effect.

I not only gained a new confidante, but a new family, too. Sheikha and Ali became the core of my social system and continue to be so, to this day. Weekends were spent being entertained at their house, where they welcomed everyone with warm hospitality. I witnessed their children grow up and become impressive and thriving adults. We cheered each other's successes, stood by each other at times of need, and consoled each other when we lost our parents and loved ones over the years. Sometimes Sheikha and I would travel alone for a few days just to get away from our busy lives and reflect on matters of mutual interest.

Eventually, Sheikha and I ended up in the same department. (Later, Sheikha became part of my team and played a critical role in projects for women's development, and we continued to work together until our mutual retirements, in 2017.)

In 1999, my manager was able to convince the vice president we had a shortage of experienced Saudi professionals on our staff.

Sheikha fit the bill in terms of experience and background—that master's degree which had first brought us together.

Salim eventually retired, to be replaced by Mr. Saud (not his real name), a moderate and reasonable gentleman. Saud was the product of a Western education and a prominent, open-minded family. I figured, finally, I had my shot. My priority was now to get the American Compensation Association certification because it was a major criterion for advancement in my line of work.

Under Saud, gaining permission proved easy, given his belief that women deserved equal career opportunities. I breathed a tremendous sigh of relief. I traveled alone and my first stop, before venturing off to other cities for my ACA exams, was Aramco's Houston headquarters, which house the Services Company subsidiary for engineering, procurement, research and development, and management—and is an important conduit connecting Saudi Aramco with its partners and customers in the U.S. The impressive office was itself a stunning statement of Saudi Aramco's global influence and prominence. Our undisputed standing in global markets was reinforced when I interacted with our international staff, who treated me with utmost respect, despite my junior position. Robert Manlove, the head of the remuneration division, brought me up to date on the company's

American business and, after hours, he and his wife, Harriet, took me to the best restaurants Houston had to offer.

One of the key perks of my job, as it developed, was that I continued to visit all corners of the States, as well as the U.K., Europe, and Asia, particularly Japan, South Korea, China and Hong Kong. On these travels, I saw myself as a representative of a greatly unrepresented segment of women in my country, and I wanted the world to know that we professional Arabian women existed and were leading our own lives. I was not out to be labeled a "feminist," as the term was not only frowned upon at home, but sometimes met with harsh consequences. Still, the one question I was asked most frequently was, "Why can't women drive in your country?" Alas, I never had a convincing answer. I'd point to creed and religion, but it really boiled down to one reason: Men wanting to control women.

I loved business travel chiefly because of the way I was treated as an equal in my dealings with our partners. This made me feel proud and whole as a woman. Then again, I was saddened that my professionalism and knowledge were better appreciated by foreigners than by my own people. Abroad, no one resented my presence, no one refused to shake my hand. That motivated me to give more of myself and strengthen Aramco's ties with our partners. However, I would be lying if I said all my business meetings were smooth and graceful. During one trip to Tokyo, a local oil executive looked irritated from the moment I walked into the room as the head of the delegation from Saudi Aramco. His answers were brief and stern, and he was not forthcoming in discussions. When I asked him how many professional women were in his company, he smirked and answered, "More than a hundred. I bet you don't have half that number." He looked at his colleagues, whispered in Japanese, and then they all looked at me and laughed. (Later I was told he thought it amusing that the question had been posed by someone who came from a country that so severely oppressed women.) "A little more than four thousand!" I answered as I watched his face freeze. The moment grew so awkward that I quickly complimented Japan's allowing women to vote, something my country did not. This did little to win him over, and he spent the rest of the session avoiding any direct discussion with me. The next day, he sent his regrets that he could not attend the second meeting. I never saw him again.

For the most part, business travel was a breeze, with a dedicated travel agent making all arrangements for (depending upon your position) first- or business-class flights, five-star hotels, fast-track lanes in airports, airline lounges, and transfers by car and driver. Expenses went on the corporate credit card. The company considered it important that its representatives reflect Saudi Aramco's power and influence in global markets.

We also were required to educate ourselves in the local culture.

After all, we were ambassadors of the company.

It usually takes three to five years to complete the requirement for the ACA certification, and many of my colleagues had to repeat the exams or remained unable to complete the requirements for one reason or another. I got my ACA certificate within two years.

It was at this point I noticed a discernable difference between my performance rankings, which were excellent, and my rate of promotion, which was not. What took male colleagues three and four years to achieve took me six. To add insult to injury, the company told me that it purposely limited career opportunities for women so that we would not hit the ceiling early on in our careers and stagnate.

Even David's words started to hurt: "Don't worry, Huda. You will reach the corporate advisor level before you retire."

Retire? I was in my mid-thirties! I still had more than twenty-five years ahead of me before I retired. You do the math. What a depressing thought!

Even with that, the corporate advisor level was as high as any woman would be allowed to rise in the company.

And there were very few of those.

Nevertheless, I did not let the injustice in our system distract me or dampen my energy. And my positivity helped me excel. I remained cheerful and jubilant, unconsciously raising my frequency and opening up my heart for inspiration and creativity to flow into my work. My hopefulness about the future helped me view every challenge, every setback and every victory as a learning experience. I was happy and optimistic. I relished the tiniest detail in my day: the seven minutes commute to work, the pictures on the beige walls of our office building, the smell of the coffee in the morning, my tuna sandwich at lunch time, my brisk walks in the evening, the old security guard at the gate, and everything that made life breath and tick with rose colors around me.

"The will to win, the desire to succeed, the urge to reach your full potential ..." said Confucius "these are the keys that will unlock the door to personal excellence"

16. ENGAGEMENTS

In spite of David's alarming words and my sluggish career progress, I was determined to make the best of my current situation. How gratifying it was to acquire new knowledge every day, for not only was that power in itself, but the fruits of this knowledge would also mean future freedom. The lessons learned here would guide me to make better choices in life and free me from the traditional psychological limitations that strangled my potential. After all, gaining wisdom and fortifying my independence were my chief priorities, even if this might be at the cost of not meeting a proper partner who would take delight in my non-conventional attitudes. And while my female friends and colleagues made marriage their number one priority—and were getting married one by one before my very eyes—my priority was protecting my autonomy and identity.

Under no circumstances do I wish to suggest that I never had any intention of marrying and "settling down"—so long as that settling down did not quash my identity and take control of my life. My path took me to four serious marital engagements. In every case, the men ticked all the right boxes: They were Western-educated, accomplished, cultured, and came from good families. And yet, every time we came close to saying "I do," I didn't.

All four engagements—perhaps a better word would be "entanglements"—failed for the same reason: There was no meeting of the minds. The men wanted control of the relationship; they were not impressed by—or willing to abide by—my autonomy, and not prepared to allow my identity to thrive. They each wanted a conformist and, in the end, were not supportive of my accomplishments. Worse, as I discovered, my defiance unleashed their personal insecurities born of their inadequacies, no matter how hard they had been trying to hide them. These traits were all too common in my world, even among cultured and educated men, who could not let go of the belief that they were superior to women. How could they not think this? Their states of mind were reinforced by every sort of available stimulus, from their mothers to the media.

Fortunately, I had a personal alarm system, though at quite a cost. Whenever marital arrangements grew serious, a dark mood would descend upon me, accompanied by nightmares and hazy thinking. Fear of losing control of my life became an obsession. Why would I want to surrender all my choices—how to live, what friends to make, what dreams to have, which places to see—I would think to myself day and night. Where would this put me? Someone else in charge of me, watching me, scrutinizing me, judging my words and thoughts, breaking my heart and spirit? Not for a day, or a week, or a month, but for a lifetime. No, thank you. Too many women in my world put up with that. The only reason I could think of was to have children. But even that was not reason enough for me. As someone wise once said, "I want what I bring to the table, so trust me when I say I am not afraid to eat alone!"

Carl Jung tells us that sometimes when two people are in a long relationship they start mirroring each other, causing one of them to lose their identity. The one being suppressed then begins to resist and resent the other and forces that partner away, so as to reclaim his or her own identity. In my part of the world, the role of the suppressed is usually, if not always, played by the woman, given the marital trap with no exit that she is placed in. No, divorce is not an option for many.

I wished neither to lose my identity nor to have to fight to reclaim it.

Try as I might to toe the line and be like my sisters, my friends and other women around me, I found myself in doubt. Today, when I look back, I feel grateful for the mistakes I made, not once, not twice, but several times. By taking these detours in my path to self-discovery, I was able to test the validity of my ideals and ascertain what were my true desires. "Mistakes," James Joyce said, "are the portals of discovery." What I discovered was that I had been hijacked by my self-importance; I wanted to stand out and make my parents, my friends, my colleagues and my managers proud of me. I also wanted to be a worthy *married* person. My heart recognized the truth—but my ego would not surrender. I craved the spotlight and external validation by trying to belong, playing the game, and identifying with the typical type of success sanctioned by social values. When the whole world believes there is only one formula for a perfect life, doubts develop should you have your own unorthodox beliefs. So, who was I to question my quest for a perfect life, perfect husband, perfect marriage, perfect children and perfect job?

How did I answer myself, I who had tried to excel at everything I had ever put my mind to? Every time another relationship failed, I took comfort by telling myself that perhaps it was not the right time, man, or circumstance—only to repeat the cycle once again, in what seemed an endless existential game of captivity and liberation.

In Sanskrit this is called "samsara," the cycle of death and rebirth to which life is bound until the soul learns the lessons of its destiny.

My chief lesson through all of this was, I cannot be caged.

I first met Marwan at work in the early 1980s, but it was not until I returned from the U.S. that our friendship deepened. Simultaneously, Mother had turned up the volume on her marriage lectures. She couldn't believe that in my six years at Aramco I had yet to meet a suitable mate. I was the last of her daughters not to be married. Mother was also hinting, not so subtly, that she would again like to set up an arranged marriage for me. I told her to forget it. Furthermore, I let her know, if she tried, I wouldn't show up.

So, there was Marwan (like the other men I am writing about here, that was not his real name). He was genteel and courteous, tall and solidly built, with piercing eyes, full lips and a roguish five-o'clock shadow. Obliging to a fault, he never knew the meaning of the word "no," and he quickly became part of my tightly knit circle of friends. Our group met after work practically every day of the week, and found ourselves playing racket ball, cards, or chess, or listening to music, or walking around the golf course, or discussing politics. Marwan was a walking encyclopedia when it came to current events, and he thrived on the attention he received as he tossed impressive facts, figures and theories at the rest of us. But underneath that ebullient personality he concealed feelings of dejection.

Showing concern for my well-being, Marwan called me two or three times a day at the office and at home, and I could sense that his feelings for me extended beyond friendship, although his feelings for me were much stronger than mine for him, which put me on guard. He was a good friend and nothing more—that is, until Mother intervened, playing the "You have been single too long" card.

So, I thought of Marwan. Why not? We got along. Had a good time. He made me laugh. He cared. He was safe. He was friendly. He was generous. He came from a good family. Better to marry a best friend than a stranger. Why not? My parents would be thrilled.

No sooner did Marwan notice I was open to his romantic signals than he proposed. I said yes—but we both agreed to keep the news within our little group until we felt comfortable with the venture. Marwan was over the moon. He spoiled me as never before, with flowers and chocolates every time he showed up at my door. I don't think there was anything he would have denied me.

So, why wasn't I bursting with joy? Instead, my chest tightened every time I thought of us as a couple. I could not bring myself to be in love with him, and something inside told me this was not going to play out well. This is what happens when one rushes into a decision, especially one based on what my head told me, not my heart.

What I discovered, only on the surface, was that whenever Marwan got close to me, I moved away. I did not know why I resented his affection and am afraid I did not deal with it in the most pleasant way. I became a total bitch, and my fondness for him soured into revulsion. I made fun of him in front of our friends, only he was too kind to say a word about this. Marwan was not one to protest. He was as sweet as always. So, what made me so ruthless?

Worrying about my nasty behavior, and trying to analyze it, kept me awake at night. Was I testing him? Trying to push him away? I didn't like the person I had become, but why didn't he stop me? I became suspicious of his behavior. No respectable person would tolerate being treated the way I treated Marwan. Was he playing some sort of game to trap me into marriage?

I opened my eyes and started discerning something dark and complex hiding behind his gentle and placid image. It was the words he used jokingly that alarmed me. "Soon you will be tamed", "Someone should put you on a leash." I suspected that his words could be a reflection of his inner thoughts and propensity. Furthermore, I was not in love with Marwan and pretending passion was no way to begin a lifelong commitment. Mother used to say that love comes after marriage with good companionship, but that was not a philosophy I could buy into. I believe commitment requires one hundred percent conviction.

Not wishing to be responsible for shattering Marwan's heart, I wanted him to initiate the breakup, only he refused. That was when the little voice inside said run while I was still on safe ground.

When I finally delivered that ultimatum that I would be his friend but not his fiancée, he did not ask for an explanation, but neither did he so much as pretend to hear me. He wanted to be with me at all costs, he said, insisting that we could work it out. Heaven knows, he kept trying.

Marwan knew from the start that I was not in love with him, but that did nothing to dissuade him. I told him outright I would never reciprocate his tenderness, and he claimed he didn't mind. For the longest time after I'd stated my position, he still kept trying to hold the engagement together, so I stopped seeing him and taking his calls. That's when it happened.

He came over when friends were around and announced that he had accepted my decision. When the friends left, however, he exploded. The terrifying rage he displayed—tossing things in my house to the ground and shouting in the worst language—was loud and ugly. All this time, this hideous side of Marwan had been hiding in wait behind his veneer of conviviality. For the first time in my life, I was confronted with someone capable of violence. He said he did not want to hurt me, *he said he wanted to own me.*

I said nothing, not wishing to agitate him further. Finally, he stormed out, sobbing. As he was leaving, my phone started to ring. It was my neighbor, concerned for my safety because of the yelling.

As time went on, Marwan and I made amends of sorts, but our friendship was never the same, and we never socialized again. He met a beautiful woman a couple of years later and they got married and had three children, but it was said he was obsessively jealous and controlling, and eventually she left him. He refused to divorce her, so they lived separate lives.

My hunch did not fail me.

Faris (not his real name) and I met when we were teenagers in Riyadh during a social gathering with relatives and friends. His parents were close friends of my parents. We then went our separate ways while the elders kept up their friendship. I next saw Faris at a dinner Mother was having at home during one of my weekend visits in 1988.

Faris was an avid reader (check) and a world traveler (double check) who approached life with an inquisitive mind (triple check).

He resembled James Joyce with his gold rimmed round glasses, wide forehead and prominent chin. His parents lived in Europe for a time, so he spent most of his childhood abroad with his family. I was fascinated by his keen intellect and philosophical convictions. And he was intrigued by my being like no one else around.

We connected immediately, and as the evening drew to a close, we exchanged phone numbers. We said our goodbyes when I caught, from the corner of my eye, our mothers winking at each other and beaming with hopeful smiles.

Shortly after, Faris and I started talking every day, finding our commonalities, sharing books, and planning clandestine dates. We became genuinely fond of each other. When he proposed, I said yes. The only people we told were our parents. Mother was besides herself with joy, thinking that, at last, her rebel beast of a daughter had been tamed. "I can die in peace when my time comes without worrying about your future," she loved to say.

Once again, though, my mind told me Faris was the one, but I felt no emotional tug. I was convinced my heart was silent because it was ready to watch my next move before performing a rescue operation.

In the following weeks, Faris and I discussed career moves, relocation and residence. Faris knew my job had significant potential, a fantastic financial future and long-term security, and was willing to quit his job at an IT company in Riyadh and move to Dhahran. He was not planning to seek a job at Aramco or any other company. He wanted to be free to read and study . . . and accompany me on my business travels.

As our marriage plans started to solidify, his true self became evident. Why had I not seen through his sweet talk? Underneath it all was jealousy, insecurity, even paranoia. Suddenly, he was taking swipes at my style of living, with such self-important comments as, "Women with liberal attitudes can't be trusted." He told me I should not attend business meetings alone with other men, because they could be wicked. "Once we get married, I will escort you to those meetings. It is my duty as your husband."

Faris had major emotional issues; paranoia was one of them; the other was a grandiose sense of self-importance. Why did I not detect his shortcomings early on? Was I again in denial hoping he would cool down after marriage or maybe I could fix him? Or was he so skillful in hiding his inadequacies to entrap me?

I did not recognize the man that I so much admired and looked up to. At first, I thought it was the strain of preparing to marry that prompted his condescending outbursts, but when my familiar nightmares returned, I knew the proper course of action. I called and told him I didn't want to get married and we had better split up. I honestly wanted the relationship to work, I told him, but the fact that we were both unwilling to compromise made this a very bad match. For once, Faris went quiet. He gave me no argument. He did not protest. He realized that he would never be able to conquer me, and I would never be submissive; it was a futile venture, it was a wise decision to terminate it and save everyone the pain and suffering.

Our mothers were a different story. They tried to intervene and mediate, but I did not give room to anyone to meddle in my business. I also didn't inform Mother of Faris's issues where women were concerned, feeling it would not be proper to say anything negative about anyone's psychological makeup.

So, I took the blame and told Mother that I was the problem and was not ready to get married.

The sad, or maybe amusing, thing was that Mother truly believed I was possessed. "It was an evil eye that casted an evil spell on you out of jealousy and envy," she used to say. After the failure of the next two engagements, she was dead certain that I was bewitched!

Majid, a wealthy businessman in Dubai, had divorced his British wife a few years earlier—this was winter 1991—and had his eye on me. He had been an acquaintance of our extended family and would occasionally visit during Eid holidays (Islamic holidays), which prompted my mother, aunts and sisters to whisper the magical M word in my ear. "A lifetime opportunity" is what they called him, also politely reminding me I was not getting any younger. Mother was convinced Majid had been "sent by God." Somehow their persistence was working to convince me. "The more you hammer the iron, the weaker it becomes," goes an old Arabic saying. Besides, they were all married; perhaps they knew better. I said yes to Majid's proposal.

"Don't screw this one up, Huda," I told myself, knowing that myself had an entirely different message to tell me: "Don't do it."

Majid was fourteen years older than I, distinguished and handsome, and constantly tanned. Perhaps Mother was right, long-lasting love comes with good companionship, and though I could look lustfully at Majid, I was not in love with him. Nevertheless, he and I decided to take a trip to a more open environment, a place where, though chaperoned, we could hold hands, and we chose Cairo, where my father was residing. While there, we discussed our wedding and European honeymoon plans, due to take place in the summer of 1992.

We continued the conversation by phone on a daily basis after I returned to Dhahran and he to Dubai. He said that once we got married, he would take care of me and I would never have to work again because he wanted me to be a beautiful housewife, raise the children, cook for him, and wait on him. Apparently, he'd had his fill of independent Western women with his first marriage and was now looking for something "normal", meaning traditional. We would live in Dubai. Neither prospect, being "normal" nor "become a beautiful housewife", was what I wanted. I shuddered but I remained silent.

I painfully gave notice to Aramco and shipped my books and valuables to my new residence. Management tried talking me out of this, suggesting I take time to think over my decision. For that reason, they offered me a one-year leave, rather than termination papers. I think, at this point, they knew me better than I knew myself. I told them there was nothing to think about. My wedding was in two weeks, and I resigned and flew back to Riyadh, where the ceremony would take place.

Two days later, with the gown, the guests, the venue, the food and flowers, and my honeymoon trousseau all set, I woke up. Yes, the old nightmare. "Do I really want to be a housewife and just look pretty and wait for my husband to come home so I can serve and obey him?" I asked myself. "What the hell am I doing?"

After the second sleepless night, I called Scott and Barrie, knowing they would be in their offices early. "I am coming back," I told them. No other words were needed. My resignation had not even been processed.

My next call was to Majid. I told him I wanted to postpone the wedding so I could have more time to think. He was not surprised, and he very calmly told me that if I wasn't ready now, I never would be. How wise he was. There was no quarrel and no blame.

And then I told Mother. She cried so much I feared she might have a heart attack. Then came the steady stream of aunts, sisters and friends to convince me I was making the mistake of my life. The atmosphere was funereal, there was so much wailing going on. Faris's mother even chimed in, telling my mother to take me to a psychiatrist. She truly believed something was wrong with me and I needed professional help. This was the third time I had dropped out of a marital agreement; fourth if we count my actual marriage at fifteen.

Mother barely lifted her head out of the Quran, from which she recited loudly whenever I entered the room. I felt sorry for her, but I felt no guilt; this was my life. When the news reached Father, he was preparing to leave Cairo for the wedding in Riyadh. He was surprisingly supportive. "Don't let your mother or anyone else to put pressure on you," he told me over the phone.

When I told him that I was returning to Aramco, he gave me his blessing.

I was packing to head back to Dhahran when Scott called, suggesting I take a few weeks off to cool down from this ordeal. But I had to escape the daily melodrama taking place in Mother's house. She kept looking at me to see if she could detect any signs of the Devil. When I did return to work, colleagues were surprised by my lack of sadness. Indeed, they were shocked to find me in such high spirits.

After all, one would think that I learned my lesson. Not really. I had to go through the experience one more time.

I had to be absolutely sure without any shadow of a doubt.

Rami and I first crossed paths in 1990 when friends held a social event in Dhahran. He was all about having a good time, could be cynical, even reckless, and definitely a rebel. In short, a lot of fun. I was fascinated. And we were about the same age. Cut to 1994, when we participated in a company project, he from Finance, and I from Human Resources. We grew to like each other. He wanted a family, and the pressure on me from my own to settle down had grown exponentially since the debacle with Majid. Rami proposed, and I thought, what could possibly go wrong? We were good friends, shared interests, had good times together, and worked for the same company, meaning no one would have to move or change jobs. I said yes.

No sooner had I agreed to marrying him, than the little voice inside me did not whisper. It shouted loudly. Only I couldn't figure out what the trigger was this time. I didn't look upon myself as harshly as Mother did, but I was annoyed with myself.

I tracked down the basis of the problem between Rami and me: our positions in the company. Mine was higher and with better prospects, and that great cultural divide—of alleged masculine superiority—was coming between us. Much as I wanted this relationship to work, as even I was becoming self-conscious about my track record in the romance department, I was not willing to relegate myself to number two in our sacred union. I wanted to be equals. This did not go down well with Rami. He let his temper fly, revealing his jealousy over my triumphs and a cruelty he had hidden well under his boyish exterior. In our culture, some men find it disgraceful if the wife is more successful than he, be it her position, salary, or stature. No marriage has a chance in such a situation; divorce would be written on the wall from day one. Rami demanded my unconditional support, even if it meant sacrificing my career. He then started attacking my looks and intellect. He made it easy to break the engagement.

Father never thought Rami was a good match and wanted me to terminate the relationship, based only on what I had told him of Rami, whom he never met. I was astonished; Father had never interfered in any of my personal or career decisions. Except for not allowing me to travel aboard for college, he generally blessed whatever path I chose. But this time, he sensed something he did not like and had to make a move.

Mother had mixed emotions. All marriages have their problems, she'd say, but eventually the partners will be rewarded with good children. Then again, she could not oppose Father's stance.

Rami's parents, it turned out, were also not happy with our plans. They resented the fact that I was a divorcée. So, the matter was dropped.

When Rami and I encounter one another by chance, which we still do, we show a liking and respect for one another.

I believe that the universe brought me together with these men to teach me valuable lessons about myself—and, if I might say, the same was true for them. There was nothing wrong with any of these five men, including my ex-husband. They all had beautiful souls and decent characters. They were simply behaving in line with their cultural programing. My success, autonomy and financial independence brought their personal insecurity and inadequacy to the surface. No matter how much they tried to hide their tendencies behind their thick masks, their chauvinistic nature would leak out at any trying moment. Once I scratched the surface and could clearly see their true nature, I ran as fast as I could and never looked back. "It is better to be alone than in a bad company," said George Washington.

Somehow, I managed to bring out the hidden demons in them, even momentarily, as if I were seeking a sign—not that I wish to place the burden entirely on them. I also contributed to the unfortunate disbandment of these engagements, by not being true to myself. I honestly strived to become a good partner by trying to emulate Mother and my sisters and seeking approval and love. Only, that was short-lived. I could not abandon the girl inside and was compelled to bring my full being to the table. I thought I could compromise. The men thought they could compromise. But then we realized that the wholeness and happiness of a partnership could not be fulfilled with acts of pretense. Both partners had to drop their masks and be who they were.

We all have demons inside and most of us are unaware of them. Until we come face-to-face with them and understand how they influence our values and attitudes in life, and how they affect our relationships, we will never be able to master ourselves. Baruch Spinoza, the Dutch philosopher, said, "I can control my emotion and passion, if I can understand their nature."

Very few of us stop and reflect upon the motive behind our thoughts and emotions. Typically, we are more preoccupied by other people's behavior than our own —judging and condemning what does not reflect our own ideology and standards. Rarely do we look in the mirror and deal with our demons and shortcomings. We only see what is wrong with others. We tell ourselves we are alright, there is nothing wrong with us, it is always someone else's fault or problem.

"What the superior man seeks is in himself," Confucius said. "What the ordinary man seeks is in others."

By the same token, I have not given up seeking love.

That would be like giving up life.

17. MOTHER

The more I relished my independent life in Dhahran, the more the visits to Riyadh became difficult. My monthly trips were to see my family, and usually I would spend no more than the weekend, though I understood how important these trips were to Mother. She not only enjoyed the opportunity to feed and pamper me, but she saw my visits as a tangible example and sustainment of our strong link and our love. Even so, Riyadh's mundane pulse drained me, and my journeys home left me wondering if I had ever felt happy there. The city represented someplace where I had merely existed, frustrated and overwhelmed by not belonging. Terrible memories, too; not just of Wahid, lost friendships and a premature marriage, but of the general sense of feeling caged in. The simple fact was, I did not like living in my parents' house. I did not like being crowded, with no privacy, and forced to follow someone else's lifestyle.

Little did I know that my worst memory of Riyadh was yet to come. Mother and I were having tea on one of my regular visits in 1995, and I could tell something was amiss. She looked disturbed and not her usual genial self. I kept studying her face for any clue of what might be the problem, and if I didn't know Mother better, I would have said that I saw fear. Finally, the teacup seemed to freeze in her hand. After a silence, she unloaded her secret to me.

"I have a large lump in my breast," she told me in a nervous whisper. "I have overlooked it for some time, but now it is growing fast."

I realize, now, that in that instant we both plunged into a state of denial. Mother was rarely ill. I can't remember ever seeing her sick in bed. Perhaps she had not been well at times, but she would never let it show. Mother would never allow us to think she was suffering. She would shield us from that. Mother was too strong to get sick. Mother was invulnerable.

"Probably it is nothing," I told her. "But you should get it checked as soon as possible." I so disavowed myself of thinking that something could happen to Mother that I really did not give her self-diagnosis much thought. Her lump would go away as mysteriously as it came on. "Mother is strong. Nothing can happen to her," I told myself.

To compensate for only having two brothers and no sister, Mother spent her life gathering many girlfriends around her, and she was close to her cousins, not that she would ask for their help in any time of need. Mother was too proud and independent. But there never was a time of need. Mother always found a way. When she enrolled in night school in Kuwait, attending classes three times a week, wanting to improve her life, she would go for two hours after supper and leave my eldest brother in charge of the rest of us. I was no more than twelve when she would ask me to review her homework and assist with math and grammar problems. In 1970, Mother took driving lessons so she could drive the six of us around, after my younger sister Asma got off the school bus and was hit by a car. Father was not around to drive us, and the only means of transportation were taxis. The only thing that got in the way of Mother driving was our move to Riyadh.

Nothing could stop Mother.

Surely, not cancer.

Shortly after our conversation over tea, a doctor confirmed Mother's tumor was malignant and, following its surgical removal, she embarked on a treatment of chemotherapy and radiation. This went on for about a year. Never once did she complain. Father was in Cairo and never made aware of her condition. I believe Mother was afraid of his reaction—afraid that he would remain passive and not react to how serious her illness was. She saw no need to add to her pain.

For a time, Mother improved, and for that, Mother thanked God. She also sought traditional advice from the older women in the community regarding herbal treatments and diet, which, combined with her positivity and cheerfulness, doubtlessly added years to her life. Although we all secretly knew she was living under the sword of Damocles.

Four years later, her faith unshaken, Mother relapsed. This time the cancer was ferocious and spread to her bones. The doctors started her again on chemo and radiation, but she refused to stay in bed, believing that would be a sign of giving up. I stepped up my visits to see her, despite my heavier workload in Dhahran, yet remained in as much denial as I was in when she first discovered her lump. My sisters, fortunately, were near to lend support, and my elder sister Ateka, who had divorced, was living in Mother's house with her two children, so Mother was never alone.

But the cancer started winning, and we could see her wither and withdraw inside. She finally decided to alert Father, who, now in his nineties, was becoming weak and fragile and ready to come home to Riyadh. I'm not aware how he took the news when he first heard of Mother's illness, but by the time I saw him he was impervious and impassive. Emotions were for weak women in Father's world. He wasn't even moved by death; it was our fate, so why make a big deal of it, he said. He did not attend his own mother's funeral, although he was in the midst of travel and easily could have changed his plans. He said that canceling his trip would not bring her back. Although he was back to living in the house he shared with Mother, the two maintained separate living quarters.

I could not stand idly by. Thanks to the Aramco office in Houston, we got Mother into that city's MD Anderson Cancer Center, with my pilot brother, Muntaser, the eldest, escorting and staying with her in Texas. I remained in Dhahran, hoping to hear good news, but that was never the case. The Houston physicians acknowledged that the doctors at King Faisal Specialist Hospital in Riyadh had provided Mother with proper treatment, but her cancer had advanced to Stage Four, and there was little anyone could do. She returned home and carried on with her life for about ten months, after which she became permanently bedridden in her room, drifting in and out of consciousness. Finally, it was time to take her back to the hospital, where she slipped into a coma.

I had taken time off from work to be with her and I slept in her room at the hospital. Her doctor was impressed that she held on for as long as she did. "She does not want to let go," he told the family. All six of us children were there. "Is there something about her life, or someone, that be making her hang around? Any unresolved issues?"

We were not aware of any. Mother simply loved us too much to let go. True, none of her children had perfect lives—lives don't come that way—and she likely also thought we all needed her help. I would not have my career if she had not brought the newspaper ad to me. Who made sure I was living properly in Dhahran and was circulating with the proper kind of people? Since I was the one who did not have a family of her own to take care of, as her other children did, the responsibility fell to me to be the grown-up. I had to be the one to tell Mother it was perfectly all right to let go.

I woke up early that day. I lay down beside her and held her close. She looked so frail and pale in that hospital bed, which seemed to grow larger and envelop her. The suffering inside showed in her face, even behind her closed eyelids. But the hurt was not strictly from the disease. "I am not dying of cancer," she said toward the very end. "I am dying of disappointment and defeat."

Mother had deserved a better life. I pray she found it in the next one. As she was slipping away that morning, I kissed every corner of a face that had been stamped by the brutality of time. Coming as close as I could to her ear, I whispered a verse from the Quran that is usually cited when one is near death: "O, comforted spirit, return to your God content and gratified; and join my devotees, pass into my heaven."

I told her I loved her and asked for her forgiveness. One by one, my sisters and close friends arrived a few hours later with soup and pastries to break the fast with the sunset prayer, as this was during the holy month of Ramadan, when all Muslims are required to fast from sunrise to sunset. A few minutes later, surrounded by her loved ones, Mother gasped her last breath, and her soul was set free to ascend to its next destination. It was around six in the evening, Saturday, December 16, 2000, the twentieth of Ramadan 1421 in the Hejra calendar.

Mother was only seventy-four.

Father was home when we returned from the hospital that evening. He received the news as if he were expecting it. His only words were, "God bless her soul. May she rest in peace. We are all walking the same path." He did not shed a single tear.

We immediately notified our aunts, uncles, cousins and close friends so they could arrange to come to the funeral the next day. In Islam, the dead are buried within twenty-four hours of their death—there is no viewing or visitation—and the services for Mother followed specific ritual. The day after Mother passed, about forty of us went to the mosque where her body had been brought so that the women could wash and prepare her for burial. My brothers and the other men waited in the men's section of the mosque to perform the funeral prayer, asking that Allah have mercy, not only on the deceased, but also on all deceased Muslims. Father stayed home. Mother's body had been placed on a large table covered with a light cloth when I walked in and saw her in that surreal state. A hefty woman in charge of the bath was waiting to guide and assist about five of us as the other women went off to say their prayers. She handed us wash cloths, started pouring heated water over Mother's lifeless body, and showed us how to protect Mother's dignity as we prepared her. I had never seen a dead body before, let alone touched one, and this was my own mother. Melancholy overwhelmed me, to the point I could barely hear the invocation over the weeping by the women surrounding me.

Mother looked as if she were asleep to me. I was not yet ready to cry. I had to be the strong one for the others, especially when one of my aunts let out a loud wail and fainted to the floor. She was taken to safety with the women in the prayer room.

When we finished washing Mother, it was time to shroud the corpse in a simple white cotton cloth. Before covering her face, about fifteen women came in one by one to pay their respects. I kissed Mother's eyes and forehead before her face forever disappeared behind the white cotton cloth. She was then wrapped in her abaya before my brothers and the other men came in to carry her on a wooden stretcher to the men's section so they could perform the funeral prayer. We joined in the women's section and recited the supplication following the voices of the men. The funeral procession itself included only men.

Mother was taken to the cemetery and buried in her abaya and shroud without a coffin, in strict adherence to Islamic tradition. Women, because they are considered unable to control their emotions, are not permitted to attend the burial or visit the graveyard. Wailing and crying loudly are discouraged, as they are viewed as disrespecting God's will.

To this day, I do not know where Mother was buried, and I have never visited her grave.

The mourning period started after the burial and, as customary, lasted three days. Our house was flooded with women wanting to pay their condolences. Men were received in my brother Mazen's house, and not even Father could escape that rite of passage. For those three exhausting days, all of us, segregated by gender, had to sit from afternoon until sometimes past midnight to receive well-wishers, listen for hours on end as people recited the good deeds of the deceased as a recording from the Quran played on a tape recorder. Sometimes my sisters and I would take turns to rest or get something to eat, if our appetites allowed. Dinner was an elaborate affair of traditional dishes catered by relatives and served around nine p.m. Whoever was present would partake.

After the official three days of mourning, close relatives and friends continued to drop by but their numbers dwindled until the final visitor showed up a month after Mother's passing.

Unable to deal with crowds anymore, I left Riyadh a week after Mother's funeral.

I needed to breathe again.

My world had collapsed. I was overtaken by guilt, brought on by thoughts about my not spending enough time with her, watching out for her, seeing that this did not happen. I honestly believed I could have saved her. My grief left me pale and grey from a regret that never stopped stabbing my heart and stealing the oxygen from my lungs. I felt selfish and ungrateful and deserving of my pain. I caused her death by only thinking of me and not paying attention to her, I told myself. But I was not the only one at whom I was pointing a finger. There was my boss and the company for keeping me away from her in Mother's time of need; my father, brothers and sisters for not looking after her; the healthcare system and the doctors for not saving her. My self-loathing manifested itself in self-destructive behavior. I started smoking again and engaged in unhealthy habits. And I cried for days and months and years.

Was this a nervous breakdown? Of sorts, I suppose. The slightest gesture or memory would trigger another crying jag. I could not discuss my struggle with anyone, even those closest to me. So, I buried my guilt, grief and regret deep within me and let them color my outlook with cynicism and negativity. Over the years, my relentless search for answers to the mystery of existence taught me to raise my awareness and master myself. Now, finally, I was also able to release my darkest emotions.

175

My whole life had been dedicated to pleasing Mother and making her proud of me. I followed every rule, stretching myself to the limit so I could bask in the pleasure of her praise when she singled me out to my brothers and sisters as an example of excellence. "Why can't you be good and obedient like Huda?" she would ask when any of them got into trouble. "She is the only one among you who never disobeys or troubles me."

In fact, my brothers and sisters were just behaving naturally, like all kids; I was the one putting on the act of perfection to monopolize the title of Mother's Favorite. But I now realized I was showing her something even more: that I could be as self-sufficient, independent and successful as any man around; that women could have just as dignified a life on their own as any married woman; and that we didn't need a man to be "in charge" of us.

Mother was proud and happy for me. She never doubted that I could thrive on my own; otherwise, would she have pushed me to leave home?

Now that she was gone, I started examining my purpose in life. Questions arose. Where was my reason for joy and my sense of security? What would bring me happiness now? Everything started to ache— when I opened my eyes in the morning, when I brushed my teeth, combed my hair, drove my car to work, sat in meetings. Everything I did, I did with pain and heaviness.

But the pain was good for me; it was necessary to bring me closer to my core so I could realize the impermanence of things.

I started to view my life through a different lens, letting go of things I couldn't control and trusting that everything happens for a reason. In a strange way, Mother's death sparked a remarkable sense of freedom in me. Now in my early forties, I no longer had to fulfill the expectations imposed by her and my absent father. I no longer had to actively pursue a husband, simply because it would please my parents. Neither was I interested in having children at this stage of my life. Don't get me wrong, I have a strong maternal instinct—I am the "cool aunt" to more than thirty nieces and nephews—but the impulse to have children of my own was just never there. It took time to see, but in retrospect I view this as an asset, as it allowed me to live my life as I desired. I am not lonely, nor do I lack for strong familial bonds. I love my family and take comfort that its younger generation comes to me for counsel and advice—and that my nieces, some with families of their own, prosper under their own freewill.

To this day, I cannot think of Mother without shedding a tear. Often, she visits me in dreams, sitting quietly in the corner, watching over me.

She is gone, but her energy remains with me. I feel her smiling and applauding with every achievement that moves me closer to equanimity and bliss. Her light forever energizes the hearts of the many whose lives she touched, and she reminds us that goodness is the only legacy that can withstand the test of time.

"God could not be everywhere," Rudyard Kipling said, "and therefore he made mothers."

18. PERSEVERANCE

When Mother's death left me with a hollow sense inside, little did I expect how I would set out to refill myself. As if overnight, I became ravenous for things that had never mattered before: status, power, money, influence, all the modern trappings of "success." Every element was crucial if I were to rekindle my happiness. Or so I was convinced. My ego needed to soak the hollowness inside with anything that would revive its standing in life, imagining this would bring me happiness again.

I wasn't sure what had prompted this aggressive turn in my nature, but neither was I going to let anything, or anybody prevent me from achieving my new goals, mercenary or not. After all, I had preparation and hard work on my side, along with another key ingredient: perseverance.

"Luck is what happens when preparation meets opportunity," Lucius Annaeus Seneca, the Hispano-Roman Stoic philosopher, averred.

I was now ready to match preparation with the right opportunity.

As Aramco became Saudi Aramco, the company gradually replaced expatriate managers with qualified Saudis. When the time came for my boss David, from Seattle, to retire, his shoes were filled by a colleague of mine, Sami (not his real name), the first Saudi to work in our department. Sami acknowledged my intellectual prowess, but I suspect he did not imagine that, within a few years, I would become his boss. In fact, no one in the company believed that one day women would assume managerial positions.

Of the sixty thousand employees in the entire Saudi Aramco workforce, only four women at most operated at my job level. This placed us under a microscope as far as corporate management was concerned, and the powers-that-be were not above assigning us particularly challenging projects to test us—unless they were testing their own conviction that women were not as strong as men. What characterized the handful of advanced-echelon women at Saudi Aramco was that we were all talented, successful, strong and knowledgeable, although I was the only one among us who would make it to executive rank. I am not aware of what factors hindered their paths, some of which could have been personal. But the mere fact that so few were elevated points to the rigidity of the system at that time.

When my effective output began receiving attention from management, Sami and the other men did little to conceal their professional jealousy. Never mind that I had no interest in competition, especially with my boss, our relationship was placed under a strain, and I needed to walk on eggshells.

Certainly, I could not outperform him publicly.

The last thing I needed to create was more animosity.

Keeping a low profile, I buried myself in my work, devoting long hours to studying programs and policies in our division, even those well beyond my purview. My aim was to measure whether our longstanding programs and procedures were still relevant and equitable. Advancing and evolving timeworn policies, especially those with a far-reaching impact on the workforce, would by no means be easy. However, having these improvements approved would roll out the opportunity for my advancement. A top priority was altering the company's employee performance evaluation system, which was vital to the assessment of productivity and labor costs. The first system was developed in the 1970s, with only a few minor modifications over the years, and was itself modeled on an antiquated 1950s style of command and control. Like most of the oil and gas industry in the mid-century, no room was allocated for employee input or for discussions of business goals or performance potentialities, probabilities and opportunities. Employees were left in the dark about how their day-to-day activities impacted the bottom line, and so a valuable opportunity to enhance productivity and performance was bypassed.

Moreover, the program was not aligned with the major changes taking place not only within the company but also in global markets. A new generation of workers had given rise to a new attitude, one of employees steering their own careers. The companies themselves were struggling, too, grappling with their outmoded performance appraisal systems. Consulting firms, sensing a need in the marketplace, jumped on the opportunity. A myriad of studies was published on the latest thinking in this area, and companies quickly had to play catch-up or fall hopelessly behind.

Here is where I took the lead. I not only read these studies but talked to experts in the field and communicated with major international companies to learn how they were dealing with the situation. I laid out the groundwork in a compelling presentation to management, suggesting we explore modern approaches to performance management, and to my delight, management agreed, albeit reluctantly.

"Keep it simple, Huda," I was told. "Don't burden supervisors with more work. They need to focus on their jobs and not be distracted by this human behavior stuff."

Silly me, I had thought a leader's main job was to inspire human behavior and bring out the best in their employees.

There was no magic pill for a tradition-bound company run by engineers to digest so that a radical change could take place in the management of its human resources. We are a "command and control" company, and most of our leaders simply were not interested in so-called human behavior theories. I knew it was not going to be an easy task or a stroll in the park. It required the involvement of many stakeholders, each with their own opinion and perspective on how to manage people. But it was necessary to agitate the system and shake it out of old patterns into completely new potentials. Getting these men to that point was like trying to pilot a supertanker into changing direction. It certainly was not a one-woman job.

Although numerous reputable consultants were buzzing around our corridors, each of them chomping at the bit to make a pitch for their lucrative work, my gut feeling told me if I wanted a strong, unwavering buy-in from the stakeholders, then the solution should come from within. This way, people's attitudes and the corporate culture would feed into any changes in our environment. The solution should reflect our best practices, not someone else's. And, thankfully, we had the right talent to get the job done.

I assembled a cross functional team of those with relevant expertise from Finance, Information Technology, Human Resources, and the core business. This credible solid core of professionals shared my vision and optimism, and we worked well together under a steering committee I also put together. These managers would advise and appraise the team's progress, thus assuring accountability during and after the new policies were implemented.

Armed with optimism, my team and I did not anticipate the steel wall of resistance that crashed down on us in a never-ending tsunami of criticism and cynicism. Certainly, I was aware that what we were proposing would take time, but never in my wildest imagination would I think it would require seven years.

First of all, there was no consensus among the leaders. No matter how many times we tried to iron out differences, we were either met with apathy or words to the effect, "Why fix it if it ain't broken? Let's just concentrate on our main mission: getting oil off the ground and to our customers. We don't need to be distracted by this stuff." Even my own management was lukewarm to the idea of change, while my boss Sami was fed up with having to deal with the negative feedback he was receiving about my efforts.

Most hurtful were the attacks on my credibility for being a woman, which, if not blatantly stated, were heavily implied every time someone uttered, "Why are you bothering us with this touchy-feely stuff?" The men nicknamed the proposed protocols PMS, as in premenstrual syndrome, rather than the correct PMP, for "Performance Management Program." Because I could not be dissuaded, I was called arrogant and domineering and a lot of nasty names.

The timing was terrible, too. As the business leaders were complaining to management about me, I was mourning Mother's death. This could have explained my borderline hostility; I knew I should have been thinking of her, not fretting over the blowback of my efforts at work. I ended up putting on a lot of weight to deal with my unhappiness, as food provided the comfort that was no longer coming from Mother. At first the weight gain was gradual, but it had increased as Mother's condition worsened, and by the time she died, I had put on 12 kg (26 lbs). I stopped going to the gym and attending exercise classes, mostly because I lacked any enthusiasm or energy. Melancholy and misery contributed to my weight and affected my metabolism. My clothes no longer fit, which further added to my depression. Instead of flinging on my usual pencil skirts with blouses tucked in, I tried hiding my ballooning torso under jackets, long scarves and baggy pants. The physical change in my appearance turned me into a hostile person hoping to mask my insecurities and self-contempt. I lashed out at anyone in my way, sneered at the shortcomings of others, and ferociously competed rather than cooperated with my colleagues. It was not so much a case of my work being affected—I still delivered on my duties—but my nasty behavior was reflected in my relations with people around me, some of whom avoided close interaction.

This mental and physical condition lasted for a few years, until I looked in the mirror and realized I did not like what I saw: a cruel creature unrecognizable to me. All along, my friends tried to snap me out of my darkened mood, but I suppose my grief over the loss of Mother had to take its course. I can't remember exactly when I faced reality, but spending time alone helped me reflect on my behavior, examine my emotions and regain control of my life. I gradually restored my internal balance and resumed my physical training to unblock my energy and discharge all the negative emotions from my body. I dropped about 7 kg (15.5 lbs) and purged from my mind all the negativity that plagued my attitude. I happily regained my strength to maintain clarity and focus on my path.

I could have fallen. But I did not want to let the bigotry around me steal my pain and grief. I believed if I let myself fall this time, I may never be able to stand again and build the credibility crucial for my growth. It was necessary for me to have faith in my internal strength to conquer the hollowness I felt inside, collect the pieces of my fragile being, and put myself back on course again. As they say, "What does not kill you, makes you stronger."

Faith in myself was of special importance at work, given how the growing negativity of others deeply dampened the enthusiasm of my team. Colleagues wished to distance themselves from the program, which was understandable once my project took on the stench of presumed failure. But, trying to think as I thought a leader should think, I attempted to defuse the situation. I began meeting solo or taking people to lunch to assure them we were on the right path—although, by now, I too was having my doubts.

Still, my fierce determination remained. That's when I leaned on my literary learnings. "When it is obvious that the goals cannot be reached," Confucius said, "don't adjust the goals, adjust the action steps."

The action I took was to keep approaching the management committee with creative options, and to lobby and negotiate with its members individually. I recognized their apprehension when it came to navigating unchartered waters, but I countered by showing them successful experiences in the market and the rewards to be had on the shore. Another fortunate turn of fate was that the company was just then implementing new software technology that allowed for the automation of several functions. I seized this opportunity to enlist some of the IT experts to design the most intuitive, efficient and user-friendly method that could appeal to everybody, including those who were barely computer literate. My intention was to simplify the process and minimize the time needed to complete it.

My persistence finally weakened their resistance.

In 2005, the management committee approved the new performance management program to take effect company wide. The system was rolled out in phases, with layers added as people became more comfortable with the process. I even earned a new nickname, one with a history but without the stigma it had before: "The Mother of PMP." It actually felt like I had given birth, but after seven years of labor! The project was one of the most challenging tasks I had to deal with in my career. It was not the intellectual part that was challenging. It was dealing with people and trying to have a democratic process to introduce change. Many people wanted the project to fail. I had more enemies than allies. But it was a great lesson in leadership and perseverance.

Chief among benefits of the new program I wanted to emphasize was our "pay for performance" philosophy, which closely aligned individual and team objectives with business priorities. For the first time, we had an official system in which supervisors are obligated to openly discuss a worker's performance and set future expectations and goals together with employees. Because the process was automated, information could be easily shared and fed into "workforce planning" and "big data analytics."

As a proud mother, let me further boast that it was a beautiful performance management program, and there was a flattering byproduct to its success. Saudi Aramco's performance management program set the standard for similar programs at other companies in the region.

One of the valuable lessons I learned from this experience was that if you believe in your goal, with hard work and perseverance you can overcome any obstacles in your way. "Let me tell you the secret that has led to my goal," said Louis Pasteur. "My strength lies solely in my tenacity."

My perseverance during this trying experience did not go unnoticed by the big boys. What happened next was the icing on the cake and nothing I particularly anticipated.

It was the protocol in our communication process with the board of directors that the corporate advisor presents the company's annual reward program and obtains the board approval for the required budget. My responsibility as a consultant was to support the corporate advisor by preparing all the groundwork for the board reports and presentations related to the relevant human resources topic. I would do the research, conduct the analysis, write the proposals, compose the presentation and prepare all supporting documents. I would closely scrutinize all the financial numbers and calculations, assure the integrity of our analysis and prepare tons of backup data that responded to any conceivable and inconceivable inquiries or questions that the board members may raise. All the corporate advisor had to do was memorize his part, attend the meeting, look pretty and deliver the presentation.

Sami and I were to present our CEO, Abdallah Jum'ah, with the dry-run presentation of the company's annual reward program in anticipation of a subsequent presentation in which Saudi Aramco's board of directors could approve the requested budget. Mr. Jum'ah had to hear what Sami and I had to say and okay the information before we proceed to the board.

As per usual, Sami and I had set aside a lot of pre-meeting rehearsal time with our teams to make sure everything we had prepared for the

CEO was on the money. We were in the corporate conference room setting up the PowerPoint presentation. Sami's boss, the vice president, was already in his seat, as was the senior vice president, when Mr. Jum'ah walked in and told Sami to step aside, so that I could deliver the presentation instead. The meeting was due to start in ten minutes, and Mr. Jum'ah asked me if I could handle his request on such short notice. Without hesitation, I replied yes.

"Great" said Mr. Jum'ah as he left the room to let us finish our preparation.

Sami was mortified at being sidelined. I no sooner caught the look on his face than my heart started racing from nerves, not over his reaction but at my having to face the CEO and his group. No words of comfort were about to be had from Sami, so I quickly excused myself for a few minutes, locked myself in the ladies' room, took a deep breath, and thought to myself, "I've got this. I am both willing and able." I was aware this was a once-in-a-lifetime opportunity, and one I could not blow. I had to let the CEO and his team know that women have just as much talent, courage and potential as any man, and I was speaking not only for myself but for all of us who had been overlooked and bypassed. Besides, I assured myself, I had prepared the material in the first place, so there really was no one better to present it.

In those few moments alone, I set about visualizing my speaking at the podium. Rehearsing in front of the mirror was my usual way to practice, only now there was no time. I figured the CEO was testing my armor by placing me center stage, so this required nothing less than perfection.

Entering the conference room smiling with confidence, I spotted the CEO and the HR management team already in their seats. Mr. Jum'ah nodded for me to proceed, which sent a surge of energy to my head, despite how jangled my stomach felt. Somehow, the combination provided me with just the boost I needed. The presentation lasted forty-five minutes. It felt like three seconds. The entire time, I remained in my zone: calm, poised, precise. I concluded my remarks and awaited feedback.

The first reaction came from the CEO himself. He beamed a contented smile, then looked around at the leaders asking for feedback. Ahmad Nassar, the vice president of Management Services, sat to his right and gave me the thumbs up. Having spent so much time grooming me, Ahmad was delighted to witness how his investment had paid off. Others nodded, too—high praise, indeed. This was not a group that broke into hearty applause.

With that, the CEO commended and thanked me, then told me to prepare to go to Genève so I could present our compensation proposal to the board of directors.

This was the auspicious opportunity I had been waiting for.

I barely had time to question whether or not I was the first woman ever to face the board. This time, unlike my brief preparatory moment in the ladies' room, I practiced multiple times, went to bed early the night before, and woke up at five a.m. I had my outfit all picked out and was ready to go by breakfast time, which consisted of only a banana and yogurt, as a salve to the butterflies in my stomach.

I'll spare you the suspense this time: The presentation went wonderfully. I was told that I was eloquent and compelling. Even more than the job I had to do convincing those in the Saudi Aramco conference room, in Genève I had to face an assemblage of powerful and influential men from local government (such as ministers of Energy and Finance, KFUPM Rector and head of KACST) and the international corporate world. Given their stature, I felt an extra burden to deliver my own powerful message about the credibility of a professional Saudi woman. What I projected would have far-reaching consequences— provided these men were open-minded as far as female empowerment was concerned. Yet I was proud to show what I believed in, even if only one of them was won over to my side. That was enough for me to make a difference. I can do it one mind at a time.

"The man who moves a mountain begins by carrying away small stones," Confucius said.

19. REFORM

My experiences so far had taught me that an open mind and a position of power, alone, are not enough to transform attitudes already ingrained in traditional belief systems. What really matters is having the courage to speak your truth and to take action. Regrettably, there are not that many leaders who have the courage to "rock the boat." They talk the talk, but do not walk the walk. Their primary agenda is to protect their self-interest.

In May 2004, management sent me to London to address an international Women in Business conference. The occasion marked the first time Saudi Aramco participated in any kind of event that concerned women's empowerment, and my focus was on the status of women at Saudi Aramco. While that status was lousy, I knew the tenor of my talk would have to be positive. I presented the company's enduring legacy in training and developing its people and chose to emphasize that we had finally begun to support the expansion of women's careers and deal with gender diversity, despite women making up only two percent of my company's workforce.

Included in the generalities of my speech was the fact that "irrespective of a woman's intellectual abilities, skills and inclination," education for

Saudi women restricted access to "areas that are historically dominated by men, and therefore [many jobs are] deemed inappropriate for women." I acknowledged that we faced an uphill battle, "even in today's modern age," and noted that many cultures "continue to preserve the traditional family model of the male breadwinner with a home-oriented wife"—a formula followed by millions that "still governs many dreams and aspirations."

In hindsight, I see how defensive I was, likely offering, at best, a scenario in which external pressure would be brought to bear to help change the plight of women. Little was I prepared for the audience assault on my company and me that immediately followed. One attendee demanded, "So, what are you going to do about it? Do you even have a plan?" My face went red with embarrassment, as I realized I had only described a deeply entrenched problem, without offering even the slightest suggestion of how we could dig out of it.

Grappling for a suitable explanation, I used myself as an example of how career opportunities were opening up for women at Saudi Aramco and noted that I would not be standing before them if we were not serious about change. I admitted change would be slow but deliberate and would need to start with the collaborative efforts of the government, the private and public sectors, and women themselves if we were to alter society's deeply ingrained mindsets. This turned the audience around. I received a heartfelt ovation, especially from Arab women in the crowd who knew better than anyone the challenges we faced.

One British woman stood up and said that small steps taken in the right direction should be celebrated, not criticized!

All in all, the conference shakily put Saudi Arabia's best foot forward. High-level government representatives also spoke, but theirs was the usual oration about how our religion had granted women equal rights and preserved their dignity by appointing men to serve and care for them. This was met with audience silence. When religion is brought into the equation, no one wishes to give offense or argue doctrine, especially one in which they are not familiar.

In my heart, I honestly didn't know why we agreed to participate in the first place, given our lack of strategy for moving forward.

Nevertheless, our participation in such an event was unprecedented and signalled my country's seeming readiness for change, even if it did land us in a trap as far as the international media was concerned.

First, a bit of background. The foreign press has always had a field day sensationalizing the status of women in Saudi Arabia, placing us under harsh scrutiny and amplifying our imperfections while marginalizing our achievements. The way we are dissected often reflects a lack of understanding of our history and culture. When the press criticizes the status of women in Arabia, without fail they make it a political issue. It is not; it is a one-hundred-percent cultural issue. A large segment of my society shuns change, and this includes many women who enjoy the financial support and protection provided by the guardianship system, for example. They consider it a fair deal that they would not trade for all the freedom in the world. With freedom comes responsibility, and that can scare many people. And the way religion is ground into their values, they fear that shedding traditional values would cause our society to disintegrate.

When I speak up and criticize our status, I do it out of genuine concern and love for my country, and because I want us to be among the prosperous nations. I am part of this culture and understand its issues, so my people will accept my opinion, they know my intentions are pure. But when foreigners criticize our system, they will always be viewed with suspicion and resistance. We consider them to be meddlers in our business. We have a saying in Arabic that goes something like, "My brother and I unite against my cousin, and my cousin and I unite against the stranger," meaning that it is fine for me to critique my family, but I will not stand for an outsider doing the same.

After the conference, foreign reporters sought hard evidence that we were sincere about social reform and contacted the Saudi embassy to set up interviews with accomplished Saudi women. I was selected to represent Saudi Aramco, and another woman, equally liberal, was chosen to represent the public sector. Let's call her Latifa. She and I did an interview with the BBC in a live broadcast for what I believe was a program called *Panorama*—only it was hardly a panorama at all, because the interviewer kept the conversation on an extremely narrow track, facilitated, no less, by Latifa herself. No sooner had the two of us taken our seats in the studio, than Latifa pulled out a scarf from her handbag and wrapped it around her head. Throughout the entire interview, she played the role of submissive Muslim wife to perfection. I couldn't believe my eyes or ears. Why was she demeaning herself? Was she afraid of persecution after the broadcast?

Then I realized that her being interviewed of course had to be cleared by the Saudi government, as did my appearance. But in the eyes of the authorities, I was a safe bet—not an activist and not a political threat. Even so, the interviewer put me in the uncomfortable position of having to answer for the women in my country and the government's call to reform. Not being a government official or policymaker, I could not speak about the country's position for women emancipation, no matter how many times or how hard the interviewer pressed me. I did not dare to speak my mind about the harsh demeaning environment imposed on women by the religious establishment. I did not dare to speak about the little girls' dreams that were slayed at the footsteps of their local schools. I did not speak about the young women's aspirations that were stifled by an atmosphere of harassment and ancient dogmas denying them a place to breathe and flourish. I did not speak about the undignified confinement of women's mobility and autonomy enforced by paranoid men guided by their false sense of superiority.

I did not dare speak on the matter because I was afraid. It was one thing to appear on an international news channel without a hijab, but it is quite another to criticize practices at home while in a foreign country. Of course, I wanted to scream about the horrific treatment of women in my world, but that required my being a person of influence. If I were to lose my job, I would lose my voice. Granted, it was not much of a voice at that time; to tell the truth, it was merely a murmur. But I felt I could still affect some change.

"Do the difficult things while they are easy and do the great things while they are small," Lao Tzu, the Chinese philosopher, said.

"A journey of a thousand miles must begin with a single step."

As I recall, my talk emphasized that the speed and degree of change are relative to every country's cultural and societal demands, and that the agenda to initiate a greater role for women in a particular society should be formulated from within and supported by those same cultural and societal considerations. It should not be driven by foreign agendas, which, in any event, tend to be built on misconceptions promoted by Western thinking. Furthermore, it was of prime importance to demonstrate that modern demands for overnight solutions may do little other than antagonize some traditional societies. To ensure continuous progress and long-term impact, we should instead celebrate the small steps and be sensitive to local customs and values.

As for Latifa, she kept repeating that our social systems were based on the teachings of the Quran and women enjoyed the protection and guardianship of men. She forgot to mention that the teachings of the Quran were often times misinterpreted by the religious establishment as a means to give men control over women.

Nor did she note that the Quran tells us all people are created equal and only good deeds may raise the status of one human over another.

My participation was well received by my management and the local media. Nevertheless, whether we like it or not, everyone recognizes that the current inequities will be constantly challenged by globalization trends and international efforts to create progressive economies and democratic societies. Women's issues are a reality and will continue to surface and set much of the world's agenda for the 21st century.

The events in London got me thinking about our fundamental gender issues in the company. If we were to be honest about our efforts to advance women, then we needed to take a closer look at the biases in our policies and bylaws. As I was now in a consultant position for Human Resources and responsible for stimulating change, I decided to take the lead and not leave anything so crucial to fate or time.

Also, perhaps by fate, timing was again on my side, because the country was starting to ease up on some of the rigid rules governing people's lives. In 2005, King Abdullah came to reign. Among his aims was to reduce the influence of the religious establishment, and this especially concerned the relaxation of some of the social restrictions on women. As someone who admires education, the king was also keen on investing in the training of a workforce for the future—and this, too, included women. A government scholarship program was put into effect for undergraduate and graduate students so that they might attend universities around the world, and that program, too, included women. He appointed a woman as deputy education minister in charge of a new department for female students—the first time in the country's history a woman was placed in an executive government position. In addition, he instituted women's right to vote and opened the starting gate for female athletes to compete in the Olympics. The entire Saudi Olympic team was at the risk of being disqualified on grounds of gender discrimination had it not been for that decision. The public participation of women in sport was still fiercely opposed by many religious conservatives. Sports were banned from girls' schools on the ground that it was immoral for women to display their bodies in sports wear!

As we were relieved to witness, the government was adamant in wanting women to participate in the country's workforce and domestic affairs, especially in light of the fact that the majority of Saudi female college graduates had remained unemployed while the country continued to import foreign workers to fill literally millions of jobs.

The government finally acknowledged that women, constituting half the population, are an untapped reservoir of talent, and should play a critical role in the social and economic development of the country. To signal the need for diversity in our decision-making processes, in 2009 thirty women were appointed to a Consultive Assembly and a related law was modified to mandate that no fewer than twenty percent of its one hundred fifty members should be women.

Progress looked to be gaining ground all around us. In August 2013, the Saudi cabinet, for the first time, approved a law making domestic violence a criminal offense and criminalizing that which is considered psychological, sexual, and physical abuse. It also included a provision that mandated employees to report instances of bullying and harassment in the workplace to their employer.

Slow and cautious as it still was, a refreshing period of change was set in motion for women and represented a new era for their empowerment in the private and public sectors, one that shined a light on gender equality in the Kingdom's socio-political and economic agenda. Further radical reforms to modernize social life were implemented by the brave and farsighted Crown Prince Mohammad bin Salman, or MBS, when King Salman succeeded his brother in 2015. The young MBS was a visionary leader who wanted to bring his country into the 21st century. Steps were taken to eradicate corruption, diversify the economy, embrace tourism and foreign investment, relax social life, curb the religious police and grant women rights for self-determination.

Last but not least, music was legalized in public places, schools and theaters, and women could now sing in public. Miraculously, their voices were no longer considered shameful!

Given the new atmosphere, it was time for Saudi Aramco to demonstrate their commitment, as an active agent of progressive change, by providing a more equitable work environment for women and taking their place at the forefront of this movement. Considering its pre-eminent position and reputation as a critical player domestically and globally, Saudi Aramco plays a major role in setting the pace for the desired transformation within its corporate environment.

The "wait and see" attitude had to change to one of "lead and teach."

At first, the company approach was cursory and devoid of strategic direction. Public Relations started planting women, like ornamental vases, at international events and including them in guest lists for foreign VIP visits. Regrettably, the selection of many of the women for these events was solely based on professional pretense and proficiency in English. They did not have major accomplishments or even a credible narrative under their belts. Moreover, to demonstrate the new progressive mood, photos of female employees started appearing in the company's local and international publications. Up until now, photographing a woman in public was taboo, lest we offend the religious establishment. Should our image appear in a snapshot, the Public Relations department would erase our beautiful and colorful faces rendering the photo all male, pale and stale. If you search our impressive archives, you will not find any official photos of me or other Saudi women in our earlier career years in the 1980s or 1990s. Photos of women suddenly started appearing all over the place in 2004.

This new atmosphere ignited an appetite among a large number of corporate leaders to expand women's careers in the company and allow us to break through not only the glass ceilings that existed, but also the glass walls that confined us to stereotypical jobs.

Encouraged by the shift in mood internally and externally, I leapt into a deep dive study of the status of women in the company. In my role as a consultant, I could officially scrutinize policies and procedures governing women's employment from hire to retire and highlight the substantial inequities in the system—injustices already familiar to management but never spoken of.

To better understand and eradicate organizational barriers to women, current trends were analyzed based on historical activities in our major Human Resources functions, such as job placement, compensation, benefits, training, career development, recruitment, and attrition. Although pay was equal, women were not receiving major company benefits such as the housing allowance, the right to homeownership, scholarship programs, international assignments, and several other privileges that male employees took for granted. This also included the free healthcare for children and spouses that automatically went to their male counterparts as part of their employment package.

I do not wish to give the impression that, over the years, women at Saudi Aramco had remained compliant about their inequitable treatment. For more than twenty years, we relentlessly petitioned management to correct the inconsistent policies, only to be consistently told that we should be grateful to have jobs and that this wasn't "the right time" to advance women's agenda. We never understood what the "right time" had to do with granting women, for example, a housing allowance similar to their male colleagues. We never understood the anxiety and fear that our petitions stirred behind the closed doors of our leaders. No one had the courage or sensibility to acknowledge and address the gross injustice in the system.

In December 2005, I submitted a comprehensive report to the Industrial Relations senior vice president, HE Khalid Al-Falih at that time, who clearly recognized the critical role women played in our economy. (He later became the Minister of Energy and then Minister of Investment.) The report provided solutions to overcome traditional barriers to career growth for women. I emphasized that with organizational prejudices so deep-rooted, a change in tone had to start at the top. Examples had to be set with leaders acting as role models who communicated messages about the value of workforce diversity. Emphasis needed to be placed on corporate values of fairness and teamwork that call for a full partnership between men and women, with a recognition of the collective creativity of combined male and female power. If we wanted a productive atmosphere that included gender diversity, women had to be visible in every facet of the corporation, particularly in untraditional places and positions. They were no longer to be hidden behind the doors of routine administrative work.

Nothing about my report was earth-shattering or unconventional. It was about adopting intuitive and palpable approaches to correcting the problem at hand by hiring more women, promoting more women, training more women, being more consciously inclusive regarding women and, most importantly, educating leaders and holding them accountable for tangible results. Without action from leaders, the proposed improvements could not gain any traction.

The management team led by the CEO Abdallah Jum'ah appreciated the findings, and subsequently, every inconsistency in the human resources policies was gradually corrected, with all areas of bias removed from our books. Abdallah Jum'ah wanted to ensure that women were, finally, treated fairly and given a chance to participate in the company's successes. Now that the "time is right" in terms of the country's readiness for social reform, our CEO pushed to level the playing field for women and empower them to unlock their potential.

Alas, not everyone on the management team shared his vision and was willing to participate. Many male workers continued to find it unacceptable to be in the same workplace with, or report to, a woman. Middle management was also reluctant and unsure how to handle the situation, and those of us trying to affect change knew it was better to leave them alone. We did not want to shock the system and go from famine to feast all at once.

At that time, I was not in a key decision-making position to take action and seed any fundamental changes. The only thing I could do was pinpoint the deficiencies and speak up about the company's obligation to initiate a tangible and genuine transformation in structure. When I was finally promoted to positions of authority and influence, I was ultimately able to achieve humble successes in supporting women's empowerment. For example, I established special training programs that targeted the young women we started hiring in the company. To spearhead the project, I relied on my longtime friend Sheikha, who gave the initiative her all. She worked with learning experts, content developers, external consultants and training facilitators to deliver world-class professional programs that trained women and expanded their employment opportunities.

It will take a considerable time before we see real progress in terms of diversity and inclusion. Authentic and transformative progress doesn't happen overnight, but we should relentlessly continue to plant and nourish its seeds hoping its fruits will be enjoyed by others, even if we are not around to witness it.

20. PARTNERSHIP

My cousin on my mother's side, Abdulhameed Al-Rushaid—we called him Hameed for short—also worked for Saudi Aramco, as vice president of Drilling and was one of my biggest supporters. Hameed is the son of my uncle Ahmad, Mother's youngest brother. Like my siblings and me, Hameed was born and grew up in Iraq before his family moved back to Saudi Arabia in the early 1980s, and he is like a brother and friend to me. Once a week, for more than thirty years now, it has been our routine to have lunch and spend time together with his wife, Hetaf, and their four children, who are all grown now. Before I retired, we'd talk about everything that transpired in the work week, and our get-togethers helped me start my week on a positive note. My cousin is a devout Muslim, but he approached his faith with reason and an open mind. Sometimes, he would tease me about my casual attitude toward my religious practice, or the lack of it, but he never criticized me over it. Should the conversation ever grow heated, we would consciously change the subject.

When, in 2006, I was promoted to director in charge of Employee Relations Policy and Planning, Hameed generously held a big celebration in keeping with our traditions. He slaughtered a lamb as a sacrificial offering to express gratitude to God for his blessings, a rite we perform whenever anyone has a major achievement, be it marriage, college graduation, the birth of a child, or recovery from a major illness.

We also share our blessings by giving money and food to the poor. We strongly believe that "the more you give, the more you receive."

Hameed said the promotion was only the beginning of bigger things coming my way.

"Keep believing in yourself," he told me.

"Only the sky is the limit."

As I've said, I was the first woman to be assigned to such a critical position. Another woman, Nabilah Al-Tunisi, was also promoted to a managerial position in Project Management around the same time. She later became Chief Engineer in her own right. At this juncture, we were the only two women at that level among approximately three hundred male managers in the company. We had broken into the boys' club.

It was an exciting and proud moment for me and the company to demonstrate progressive and fair-minded efforts and place women in critical leadership ranks. The late U.S. Supreme Court Justice Ruth Bader Ginsberg, known as RBG, said, "Women belong to all the places where decisions are being made ...it should not be that women are the exception."

The advantages of being in this new, rarefied atmosphere quickly became apparent. Shortly after my promotion, I was appointed to the board of directors for Vela International Marine Limited, one of Saudi Aramco's major subsidiaries, and was the first woman ever to hold such a position. Headquartered in Dubai, Vela ranked sixth largest owner of VLCCs (very large crude carriers) in the world, with a fleet of twenty-nine vessels. In March of 2008, I inaugurated one of its double-hulled oil tankers—capable of carrying 2.2 million barrels of oil—the *Sirius Star*, in its South Korea shipyard. The *Sirius Star* was built by the Daewoo Shipbuilding and Marine Engineering Company. Unfortunately, eight months after her launch, the *Sirius Star* was hijacked by Somali pirates, and a ransom of $3 million was paid in January 2009. If this scenario sounds familiar, in April of 2009 Somali pirates hijacked the *Maersk Alabama*, an American container ship; the story of its rescue by U.S. Navy Seals became the film *Captain Phillips*, starring Tom Hanks.

I was paraded at the company's local and international events and invited to high-level social functions continuously until the day I retired. It was a refreshing achievement that was welcomed by our partners, allies and the business community at large. But despite the sometimes-lavish trappings of my new job, few festivities were going on inside the office. My previous boss Sami could not handle being made my subordinate, and refused to attend our staff meetings, finding a creative new excuse every week as to why he was absent. Basically, he shot himself in the foot: isolating himself in his office, carrying out insignificant work, taking sick leave and time off, and just killing time until his retirement.

Fortunately, not everyone shared Sami's view. I had a professional staff of about fifty. Most of them had been my colleagues for fourteen years and were happy to work alongside me—or, at least, that's what they pretended. That was good enough for me. The younger ones, especially the few women, were fascinated by my role, and wanted to serve and learn, even if it meant long hours. As a boss, I was demanding, though, as everyone knew, extremely hardworking and the first to show up in the morning, at six a.m. Those who didn't live up to expectations saw their lack of eagerness reflected in their annual merit increase and performance reviews.

What I truly disliked, though, were the political games I was now forced to play. My every turn, move and decision was scrutinized on every level of the company and often shaded by deeply ingrained misogynistic attitudes. But that was nothing new. I had encountered resistance from both men and women in the past, and I always maintained my poise and humor while dealing with gender issues. Prior to this position, I had briefly taken over as corporate advisor, and I remember one of the men in the division asking my boss to transfer him out of the organization— because if his father-in-law found out that his boss was a woman, the in-law would ask the man to divorce his wife, and he would be the ridicule of the tribe.

I found this amusing and sad at the same time, and immediately gave him his release.

I did not want to be responsible for breaking up a family.

When I first joined Human Resources in 1992, I was constantly lectured on how I should not "rock the boat," even if the boat seemed to be already rocking with its own ineffectiveness. For such a long time we were trained to do things a certain way, and no one wanted to step into unfamiliar territory and try something new. People will not venture into the unknown and change long standing attitudes and traditions willingly. They feel more comfortable in their habitual environment. People reject change because of fear; fear of failing to adapt and perform in the new environment which requires extra effort to learn and acclimate. Maintaining the status quo is a safe bet to many.

I tried to walk the line for a while in my earlier years with the department. I buried my head in the sand even when some things did not make sense to me. I used to think, "Oh Huda, what do you know? You are just a novice; an inexperienced woman surrounded by these big wise men. Just listen and follow their lead." Until I had so much sand in my mouth and lungs that I could not breath anymore.

Furthermore, HR saw a new vice president come and go every two years, if he lasted that long. The job was nothing but a training ground before moving on to more exciting functions in the company's core business. Over my fourteen years with the department, I survived nine vice presidents. Not one had enough time, or perhaps enough interest, to study the organization, transform it and invoke change. Transformation is a slow process. It takes time. More than one or two years. Much more. Much more.

To pour salt in the wounds, HR was, at that time, not considered critical in the grand scheme of the company, which regarded it an administrative function. Most managers did not have time to deal with this "soft stuff," an attitude entrenched in our structure and re-enforced by decades of what is known as a silo mentality, a damaging reluctance to share information with those in different departments of the same company. We in HR were also guilty of contributing to this us-versus-them mindset by pushing people away and isolating ourselves in our protective bubble. As a result, our business relations lacked coherence and suffered.

The nature of my new position required that I interact with managers and executives and address their human resources issues, mainly those of compensation, benefits and work-related allowances. Because of how we operated, never sharing or discussing our approach to pay policies, we were viewed with suspicion. When your policy reaches into people's pockets, they become nervous and want to know why and how you came to that decision. Invariably, we would hear complaints of "not enough," "not fair," and "demoralizing."

Policy design took place behind closed doors with discussions limited to the HR vice president, the CEO and the board of directors, as mandated by internal privacy laws. Any leaking of information could compromise our position with our competitors. Neither did we want our compensation data splashed across the media. As a result, even in our own department, not everyone was privy to the sensitive information kept locked in steel cabinets. No visitors were allowed into our offices without an invitation.

The situation as it stood bothered me. I yearned for a harmonious and coherent interaction with all.

Establishing more congruous partnerships with others became my top priority.

In elevating the role of HR, I wanted us to be more transparent while still able to safeguard sensitive data. It was also timely for Human Resources to move from the backseat to the forefront of the business agenda and have our engineers recognize that companies are living organizations and social institutions influenced by people relating to one another. "Human resources isn't a thing we do," said one market leader. "It's the thing that runs our business."

In transforming our tactics and practices, I wanted to make them more participative and approachable. HR is a shared responsibility between the HR organization and the business leaders. Information needed to be shared and, where appropriate, books had to be opened. It is not the business of only our organization, it is everyone's business.

In addition, we were going through a period of increased emphasis on workers' productivity and motivation, with the former a main ingredient for business profitability. So, it was crucial that we assumed the role of business enablers and provided appropriate tools for supervisors to create a balanced, rewarding and productive work environment. It was not going to be easy to convince managers that HR was a collective responsibility after decades of separation and silo mentality.

From the outset, I was not sure how management would react to my open approach. But isn't all of life an experiment? My attitude was, "If it works, I win. If it doesn't, I will grow wiser." This reminds me of a discussion I had with one of our vice presidents who once told me that "sometimes you should be bold and do the unconventional when you believe it would add value and would not compromise the integrity of the system. If it worked, then everybody will be happy. If it did not work, learn the lesson, take responsibility, say sorry and move on." Whatever happens, the sun will also rise tomorrow! His advice remains with me to this day.

Or, as T.S. Eliot put it, "Only those who will risk going too far can possibly find out how far one can go."

In one fell swoop, I played negotiator, strategist, salesperson, promotor, coach, cheerleader, and peacemaker with our partners. Sociability was not one of my great attributes, but, despite my discomfort, I slipped on a warrior's mask and marched into my duties armed with confidence and fervor. I learned to listen to disgruntled people without allowing them to stress me out or letting their problems follow me home.

It was time to go back to the classroom. My team and I designed a training course for managers called the "Human Resources Partnership Program," to educate some three hundred managers about our strategy and methodology and help them understand the rationale behind our policies. The course was presented in a classroom-like setting over two days with no more than sixteen managers participating at any one time. The speakers were the corporate advisors assisted by their consultants and management trainers. When time permitted, I would speak about our mission and the roles managers were expected to play in order to support our business.

Any complaints we faced were not actually directed at the programs or policies themselves, but at us. Among the adjectives used were ridiculous, unrealistic, irrational, irrelevant, conceited, deceitful, heartless, ignorant, and unfair. Fortunately, we knew better than to take it personally. We continued to maintain our poise and remained patient, cool and collected throughout the entire program. The crux of their problem was that they had not been consulted about policies that directly affected their employees, and this made them feel irrelevant. By not being able to respond to their employees' inquiries about HR matters, they were in no position to defend or support our policies. We agreed. We understood their pain and frustration.

Again, fortunately, the more conversations we held with them, the more they understood, until many finally even came to appreciate what we were setting out to do. People generally become antagonistic when you challenge their intellect with new perspectives. It is human nature. In the beginning, people became hostile because they did not understand our business. As they spent more time in the conversation, they started to calm down, then they listened, then reflected, then empathized, then understood, and finally they collaborated, or didn't! There will always be the few egoistic and stubborn personalities that will never concede and continue to argue until the end of days.

There is only so much in human nature one can change—but that is precisely why I love HR. It stirs emotions and stimulates intellectual curiosity. It's an art sprinkled with the marvels of science, behavioral science, that is. Because there is a lot of grey area in its evergreen space, one is constantly confronted with the unpredictable intangibles of human emotions and personalities. That's the beauty of HR. Engineers generally get uneasy dealing with HR decisions and the underlying abstract concepts. They prefer to work with tangible problems that can only be solved with numbers. That is why they habitually disparage the HR profession and regard the humanities as an unintellectual discipline. Sadly, they miss the point.

As planned, we opened our books for the first time and allowed other leaders to look inside. Everyone wanted to have a say in our methodology; everyone believed their way was the only right way; everyone suddenly became an HR expert. Every manager was concerned with his own situation and how our policies would affect his people, as well as him personally. Few were willing to look at the big picture. Considering the diversity of Saudi Aramco's workforce—eighty nationalities, more than twenty payrolls, four-thousand-plus positions in three hundred departments, and approximately sixty-five thousand employees in nearly fifty locations worldwide—the challenge was to balance segmentation with inclusiveness, competitiveness with cost effectiveness, and short-term needs with long-term targets.

My team and I were stressed out and exhausted, but also gratified. The program was a magnificent success. It subsequently cascaded to more than a thousand division heads. We helped people speak our language. We created coherence.

In the meantime, the third floor, home to corporate management, was quiet. No hissing noises. That was a good sign.

The positive feedback from line organizations had already dissipated the old guard's reservations.

Our plan worked.

✦

Our relationship with leaders solidified, we now had to win over the workers. The best method: make them feel appreciated and respected and they will walk a thousand miles for you.

Up until then, the relationship between management and employees was very formal, with no participative culture before the recent introduction of the Performance Management Program. Communication about the reward programs was flimsy and infrequent. Yes, everyone knew how much money they would get at the end of the month, but most workers didn't see the big picture of their assets with the company. Communication would now have to be key, so everyone would know what tangibles and intangibles—what we in HR called "employment value proposition," or EVP—contributed to their and the company's success.

We understood that the foundation for retaining talent in any environment is to create and sustain a vibrant participative workplace that people feel proud of, which provides a strong sense of belonging. Research shows that salaries and benefits are only one aspect of employee contentment. Equally important are opportunities for growth, training and development, long-term financial security, health and well-being, and other perks that don't appear on the pay stub, and one should not be a substitute for the other. In fact, that could prove a costly mistake.

To reach our workers, my team and I relied on the wonders of technology, which gradually came to handle HR transactions. With our sister organizations in Finance, IT, and Personnel, we developed a customized program that monetized the value of every element of the employment package for every employee. The program also provided tools for the employee to build a scenario of their future financial position based on years of service and anticipated salary increases. The reaction was even better than expected. For the first time, employees could grasp a full picture of the financial return on their time and effort with the company. It also facilitated our recruitment and retention efforts by assuring employees of their competitive status in relation to others in the market.

Simultaneously, in a giant leap forward, Personnel delivered their magnificent HR online system. The system plugged in people and organizations to HR data for the purposes of facilitating communication, learning and planning. Its major accomplishment was in humanizing our relations with the rest of the company.

Our new HR model was emulated by other companies in the region as "best practice" in HR. But what was most gratifying to us was the change that we witnessed in our partners regarding their HR departments' role in nourishing the aspiration of their talent. I can't say that our partnership was all smooth sailing with no bumps on the road. That would be unrealistic and naïve. We will always have competition, resistance and challenges; and we welcome that. Competition keeps us on our toes. It pushes us to do our best, to never be complacent, and to always keep reinventing.

A few years later, HR was finally elevated to its rightful seat on the CEO's decision-making table. Developing and retaining people with cutting-edge capabilities became a priority and hot topic in the leadership agenda. Talent is truly one of the company's most important competitive advantages, not only locally but globally.

In a *Forbes* magazine article dated October 15, 2020, titled, "*The World's Best Employers*," Saudi Aramco ranked number one in the oil and gas industry, and No. 26 overall, from among seven hundred fifty companies in fifty-eight countries.

21. LEADERSHIP

The risky nature of the oil business commands that we play it safe. Particularly in selecting leaders. This was clearly the case in 2009, when my boss, the vice president of Management Services, Ahmad Al-Nassar, announced his plans to retire. We had both hoped I would step into his job, but in the back of my mind I knew, as a woman, I did not fit the standard profile of an executive leader at Saudi Aramco, which did not permit diversity. So I was a risky bet!

No one disputes the fact that we have had remarkable brilliant leaders, responsible for sustaining the successful performance of the company over nearly nine decades. But they all looked the same, thought the same and talked the same. No one was willing to take a risk and deviate from the standard formula! Diversity, as far as the company was concerned, was just a word in the dictionary, and that dictionary had been collecting dust on the library shelf for the past nine decades. Predictably, a gentleman from Finance replaced Ahmad.

I was fifty-one years old! And had twenty-eight years of solid experience. But still I was told I needed more preparation before I could assume so responsible a position. How ludicrous!

As an intermediate step, and in recognition of my work efforts, I was promoted to General Manager of Training and Development. Another celebration was held to mark the achievement, not only for me, but also for the company and the community for breaking down another barrier in the fight for gender equality. Money and food were distributed to the poor to mark the honor. A woman appointed to GM did not happen every day.

It surely didn't. Not to diminish the fact that the position was a big deal—it was, as the numbers bore out. I was now the top company official with direct responsibility for corporate training. In all, my staff totaled sixteen hundred members, of which more than five hundred were teacher-trainers. We operated twenty-three training centers throughout the kingdom, in big cities and remote locations alike. The course rosters included more than six thousand trainees—all of them male—and nearly two thousand undergraduate and graduate students in North America, Europe, the Far East and locally. We provided leadership and professional development programs to some ten thousand employees while tracking the competency development of twenty thousand more. We also provided ongoing maintenance for one hundred forty-one Saudi Aramco built government schools, and extended summer training programs to local students and teachers to enhance their soft skills and English and math proficiency. In addition, we maintained numerous partnerships with local and international educational and training institutes and many educational outreach projects with the local community. Basically, the job carried enormous responsibility for preparing and building the capabilities of the current and future workforce of the company.

Because my duties were spread over many locations, I often traveled by car or company plane to acquaint myself with the staff at the training centers, where, to date, no woman had ever been granted access. In the beginning, my visits to all-male centers were a culture shock and a blow to the belief system of many of the men who worked or studied at these centers, the majority of whom were very traditional.

Here is an amusing story in this regard:

It was 7:00 am when I stepped out of the front door of the main administration building on my way to a meeting with my new staff. Sayyed, a Pakistani driver, held open the back door of the white Cadillac parked at the foot of the main entrance. Sayyed was one of our executive drivers available to drive me around when I needed transportation to attend a business meeting or event outside the perimeter fence. I was on my way to visit, for the first time, one of our all-male training centers in Ras Tanura, which was about ninety kilometers from our headquarter in Dhahran, and one of the most important industrial cities in the Eastern Province. Father worked here in the early 1950s, and the one-time small port now housed a Saudi Aramco compound that was home to thirty-two hundred workers. The industrial complex includes the largest oil-exporting terminal in the kingdom, a major oil refinery, and off shore oil rigs and production facilities. To support its operations, the company built a residential compound on one of the most gorgeous white sand beaches in the area. Wherever we have a major operation like this one, we usually build a training center to supply the plants with the relevant skills and capabilities needed to run the operation in a safe and reliable way.

As my driver, Sayyed, pulled up to the gate outside the industrial training center, a skinny, young security guard rushed out of the security cabin ready to open the gate for the executive car to pass through. As Sayyed came to a halt waiting for the gate to open, the security guard peeked inside the car to greet us and then froze in his place with a shocked expression over his face. His smile was replaced with a confused frown as he signaled to Sayyed to roll down his window.

"Women are not allowed to enter the center," he barked at Sayyed while avoiding eye contact with me.

"Open the gate," Sayyed shot back. "This is the general manager." As if Sayyed's word wasn't enough, he pointed to the executive sticker plastered on the front windshield.

The guard wouldn't budge. He said he was only following instructions, despite Sayyed's telling him I had a meeting.

"Please turn the car around and leave," the guard insisted, unfazed by our executive standing.

Sayyed looked at me and awaited instructions. I told him not to move the car. Many of our plants and remote location facilities were off-limits to women so this was no shock to me. But I was irritated because I had already secured special permission to access the area since I was the head of the training operation.

The impasse was momentarily put on hold after I patiently explained to the kid who I was—the head of the very facility he was guarding—and what I was here for. I showed him my ID and asked him to check with his supervisor, for surely he must have received instructions to let me in. He slipped back into his security hut, while I grabbed my mobile and called the vice president of Industrial Security in Dhahran and said, half-kidding, "Mohamad, you've overtrained your guards."

"I don't understand," Mohamad said, clearly confused. "What happened?" I filled him in, and Mohamad told me to hold the line as I overheard him chew out a manager. It seems that the directive granting me access had gotten lost in the shift rotation of the nearly five thousand crew members. Apparently, it was not deemed urgent.

Seconds later, the security guard was practically tripping over himself as he ran out of his hut—with his colleagues and supervisor on his heels. They were all smiles and apologies. The gate was expeditiously opened and Sayyed sped toward the building where I was expected, which turned out to be only a few small steps from the front gate. As we approached the building all the managers and administrators came rushing out of the front door to meet me and apologized for the misunderstanding with the security guards. It seemed they were watching the entire escapade unfold with great amusement from their windows, and most probably thinking, "Why is she here? This is no place for a woman."

This was not an isolated incident. In fact, the vignette pretty much epitomized my three years as GM of T&D. These sorts of stalemates became habitual, but always apologetically resolved. Constantly surrounded by men, and often hundreds, if not thousands of them, I carried on, never feeling personally uncomfortable, except in one glaringly obvious regard: There was never a ladies' restroom.

Being a strategist by nature, I would make sure on those days I was to visit the centers that I would carefully monitor my intake of coffee and water. In most cases, the administrators would convert one of the men's toilets by sticking a temporary sign on the door indicating the facility was for women. A janitor would be guarding the door to make sure no man came near the facility or attempted to enter by mistake. But I preferred not to resort to that, if at all possible.

More to my liking were the monthly Executive Management Safety Reviews, or EMSR for short, and they were exactly what their name implied: a CEO-led inspection of one of our operating areas, and a chance for me to learn firsthand about the intricacies of our oil and gas production facilities. The reviews took place on the first Monday of every month, starting at six a.m., and the forty or fifty of us would journey to our destination either via private plane or motorcoach, depending on the distance. Those who ran our refineries and plants were the best in their field and, yes, many were intrigued by the presence of a woman for the first time at their location. If anything, they took extra care to make me feel comfortable and the security guards would vigilantly monitor my surroundings to make sure no one bothered me—and, sure enough, given the guards' and CEO's presence, no one ever did, although I would get quizzical looks. Some operators also refused to make eye contact or shake my hand, and I would overhear them muttering under their breaths prayers, asking that they be protected from temptation. "God forgive me, God forgive me, God forgive me," they would echo until I disappeared from their field of vision.

The composition of the T&D staff was an interesting mix of conservative expatriates from the Middle East, the U.K., the U.S., and local tribal men, none of whose backgrounds prepared them for a female boss. Some of the managers also carried the extra burden of my not having any experience in their business, and I understood where they were coming from, so I was ultra-sensitive in handling them. After all, I would have been lost without their knowledge and could not run the operation without their loyalty.

My philosophy toward carrying out my duties relied on the "servant leader" principle, which calls for the engagement of people by attending to their needs, so they, in turn, become invested in attending to the organization's needs. This way, everybody wins. It is an attitude dating back to ancient times, when Arab rulers sought to exercise fairness and compassion. Abu Al-Ala Al-Ma'arri, a tenth-century philosopher and poet, said, "The people's leader is the servant of those he rules," while a popular proverb went, "The master of people is their servant." In the West, in the twentieth century, it was Robert K. Greenleaf, the founder of the modern Servant Leadership movement, who coined the term "servant leadership." Greenleaf founded a namesake Center for Servant Leadership in 1973, in South Orange, New Jersey. Greenleaf's teachings note that the servant leader is inspired by serving people first, which takes precedent over leading. He also said the "leader-first and the servant-first are two extreme types. Between them there are shadings and blends that are part of the infinite variety of human nature."

Another proponent, Joseph Jaworski, author of the 1996 *Synchronicity: The Inner Path of Leadership* and a lifelong devotee of leadership development, said that the authentic presence of the servant leader works like a magnet to draw in people. "Leadership," he believed, "is much more about being than doing."

I never viewed leadership as a power trip. The domain of authentic leadership goes beyond formal power hierarchies of "leaders" and "those who are led." It is about being the best you can be for others, not for yourself. Lao Tzu viewed leadership efficacy as a meeting of equals, saying, "To lead people, walk besides them." Leadership is about creating a collaborative environment in which people work toward achieving a common goal and participate in shaping the future. Ultimately, leadership is about serving others with compassion, fairness and responsibility, and creating a vibrant space in which everyone can thrive and prosper.

My mostly male staff had to adjust to my hands-off approach. After all, we were a "command and control" company with sharply drawn lines when it came to authority. By contrast, I shared power, delegated and regarded my directors as colleagues. My door was always open, yet I had little time or patience for involving myself in the micro processes within our formidable operation. Leaders should not waste valuable time allowing small stuff to distract from their main mission: guiding people, not managing them. I had sixteen hundred people qualified to take care of the small stuff for me.

As I adjusted to my role, I felt more comfortable showing my feminine colors and being flexible, nurturing and socially interactive with my team. People were empowered to implement their own ideas, and my power was not derived from my title, but from the trust of others. To earn their commitment and respect, I fed their sense of ego and self-esteem and made them proud of their achievements. I won them over. Not all of them, but at least the ones that counted.

The ego is funny, capable of projecting a grandiose image of oneself with a childlike neediness for attention and praise. Its insecurity is governed by fears of losing identity, becoming a nobody, and vanishing into the void. I didn't need to have studied psychology to understand the intricacies of human behavior, not when my studies of classic literature made a deep analysis of the complexities of character.

That helped me see how people's range of personas, including my own, reacted under certain circumstances and prepared me to deal directly with those colorful egos I encountered on a daily basis.

By delving into Saudi Aramco's operations and history and considering my studies of the latest trends in learning and education, I concluded that the organization needed to be uplifted and upgraded. Our outmoded business strategy was not aligned with the corporate vision. We had the resources, so it was time to transform our dusty old training centers into lively learning facilities, where employees became the driving force behind their development and growth. To do this, my team and I sought to introduce blended learning approaches that would integrate technology, simulations, action learning, knowledge sharing and relevant digital prowess.

Teaching and learning should be an engaging active process connected to real life, and relevant to the digital workplace. To create a lifelong learning culture, it was necessary to abolish the old pedagogy methods in which the teacher serves as an authoritative figure who simply pours lessons like water from a single container into an empty receptacle and expects sudden miracles. Socrates said, "Education is the kindling of a flame, not the filling of a vessel." To kindle an actual passion for learning, it was necessary to transform the teacher into a facilitator who enables students with a freedom to think independently and make the learner the center of the learning experience. Plato described such a power shift as, "All learning is in the learner, not the teacher."

We also wanted to spread our know-how in people development to the local community and participate in the newly emerging efforts to reform education in the country. This required prioritization on my part, and quickly. I lined up several projects to address the transformations taking place in structures, processes and the staff, all of which required a substantial investment of money and people. (At the same time, we were recovering from a two-year fluctuation in the oil market, from $147 a barrel in July 2008 to a $34 low in February 2009 and had to economize when it came to spending—or, really, not spending.)

Brain-storming sessions with my team were called for, and we focused on four main topics: safety, professional and leadership growth, women's development, and community outreach initiatives, as well as the expansion of existing efforts to connect with local and international academic institutes.

In terms of safety, our chief concern was the unspeakable number of traffic accidents. Saudi Arabia ranked twenty-third on the list of countries with the greatest number of driving fatalities, most involving young men. At blame were excessive speeding, use of mobile phones, inattentiveness to the road, and weather conditions in the form of spring and summer sandstorms and fog and mist in autumn and winter, especially in coastal areas. Regardless, the fundamental problem was rooted in the absence of a safety culture in our communities. Practically once a month, we would lose one of our trainees to a traffic accident, not to mention men (women were not driving yet) between the ages of eighteen and twenty-four who were injured and/or incapacitated at an alarming rate. Many of these victims were the only source of income for their families. Urgent attention was required.

Transforming behavior is not an easy task, especially when it is supported by a deep-rooted belief system and culture. Transformation is naturally triggered when one experiences real-life trauma. However, you can affect behavior change very slowly when knowledge is converted into emotional stimulus in the subconscious. This meant employing experts in the science of transformology—the stripping away of mind blocks—whose success depends on the deployment of emotional effect programs, education and consequence management. Those trainees with high-risk propensity were targeted with special training interventions.

To monitor the driving habits of our trainees, we installed Driving Monitoring Devices in their cars, and those with reckless records were counseled and, in severe cases, even terminated. A clean traffic violation record became a major criterion for recruiting trainees. Newcomers had to attend Safety Boot Camp before starting work for Saudi Aramco, with a traffic safety point system established to reward good behavior and penalize unacceptable ones. There was also a call for a structured and formal program to propagate, internalize and sustain the knowledge and safety behavior throughout the local community. For that, we enlisted parents, teachers and government officials. Traffic safety topics were introduced so students would have a safety culture ingrained in them from a young age, in a program that was soon adapted nationwide.

We were lucky to have the Industrial Relations senior vice president, Abdulaziz Al-Khayyal, as our champion for this monumental initiative. Through his connections and influence, we got the relevant government entities on board to support our initiatives in the community. The collaboration and efforts of various industrial relations organizations culminated in the formation of the Saudi Aramco Traffic Signature Safety Program—the company's flagship initiative for propagating a safety culture in the community. The program, under the leadership of Sultan Al-Zahrain, another gentleman passionate about the subject, became a major source of learning and knowledge transfer for the government traffic safety strategy.

All the pushing and shoving paid off.

Within five years, we reduced our traffic fatality rate among trainees by fifty percent.

Transforming culture is a journey that requires the collaboration of everyone involved. Culture is a collection of habits and belief systems reflecting people's past experiences. Change the experience and, over time, you will change the culture. You also need to teach young people how to learn and adopt new habits that will lead them to a prosperous future. Building a learning culture would be my next item on the agenda.

Seeking to invigorate professional development, in 2010 my team and I launched a Saudi Aramco Professional Development Academy, or SAPDA, which in Arabic (pronounced Sa'abda') means "I shall begin." This was to initiate recently hired college graduates into the corporate world. We wanted to capture the hearts and minds of the young talent and fresh graduates, and introduce them to a lifelong learning culture from the first moment they step foot in the company. We wanted to engage the new professionals in an intensive induction program from day one, and build strong foundation and uniform understanding of the company business, culture, values, safety, and strategic imperatives. SAPDA provided seven weeks of full-time courses consisting of three components: integrated-action learning, field visits and network building. The academy also included a community services arm so that students could volunteer their time to aiding others.

From personal experience, I knew new approaches to long-standing programs often met with resistance. I also knew that you did not need the full crew to sail the ship. And while opponents may try to sink the ship, a good captain never gives in to negativity and criticism. I was also aware that the lengthy SAPDA program might rankle some members of management who wanted the new recruits to dive into the water of the work week right away, and sure enough, they grumbled and protested. "Onboarding should not be more than three days," they said, trying to pressure me to shorten the program. I stood my ground. A lifelong lesson could not be delivered in three days. There had to be, especially among young people, time for reflection when it came to assessing their fullest potential, coupled with a period to unlearn old beliefs and to relearn new concepts relevant to modern thinking.

I knew what I was talking about. A secure foundation of background knowledge is required if one is to master a greater amount of knowledge, a precept advanced by what is called the Matthew Effect, named by husband and wife sociologists Robert K. Merton and Harriet Zuckerman in the late 1960s. It is a belief that the smart get smarter, or, if you will, the rich get richer and the poor get poorer—in knowledge. Expertise grows exponentially, and heaven help those who fail early at a subject—for instance, reading—because that will prompt a lifelong distaste for that subject, just as a favorable introduction to the subject will do the opposite. Therefore, the more we know, the greater our ability to learn more and the faster we expand our foundation of knowledge.

SAPDA called upon the new graduates to learn about broad subjects and thereby add to their intellectual capacities. People with restricted specialties do not make for good leaders, so we wanted to show our pupils how to develop the skill of communicating clearly and persuasively, the talent for argument, and the ability to think on one's feet. This was not something that could be conveyed in three days. Not even in three years. But we could at least, in the longer timespan, effectively plant the seed that would ignite their intellectual curiosity. So, the managers conceded, on their terms—insisting that training should last no longer than one week, or ten days at the most.

I made my case and won the argument. Seven weeks, it was—and the results were clear.

In 2014, SAPDA was awarded a Certificate of Merit by the International Federation of Training & Development Organization.

However, a few years after I left T&D, the program duration was sadly reduced from seven to five weeks!

Regarding leadership training for supervisors and professional staff, a large part of our stagnation had to do with infrastructure and content. Thirty-six years old, the six-classroom Leadership Center in Dhahran, where most of our people skills training took place, desperately needed a modern expansion to serve some eighteen thousand participants a year and allow us to eliminate the unwieldy waiting list for courses and increase our offerings. We also were looking to increase the annual workforce by another ten thousand. At the same time, the company was no longer the same company it was a decade or two ago. We had not only grown substantially in scale but also expanded from our core foundation. We had shifted from relatively simple and straightforward wholly-owned activities in our domestic market to international and local joint ventures requiring sophisticated leadership skills.

In terms of our people, the proportion of younger employees in our workforce was rising, and they brought with them a new set of life experiences and very different expectations from those of previous generations. At the same time, a recently launched corporate transformation program contained an ambitious agenda to transform the company into the world's leading energy and chemicals enterprise, and our people needed to keep pace.

It was our CEO, Abdallah Jum'ah, who set the tone for the new leadership center. He decreed that instruction be delivered in a pleasant, tranquil setting distanced from the hustle and bustle of the headquarters in Dhahran. Ras Tanura was selected. The location was breathtaking, right on the shores of the Arabian Gulf with a white sand beach, azure sea, blue sky and palm trees. The beachfront setting could not have been more ideal, even if, at first, there were those who complained about the fifty-minute driving distance from Dhahran. There will always be voices of dissent, just as there will always be sandfleas.

The new center featured twenty classrooms, a four-hundred-capacity auditorium, multipurpose halls with room for three hundred, two computer labs, an exhibition area and a lounge. In all, twelve hundred people could be served at any one time, as opposed to two hundred fifty in the old center. In addition, housing accommodations were provided to the participants attending residential programs to reduce the amount of commute and protect people from long drives after an exhausting long day which included evening activities.

The only thing lacking was a progressive, holistic, future-oriented leadership development strategy. We decided to follow examples set by leading international companies and our team visited the headquarters of General Electric, Shell, British Petroleum, Schlumberger, Weatherford, and a few others. We hired additional staff and instructors and, to set a new direction in the learning process, got management involved, both inside and outside the classroom, as a means of sharing and passing on their aspirations and knowledge to the younger generation.

The cost was anything but modest, but as Peter Drucker, a prominent management consultant, said, "If you think the cost of training is high, consider the cost of ignorance."

The center was inaugurated on September 29, 2010, and marked a new era in the company's long, proud history of developing its most valuable and enduring resource.

No, not oil.

Our people.

The third priority in my development job had to do with a subject dear to my heart, women in the workforce. Given the recent social reforms, the company started hiring more women right out of college, and because there was no history of women in a mixed workplace locally, the environment was completely alien to them. Most had never so much as traveled out of the country or had been exposed to anything beyond what was available locally. They certainly did not know how to present themselves professionally, act independently—or interact with male colleagues.

It was disappointing to see: a new generation of women who were timid, felt inadequate and, in some cases, terrified. Some were embarrassed and offended by our mixed workplace and veiled themselves from head-to-toe. Others were flamboyant with a colorful appearance fit for the red carpet or a beauty contest! I knew that, unless they toughened up and took their jobs seriously, they would not progress much in their careers regardless of their potential and intellect. They needed guidance on how to look and behave professionally, and how to set boundaries and deal with harassment in the workplace. I thought back to what I had learned long ago from Moneera and her assertiveness training and wanted to take this opportunity to give back. The result was two professional growth initiatives, launched two years apart, in 2010 and 2012: Women in Business, for newcomers, and Women in Leadership, for those in mid-career.

Management met my explanation of my plans—I sought merely to inform, not ask permission—with trepidation. Although they welcomed the initiatives and agreed it was timely, they were nervous about the reaction it might create in and out of the company. Were we training women to be rebellious? Disobedient? Aggressive? Troublemakers? Would this initiative make women demanding and give us more headaches than we needed? These were the sentiments among some of the senior leaders, who were all men of course. They wanted to support women's empowerment, but were hesitant to champion any of my initiatives. I am not sure if some of them truly understood the meaning of "women's empowerment"!

When I requested a face-to-face meeting between thirty of our professional women and a couple of our senior leaders, so that the women could hear for themselves that the company was serious about empowering women, the men balked—but they showed up. Afterwards, the women expressed their appreciation for the opportunity. The men did the exact opposite, dismissing the meeting as unnecessary, when I think what they meant to say was that they felt uncomfortable being cornered in a roomful of women.

Bringing science to the table, I enlisted a friend from the New York-based McKinsey Consulting, Dr. Julia Sperling, a lead partner in the firm known for helping corporations and governments organize themselves. Working with my team, Julia laid the foundation for women's development programs at Saudi Aramco and, knowing my devotion to the project and having her own enthusiasm for the topic, declined to charge for her efforts. She said that her reward was seeing women succeed in claiming their rightful place in the world.

The new development programs helped women open their minds to new possibilities and learning opportunities, and develop their personal identity, courage and character. For women to succeed in our male-dominated business environment, they needed guidance, and a lot of it, to develop and cultivate their minds to their fullest potential and to liberate themselves from prejudice, intolerance and old doctrines about their capabilities and potential.

Key to the learning experience was mentoring by other accomplished women in the company. At every session, I chose two or three senior women to lead an open roundtable discussion with the participants. Their participation, sharing their experiences and providing guidance to the young participants, was a key element in the learning environment. Leading women such as Sheila Rowaily, Mae Mozaini, Sheikha Althakafi, Fatema Awami, Amira Mustafa, Lubna Younis and Soulafa Al-Nassar, presented role models from different technical backgrounds and experiences. In introducing them to the young women, I explained how they had paved the way in leveling the playing field so that they, the young ones, could come in and succeed. I coached them on projecting a compelling, winning and credible professional image and said, "You don't need an impressive degree and technical expertise or to show off masculine qualities in order to succeed. Look at me. I came here thirty years ago with a degree in the humanities. I knew absolutely nothing about the oil business. Everywhere I looked all I could see were rough, tough men. But I worked hard and remained focused, and I beat the odds. You will, too, if you want to, but you will have to work for it. Success comes at a price. It is not free."

The exposure to the senior women made the younger ones feel confident about themselves, and the program was labeled a success. We expanded the sessions to the local community, and I am proud to say they were subsequently adopted by the Chamber of Commerce. We were also requested by the women's universities to help them with strategies to prepare senior students for the job market. We opened our doors to professors, teachers and senior students to visit our facilities and learn from our experience. We freely shared with all who asked.

In the twelfth century, the Muslim philosopher Ibn Rushd said, "Much of the poverty and distress of the times arises from the fact that women are kept like domestic animals or houseplants for purposes of gratification."

Nine centuries later, we awakened to the fact that transformation cannot take root with the efforts of only half the population. We need to apply the strength and capabilities of all.

A race cannot be run on only one leg.

We need both legs to reach the final destination.

My fourth priority was to expand our community outreach initiatives by linking them to the world of academia. The country was embarking on a monumental initiative to reform general education, and Saudi Aramco happily provided some of our talented education experts to support the government's efforts.

Beginning in the 1940s, Saudi Aramco had developed some of the kingdom's first educational institutions. Developing local skills was imperative to secure economic progress, safeguard against swings in the labor market, and provide an ongoing flow of talent. Like many companies in the industry, we faced the challenge of closing the gap between the outcomes of the education system and the industry need for qualified graduates, especially in technical and industrial fields. To address this challenge, we partnered with reputable academic institutions both domestically and globally, with the intent of developing teaching capabilities, as well as designing and delivering smart educational environments starting with kindergarten up to high-school level. We wanted to create intellectual curiosity and passion from a young age for STEM (Science, Technology, Engineering and Mathematics) skills, and also develop character and soft skills. Our partnership with academia, government, private sector suppliers and other stakeholders has allowed us to influence policies, gain access to talent and ensure the skills of the next generation meet the business needs of the day.

Two of our partnerships for which I was proudest were with the U.S.-based MIT (Massachusetts Institute of Technology) and the CEE (Center for Excellence in Education). The MIT alliance helped enhance teaching methods and facilitate students' engagement by introducing MIT BLOSSOMS (Blended Learning Open Source Science or Math Studies), founded by Dr. Richard Larson and Elizabeth Murray, into public schools. BLOSSOMS provided interactive video lessons in math and science, with a focus on stimulating students' interest in STEM studies. Because most of the videos were in English, our staff worked on translating the lessons to Arabic so they also could be used by hundreds of teachers in Saudi Arabia, although the videos were later posted on the MIT/BLOSSOMS website to aid teachers and students around the world.

The CEE project kicked off in October 2009, when at a business event I was introduced to Dr. Joann DiGennaro, the Center's President.

She and I contemplated the idea of establishing a Saudi Research Science Institute with a six-week summer program to match talented high-school students with a university professor who taught in the area of the student's strength. Joann put her own formidable strengths to work at cutting through the local politics and bringing her initiative to fruition. In the summer of 2011, we secured agreements with King Abdullah University of Science and Technology to host the program in its campus, and the Saudi RSI became the sixth national RSI program to thrive outside of the United States.

There were other programs, too, with such titles as TryEngineering, the Siemens Science Discovery initiative, Mathletics, and summer youth courses, to name a few. All these programs were designed to awaken interest in science and technology, ignite passion for learning, enhance language proficiency, develop soft skills, and introduce modern pedagogical approaches. All aimed at ultimately building the brain power of our local talent. You can read about all these programs in the company website. I was especially gratified by the productive results I witnessed in the girls' schools. Every year since 2006, we granted some one hundred scholarships to top female high-school achievers to study in competitive universities in America or Europe.

Moreover, in November 2009, we established a University Relations Division to oversee the growth in our partnership initiatives with higher education institutions worldwide. This effort was led by Waleed Somali, a sharp, energetic and eloquent gentleman, who was passionate about maintaining and sustaining strong relations between industry and academia. Our strategic partnerships aimed at enhancing academic and industrial collaboration, providing insight into new research fields, tapping into complementary technical expertise, and extending opportunities to our workforce to build their technical knowledge and share experience through part-time teaching programs.

In my position at the company, I was required to interact directly with the leadership of local universities. Once again, this posed a painful challenge—not to me, after all these years of dealing with gender issues, but to the men in charge. One example was with the management of King Fahad University of Petroleum and Minerals, which specializes in energy-industry studies. The fact that the university received significant support from the company took precedence over any reluctance to deal with me, as I was one of the conduits to Saudi Aramco's resources.

As a matter of fact, I had fun ruffling feathers, especially when it came to face-to-face meetings on the all-male campus. On several occasions I took the opportunity to voice my concerns about their discriminatory practices against women and suggested that KFUPM, given its prominent position, be bold and pioneer an effort to turn things around. I even offered to host their programs in Saudi Aramco's facilities, so that women could attend without being a physical presence on the university campus. The rector strongly objected.

Faced with his opposition, I expanded partnerships with international institutes to deliver their programs on our campus so that women could participate—subsequently signing agreements with the Hong Kong University for Science and Technology and supporting the launch of several company partnerships with, for example, the Georgia Institute of Technology, French Institute of Petroleum, Pennsylvania Institute of Technology, and Texas A&M.

Change, however faint, was in the air.

In 2020, at long last, KFUPM started granting women access, albeit limited to its academic programs.

Welcome to the twenty-first century.

It was also time to use what was then the rapidly expanding worldwide web for long-distance and online education. We relied on Saudi Aramco's impressive e-Learning Library, stocked and accessible 24/7 with more than thirty-five hundred courses and a bookstore with more than twenty thousand titles from three hundred publishers. Access was provided to outside organizations to benefit from the rich content of our library. The materials covered business, IT, legal, engineering, environmental and safety topics, in addition to content on management theories, interpersonal skills and leadership capabilities.

I enjoyed our educational outreach and what it could provide both our young population and employers, and the feedback was extremely positive. Bridging the gap between academia and industry proved one of our greatest hurdles, and we as a company often talked about the need for a close partnership between the two. Institutions of education should develop content based on an awareness of what the labor market needs and a look toward the future impact of technological advances as they pertain to job creation. Therefore, it was imperative to create and sustain a lifelong learning environment that met the business requirements of the day.

All of these educational and cultural programs reflect our belief as a company and leadership team in the value of people talent over financial capital and other resources, as the decisive factor in productivity and consequently prosperity and advancement of nations.

During my stint in T&D, as in other areas, my interest was in keeping my eye on the big picture. Rather than micromanage, a duty I left in the competent hands of my staff, my focus remained on guiding the ship to its next destination. Not everyone was impressed by my leadership style. Many believed we should "get our hands dirty" with the minor details of the operation. But I kept repeating that "the captain's seat is in the cockpit, not the engine room."

Many leaders grew with the habit to micromanage their organizations; that's the only way they know how to draw their power. To me that is a sign of insecurity, distrust and lack of faith in one's abilities and those of the staff. Command and control approach is sometimes necessary, and the authoritative style is needed in sensitive functions and risky business. But there should be a balance in the leadership style depending on the situation, the issue, and the nature of the team.

There are as many ways to lead people and manage a business as there are people in the business to manage. Leadership invariably reflects the experiences and beliefs of its leaders. That is natural. But when opposite styles compete rather than cooperate, the atmosphere becomes toxic, lacking trust and harmony in the relationships between leaders.

Learning to see and appreciate differences in people is an act of grace. No two people are meant to be the same. Embracing diversity makes for better leadership decisions, better discussions and better performance.

"Our ability to reach unity in diversity will be the beauty and the test of our civilization," said that most wondrous of organizers, Mahatma Gandhi.

Right on.

22. THE LAST DANCE

"Where do you see yourself in ten years?" The question, posed in 2004, came in the midst of a talent assessment exercise as part of a leadership development program. Without giving it a second's thought, I replied, "I will be the head of Human Resources in Saudi Aramco." Don't ask me why I said that. The job was certainly not a goal of mine at that time, or possibly at any time. All I can say is, something inside me was spiritually aware of the path set before me, and I was as surprised as anyone else to hear about it.

When I first arrived at the company, leadership positions never had much appeal to me, given my distaste for internal politics. At the time, I thought that my great aim was to become a senior economist more involved with research and analysis, and less with people. That seemed safe, even feasible, and out of politics' way. It wasn't until I was promoted into leadership roles that I discovered that I had innate capabilities for, well, leading people.

Neither was I aware from the outset that by May 2012, which was when I was promoted to Executive Director of Employee Relations and Training, there would remain no hesitation among the big boys to moving me up to replace my boss. In fact, they were confident that I was the right person to head the company's organization of Human Resources, which is what Employee Relations and Training came to be called. I received the news through my boss's boss a few months before the promotion actually came through. When the time came, the step up simply took place as a *fait accompli*.

At that juncture, HR was divided into two parts: Management Services, which oversaw policy development, and ER&T, which handled policy execution. It was a structure handed down from our American pioneers who wished to separate the legislative and administrative branches and, this way, minimize any potential for conflicts of interest. It worked well in the past, but as our business grew and expanded, so did competition and contention between the two sides. My mission stepping into the job was to build a solid HR foundation for the company, unify all efforts by merging the two organizations into one, and report directly to the President and CEO.

Don't look for downtime in the oil business, especially with the unforgiving pace of our critical operations all over the world and in every time zone: Houston, Tokyo, Beijing, London, Saudi Arabia, and others. Combine this with the fact that executive status at a giant such as Saudi Aramco brings with it a scope of answerabilities equal to those faced by a CEO in small to medium companies. The intrusion of the smartphone also forever vanquished the notion of traditional "office hours," forcing the already twelve-plus-hour workday to expand even more. Forget about a work-life balance. There was no escape. Your life is your job, even at home. Family, friends, personal needs are all placed on hold. Your rewards are power, status and money.

Because of the sacrifices entailed and the demands placed, selecting a company's top leaders must be a rigorous, prudent process. It is by no means a one-man decision, but one that involves committees, assessments, success profiles, metrics, targeted development, and executive coaching. Saudi Aramco's investment in developing and honing executive skills is unmatched in the industry and involves an impressive network of contributors to the decision. We work with executive coaches and attend educational programs in such universities as Oxford, Harvard, MIT, Stanford, and Switzerland's Institute for Management Development, among others. I, for example, took executive lessons at the University of Michigan's Ross School of Business and University of Oxford's Saïd School of Business, as well as at the Royal Academy of Dramatic Art in London—no, not to learn acting, but to work on skills for influence and presence. There, I was taught to polish the performance of my roles and express my thoughts and emotions so that I might effectively communicate on a global stage, internally and externally.

For all the world *is* a stage.

Because of my unique position as the first woman with an executive title at Saudi Aramco, I received increasing public attention from the mainstream and trade media, the business community, and women's universities and schools, all curious about my experience. The company welcomed the publicity, as it served as a sign we were a viable contributor to the progressive business community. There was also another side benefit to my write-ups and public speaking around the globe: headhunters chased me down, waving lucrative contracts with bonuses—you name it—from big players in the field. And yet, aside from my loyalty to Saudi Aramco, I found myself no longer interested in power and status beyond what I had.

There was also another consideration. Although the attention was flattering even to one who valued her privacy, I did not wish to be distracted from my final critical mission in the company, to turn HR into a modern, world-class operation, despite what remain very real obstacles.

As usual, intolerance reared its ugly head from the depth of the oil fields. Not only was I not an engineer and devoid of any technical skills or field experience in the oil and gas operation, the whispers echoed in my surroundings, but I was a woman. Not suitable for the oil business. Not fit to lead. And while the office corridors and offsites became more treacherous than ever, to their credit, the top leaders acknowledged the situation as, one by one—and this included the CEO—they congratulated and offered me support. "Stay the course" was the sentiment I heard most often.

And what a course it was.

It was one thing when I was perched on a lower rung of the corporate ladder, but here I had risen to the rarefied atmosphere of the top rung. As a woman in a bigger position, I posed a bigger threat to men who took a dim view of women in general, not just me (which did not make the situation any easier, although I knew not to take the snide comments personally).

There was a particular cynicism among managers in the core oil and gas operations, who believed that their engineering degrees and deep field experiences outranked any of my skills. Despite what they told themselves about their presumed superiority, I threatened their status and sense of themselves, which they shielded with conceit and arrogance.

This stage of my journey proved to be the greatest test of character. The higher I rose up the corporate ladder, the more comfortable I became in my own skin, and the truer I became to myself. I could see through the illusion of power, and the thick political mask that people were hiding behind. I could not playact anymore and was myself weary of wearing the mask for so long. Time and again, I tried to play the political game but was unable to keep the mask on for an extended time. I would suffocate!

Was it Friedrich Nietzsche or Rudyard Kipling who said, "The individual has always had to struggle to keep from being overwhelmed by the tribe. If you try it, you will be lonely often, and sometimes frightened. But no price is too high to pay for the privilege of owning yourself." So true! Regardless of who first said it.

Moreover, I witnessed how rising to a position of power in the corporate world dramatically alters leaders' attitudes and veils their hearts with curtains of narcissism and conceit. They become so attached to the power of their position and its resulting privileges that they are willing to compromise their truth to protect their status.

One of the leaders stood out, with a vehemence I had not experienced before (because we don't have many of those in the company). "Not all psychopaths are in prison—some are in the board room," said Dr. Robert D. Hare, a contemporary Canadian psychologist. I learned the hard way that he was right.

In just a matter of days, Sultan (not his real name) made a leap from being a gentle, wise leader to a ruthless tyrant. "Nearly all men can stand adversity," Abraham Lincoln observed, "but if you want to test a man's character, give him power." No sooner had Sultan advanced in the company than he became greedy, and his hunger for money and power consumed him. Feeding that hunger also fed his sense of self-worth, so that no one dared challenge him on anything. "The need to always be right is a sign of a vulgar mind," said Albert Camus. I dared to speak the truth. He retaliated.

The two of us had shared a respectful relationship earlier in our careers. I admired his strong intellect, and he cheered on my assertiveness and determination. But now he viewed those same attributes in me as impertinence and did his best to marginalize me when he could not manipulate and cage me in. Undermining my authority at every opportunity, he made autocratic decisions affecting my organization without consulting with or even alerting me. I could not understand his mental construct. Suffice it to say that I spoke up when I disagreed, and spoke up when I saw inequities. I spoke up with honesty; and expressed my views openly and boldly. I thought to myself that if I was going to be held accountable for the organization performance, then I should be in control of how to deliver my business. He did not like it. One of our senior leaders once told me "Huda, your courage is a double-edged sword!" He said, "It can bring you victory, but sometimes it could lead to unfavorable consequences." Nevertheless, I believed in Socrates' wisdom that courage is "the greatest quality of the mind next to honor." Sultan used the power of his position to block any chance of future advancements as well as negating recognition of my achievements, something he was in a position to do. He justified his actions by accusing me of not being a team player.

This was the first time I faced an ugly confrontation on so large a scale, and hardly what one expected after years of faithful hard work in a firm.

I chose not to give in to Sultan's drama or the politicized atmosphere he created. I was too close to the finish line to allow him to derail me. Again, I could not confide in anyone about Sultan's underhandedness, not even the top-level company men who were my staunchest defenders. The last thing I wanted at this point was to be perceived as too weak to fight my own battles.

I was a peaceful warrior who was always hopeful that conflicts could be resolved subtly and at no cost to anyone's pride. That's not always feasible. In fact, had I clung to my earlier hope of living and working in a utopian dream, I never would have been able to survive the disappointments, or learn from them.

"Life is not about waiting for the storm to pass," said the twentieth-century British writer Vivien Greene. "It is about learning how to dance in the rain."

Throughout this ordeal, I thought I was strong enough to handle stressful situations at work, because taxing conditions were nothing new and I always faced them. But what was also required was paying attention to my physical health, not only mental health, because, suddenly, I started gaining weight again and losing sleep. Nightmares developed and, even more frightening, I was falling out of bed as if some force was pushing me and yelling at me to wake up.

The situation was exacerbated when I developed balance problems while taking simple steps. One fall resulted in a break in my collarbone, followed by twists in my feet and toes. Stress was the cause; energy to my internal system was blocked, and the function of my vital organs was severely disturbed.

Tensions at work also led to a myriad of other maladies, from the inflammation of my joints and intestines, to hormonal imbalance, thinning hair, and the aggravation of my digestive system. My personality was similarly negatively affected. My motivation was low, and I easily became annoyed and irritated, cynical, and unhappy. I felt as if I were being ripped apart inside, and my doctor confirmed many of my worst suspicions when he compared my annual physical exams of the previous years.

The doctor said that if I didn't manage my stress immediately, it would cause grave and potential irreversible damage to my being.

I listened.

Sultan's horrid behavior toward me brought about one silver lining: It brought about a re-evaluation of my own self-image. It was not merely fear of becoming like him; I am confident that would be impossible, as selfishness has never been a guiding principle. Indeed, I suddenly found myself unimpressed by the status and privileges of my position; after all, they were not the source of my happiness and peace. I was now repulsed by how some people lusted after them. From my new perspective, prominence and affluence lost their allure and no longer defined me. My strength need not come from the validation of others. Those who allow that happen actually surrender their power, by allowing their destinies to be manipulated by others. By releasing myself from my status, I felt a sense of elation. What now mattered to me was being able to lead with authenticity and integrity. And wow, was that liberating.

Office relations can sometimes be complicated and tricky. You spend almost half of your day surrounded by people you did not choose to be with. To get the work done and protect your sanity you have to reconcile your differences and put aside personal moods and tendencies. And it gets worse as you move higher in the organization where inflated egos rule. That is when you have to perfect the political dance to endure.

My attitudinal shift also allowed me to take a fresh look at my career. Here I was, the only woman in the room of the company's highest leaders, like an alien who had invaded a sacred club. What I found interesting was that the towering giants I admired early on in my career now looked no more imposing than I did, with my five-foot frame. They, in fact, were my equals. Stepping closer to them, I could see their mundane qualities and imperfections.

Dealing with me was the first time in their lives they matched wits with a woman of equal standing. All the women they were connected to in their personal or professional lives were their subordinates or dependents. So my position as a colleague created a massive shock to their belief system and required real conviction and a heroic shift in attitude on their part. Nevertheless, I was always friendly and gracious. Some of them were so intrigued by my doings that they brought their daughters in to meet me, sometimes even their sons, to show what was happening in the workplace and to open their children's minds to new possibilities. What I found especially gratifying was that the executives also would ask me to give their girls pep talks to better motivate them in school. It made me so happy to see the hopes in their wide eyes and hear the whispers of their thoughts and aspiration "Woman can be leaders! Me too!"

As for the old boys' social club, the men routinely socialized outside of work, where they could openly hash out business challenges, resolve personality conflicts and strike deals before plans were even presented in the decision room. Obviously, I was not a part of this . . . and it was annoying, until one day I decided to establish my own network and invite a few of my colleagues in corporate and executive management to dinner at my house. They were all men, of course, and in our culture it is completely inappropriate for a single woman to invite men to her house. Somehow, that was the least of my concerns. I was mainly worried how their spouses would react to my being the only woman at the party. Rather than face their gossip, I invited the wives, too.

Not that the gathering was without its social predicament. Once the guests arrived, the women drifted to one side of the living room and the men to the other. (The spacious room had different seating areas.) I was both stunned and puzzled. Do I socialize with my colleagues in the "men's section," and risk upsetting the wives, or be a good hostess to the women and leave the men to chat among themselves? By now, I was distressed, as this had not been the intention of the gathering.

I ended up spending a lot of time in the kitchen supervising the dinner preparation and little time in the two seating areas. At least the food was a success.

I never again contemplated establishing my own social network with my male colleagues.

Our labor laws mandate that people retire at age sixty so that jobs are made available to the younger generation, who comprise the majority of the country's headcount. (More than half the population is under twenty-five.) My job as the head of HR was my final position in the company before my retirement.

Before I left, my two top priorities were to transform the corporate HR function and to help women successfully integrate into the workforce. With the company moving at full tilt with an ambitious agenda to globalize and expand operations, the workforce was the engine expected to propel the transformation. My team and I rolled up our collective sleeves to develop a progressive HR strategy in support of the company's vision and ambitious agenda. We cross referenced external HR practices and benchmarks, examined global talent megatrends and measured organizational health surveys. We also reviewed the World Economic Forum findings on the "workforce of the future" and the implications of the Fourth Industrial Revolution brought about by the exponential changes in technological advances and the impact of Artificial Intelligence. "It is quite different than the three Industrial Revolutions that preceded it—steam and waterpower, electricity and assembly lines, and computerization—because it will even challenge our ideas of what it means to be human," *Forbes* magazine spelled out. "This revolution is expected to impact all disciplines, industries and economies."

We also had to rise to the challenge of initiating the new crop of young workers who were beginning to populate our workforce and teach them the conduct and values we demanded of our people. Topics included conflict of interest, financial integrity, sexual harassment and bullying, as well as safety and the environment, and safeguarding assets and information.

What emerged from our vast examination was a dynamic and compelling strategy we named "Creating People Advantage." We identified three high priority areas including workforce planning and analytics, performance culture, and leadership development. Its aim was to differentiate Saudi Aramco through the quality of leadership and talent to give us a competitive edge over our competitors.

Equalizing policies and regulations may have been a step forward, but the number of women in the Saudi Aramco workforce continued to be embarrassingly low, under five percent. The country had already embarked on major efforts to empower women and correct the existing social and economic imbalance. Government, public, and private programs and policies were restructured to create more jobs, and reform any laws obstructing women's greater participation. There was nothing stopping us from proceeding at full force to enhance workforce diversity. But some lingering factors impeded the company's advancement in this area, including resistance to gender diversity from some old-school leaders, the country's lack of engineering schools for women, and the discomfort of women themselves when it came to working in our mixed environment. Something urgent had to be done.

I established a Women's Development and Diversity division, later renamed Diversity and Inclusion, to monitor, address and report on our progress with women's empowerment. The new division provided mentorship and coaching programs as it also assessed progression, or regression, in core talent management areas that included recruiting, training, promoting and leading. Results were shared with CEO Amin Al-Nasser and his corporate team. Amin was wholeheartedly supportive of our efforts and urged company leaders to show a visible commitment. Support programs and facilities, such as a daycare center, were also provided to attract and retain women at Aramco.

In 2014, we established the company's first Women in the Workforce Forum to provide networking opportunities with partners in the market and community to analyze solutions that could be mobilized into action. The forum proved so successful that it was turned into an annual event. We also ventured beyond the company's boundaries and into the community, where we encouraged more women to join us and more companies to hire women.

Progress was slow but steady. Scholarships for women so that they might pursue STEM studies in the company increased from twenty to thirty percent, and the percentage of women in our employment candidates' pool for professional jobs rose to forty percent. As for women in leadership positions, we still lagged in this area.

But at least we got the wheel turning.

So, why was I not dancing in jubilation? Here I was, at the pinnacle of my career. I had status, power and wealth. Yet I found myself itching to disengage. Try as I might to avoid it, I was still subject to that old affliction of letting others define my success. The happiness I so convincingly feigned was as thin as a crust of dust and unable to conceal my internal unease and anxiety. I had to play the game and hide behind a thousand masks to get through the journey. It was like trying to dance Swan Lake while implanted in a potato sack.

How many times during my four decades of work was I screaming inside to give up the suit and surrender my corporate life? Only that would have been giving up the most valuable test of my character as a woman and totally against the plan my soul came to this world to fulfill. "Life is the sum of all your choices," said Camus.

In retrospect, I can say I am pleased with my major life choices, be they good, bad, or mad. Some were made consciously, while others were guided by passion and intuition. They made me who I am today: comfortable in my own skin and leading my life with honor, peace and authenticity. That what defines success to me, not worldly possessions or my bank account.

I don't wish to give the impression that money, status and power are unimportant. On the contrary, they are natural desires necessary to secure a comfortable and dignified life for people and their dependents. But when they become one's ultimate goal in life, the impoverished soul sinks in the deep hollow inside that even all the riches in the world cannot satiate. I have enjoyed these worldly rewards at different stages of my life and considered them vital for my prosperity and psychological development. But with time, they became like old toys—monotonous and stale, with no satiation point, mere objects unable to provide perpetual joy and peace. That's when I realized running after them would never pacify the void inside. They were only, I realized, the lesson-filled means to take me in the direction of a more fulfilled life. It became natural that, once they lost their original allure, my attachment to them declined, leading me to seek a new philosophy that transcended material rewards beyond the circumscribed reality of my world.

I am proud to say that, at last, I was happily at peace with myself, a conclusion I reached when I realized I was serving people with my own genuine power, not my power of position. Helping others find direction, whether it be schoolchildren who came to visit my office or the women in my purview and beyond, is what made my heart dance. What drove me was fulfillment, not achievement; inspiration, not ambition.

From the time Mother, God bless her, first came into my room with the newspaper ad, what I feared would be my worst nightmare had turned into my dream job, and I was enormously gratified to be serving a company with a global influence, respected reputation and caring nature.

As for the challenges en route, they taught me that we would never be able to discover the gifts that lie dormant deep within us had we not the courage to sample life with all its distinct flavors: bitter, sweet, and sour.

Don't pick and choose any one of them, simply receive and experience. The positive experiences give us hope and help us persevere; the negative experiences give us lessons and help us grow wise.

"The dark thought, the shame, the malice—meet them at the door laughing and invite them in," said Rumi. "Be grateful for whatever comes."

"Because each had been sent as a guide from beyond."

23. REFLECTIONS

The last thing I wanted was a retirement celebration. My plan was to slip out quietly, the same way I had entered, even though I was now an entirely different person. But, for once, this radically transformed woman was not to have her way.

Amin Al-Nasser, our President and CEO, insisted on the traditional public ceremony to honor my achievements, just like the ones held for every executive who ever preceded me into retirement.

Retirement. Sometimes viewed as the finale for someone's productive life. To me, however, it was not an ending; it was a progression to something with deeper meaning about who I was, my being.

The morning of December 28, 2017, was cool, but my every feeling toward my surroundings was warm. Nearly four decades at Saudi Aramco. Standing at a podium, for some reason I blurted out before hundreds of colleagues, relatives and friends that I did not plan to write a book about my journey. It could have been my imagination, but I could swear I heard a discernable sigh of relief from some of the men in the audience.

It was true: Never had I seriously entertained the idea of sharing my story, be it for myself, my family, or the global community with whom I'd interacted in my career. But as an old saying goes, "Don't tell God about your plans, for he will laugh at you."

Despite my declaration, for two years after my retirement there were gentle signs (or nudges from the universe) that kept appearing from a variety of sources—dreams, astrological readings, subliminal messages in movies and books—as well as people pressing me to tell my tale. I waved away these suggestions as silly and meritless. "I have nothing special to say," I would reply, as if proving how mundane the things I said could be. Mine had been a lifetime of playing down my achievements with self-effacement and humility, as Mother had taught all of her children to do. But I took it to the extreme. That is, until my path intersected with that of Abdi Assadi.

I believe the universe orchestrated our encounter to open my mind so I might view my life with lucid objectivity. "When the student is ready, the teacher will appear," is another old saying, and it is far from mundane. I had started having regular sessions with Abdi, an American author, spiritual counselor and healer in New York, starting in the summer of 2019, and he would help me put all the pieces of my journey together and tap into my spiritual ability.

As part of the process, Abdi recommended I write a candid and truthful personal journal. "See where it will take you," he told me. He knew. Abdi opened my eyes to all the extraordinary corners, junctions and turns in my road, allowing me to take a closer look at my soul and speak to the inner strength that uplifted me every time I stumbled in my quest for identity and gave me the chance to thrive in spite of the unforgiving patriarchal world I lived in.

Following Abdi's advice, I began writing, with no thought beyond keeping my words locked in my desk. Still, I was pleased—and amazed— how effortlessly the memories came rushing back as I raced to commit them to the page. "This is not for public consumption," I repeatedly told myself, which made the writing even easier.

What I saw was the rebellious pattern I had developed so early on, always screaming for originality and autonomy, and how I greeted the self-limiting beliefs I was fed from childhood with my own barrage of skepticism and defiance. I rejected convention and the stereotypes painted for women in order to stymie any hope of achieving, and I choked in a world that was unkind to women by denouncing our individuality and ignoring our intellect.

I sailed my own course, recognizing the sea monsters I had to battle both internally and externally. To fend off the ferocious undertow, my vessel had to be strong and solid. But I weathered the storms.

I reached my destination.

No one instruction manual can tell you how to triumph in life. Those endless stacks of "How To" books only touch upon generalizations. We are each different, unique in our experiences. No one taught me how to fight the temptations of the ego, or how to avoid being swayed as I awaited validation by others. I had to figure out these lessons for myself, by unleashing myself from the safety net of the flock. Falling into the trap of social and cultural convention is especially easy for women, particularly in a world where their limited roles are determined before birth. And believe me there will be forces, internal and external, that will attempt to deter you from following your own path. Social and cultural forces will try to program you with their "right" way to live your life, practice your spirituality, and to be happy and successful. Society will push you to act a role already predetermined for you. You are conditioned from childhood to start wearing a mask to play the different roles that culture and customs needs you to play; and some people never take off the mask. We must never bow to this; we must snap back instead. We must be our own selves. Life begins only when we stop betraying ourselves.

"To live as a released individual, one has to know how and when to put on and to put off the masks of one's various life roles," Carl Jung said, "and then learn to live out of one's own center."

Those who don't remove the masks that conceal their true identities start believing what others see, thereby leaving their own souls to grieve and search for fulfillment that never comes. We then become "hollow" and never fulfilled. I have witnessed this with colleagues who acted out their executive roles from the office with their families and friends at home. As a result, they were never content. It happened to me when, as an adolescent, I believed my only role was to be an obedient daughter and then wife. It happened again when I reached the top and could not comprehend why I was not happy. I had everything I wanted, but I felt lacking, even miserable, inside. Finally, I understood that I had been wearing the mask too long.

Over the centuries, culture has been used to manipulate crowd consciousness into submitting to orthodox conformity and ideology. I am not referring to expressions of cultural heritage as represented in civil standards, art, technology, architecture and literature, but rather cultural concepts imposed to repress independent expressions of the mind, body and soul—concepts used to mold our behavior under a universal gauge for measuring success and happiness. This formula is irrelevant to the spirit of many of us.

Learning to discover and appreciate differences in people is an act of grace. Disrespecting differences by imposing blanket opinions is disrespecting the universe and the laws of nature. We are not meant to be measured against one another. We are a reflection of nature's multiplicity of colors and shapes, a philosophical notion upheld by Oswald Spengler when he said, "We are free and virtuous beings, until culture came to destroy us . . . with material conducts and techniques, accumulation of wealth, and left the soul bankrupt and drowning in boredom."

He added, "Culture is just a superficial artificial manmade life tactic evolved into a cage for those souls that could not be restrained."

Those in the East concurred, centuries earlier. Ibn Khaldun, a fourteenth-century Muslim philosopher and historian, said, "Blindly following ancient customs and traditions does not mean that the dead are alive.

"But that the living are dead."

As I chronicled my life, I felt like a spectator, viewing and reliving the journey with amazement. This wasn't an ego trip, but another lesson: I could see that there was nothing ordinary about my story; it was individual, at times, remarkable. I felt an obligation to share what I had learned on my adventure. Perhaps, I thought, this will give hope to others, young women, also young men, and inspire them to believe in themselves, even when voices around them grow loud and try to dash their every last hope. When such a force arises, silence all outside noise, listen to your inner whisper, and awaken your willpower to fulfill your yearnings.

Despite the detours I might have taken, and now I realize how important those subconscious detours were, when I view my life from my current perspective it seems as if I was following a divine plan all along—an itinerary meticulously designed with a main plot and separate narratives moving in a type of choreographed synchronicity. It is easy to see the big picture of your life when you view it from a higher perspective. I did not perceive its orderly form as the events unfolded; at the time, it felt I was aboard some long, chaotic ride. But as I have said repeatedly, I know there are no coincidences in life. "God does not play dice with the universe," said Einstein. We must be in alignment with what happens to and around us, and the meaning of it all will be revealed when the proper time comes.

What I realize in hindsight is that everything that happened was happening for me, not to me, including the unpleasant experiences. Every person, every incident I encountered was there by divine design and for a reason. It was not like the universe was conspiring against me. The universe was giving me what was necessary for my soul to reach an awakening. It was responding to my every thought, intention and action. Sometimes our rigid self-image simply holds us back from waking up. Vedic literature describes this in a dharma that goes, "If you want to see what has brought you to this point, look at your past thoughts and actions. If you want to see your future, look at your present thoughts and actions."

Examine your life through an objective lens and you will grasp that no one is responsible for you but you. The events that weave together your life with happy and sad moments are consequences of your choices.

There are no victims here.

The hero's journey is a story shared by all ancient and modern civilizations. Scholar and mythologist Joseph Campbell popularized the monomyth when he said, "The lion of self-discovery is meant to kill that dragon whose every scale reads Thou Shalt." That myth is fundamentally about examining your inner world on an authentic journey of self-discovery, with the emphasis on self, not following the path of others, and then rising to the calling of your own soul. Follow your passion and respond to "every call that excites your spirit," as Rumi expressed. "Know thyself" is something every ancient philosopher has said since the beginning of time. Tap the potential inside, because everything we seek in life exists right inside there. I now realize that my journey was about the quest to discover myself.

I left the company fulfilled and content with my achievements and experiences. It was then time to connect all the pieces of this marvelous expedition and take it all in. "A life unexamined is not worth living," said Socrates. Having engaged with others and served the community in the first stage of my life, this next chapter could bring engagement with myself and a disentanglement with whatever failed to bring bliss. Again, from Rumi: "Yesterday I was clever, so I wanted to change the world. Today I am wise, so I am changing myself."

Retirement meant I could return to the company of my books, music and thoughts—that secure place I occupied at home with Mother before embarking on my adventure. It was like a reunion with lost lovers to whom I am indebted for exposing me to a higher vision so early in my life. Only now I am a changed person, one with knowledge and insights since I first encountered them starting in my cousin Ibrahim's library. In his autobiography, Charles Darwin wrote, "If I had to live my life again, I would have made a rule to read some poetry and listen to some music at least once a week; for perhaps the parts of my brain now atrophied could thus have been kept active through use."

To sort out my priorities, I went into seclusion. I meditated and practiced yoga with reputable teachers and spent time with spiritual healers. There are no words to express how this rejuvenated my mind, body and spirit. Gone are the fears of being a nobody not seen and recognized—a fear that can often come with retirement. I just wanted to get to the core of myself and just BE.

I started to enjoy life in the moment, not regret the past and not worry about the future. The past no longer exists, and the future we don't own. Everything outside the present is irrelevant.

My memoir, I hope, is about the determination and perseverance that underpins achievements. It is not intended to provide surefire tips on how to succeed in the business world or how to climb your way to the top. You may pick up a few ideas in the process, but that is not the intention.

My purpose is to emphasize that we are all born with the freewill to fulfill our heart's desire, no matter the circumstances of our coming into the world, and we must struggle to transcend the traps of the ego and cultural hypnosis.

We must fully trust our internal yearnings and stay the course.

Ultimately, this book is about my quest for an unbounded identity beyond the ancient walls of the desert.

It is about developing the sensitivity to appreciate the peaceful state of just BEING.

This place is a dream.
Only a sleeper considers it real.
Then death comes like dawn
And you wake up laughing
At what you thought was your grief.

—Rumi

EPILOGUE

Over the past few years, life has changed dramatically for women in Saudi Arabia. Their legitimacy and empowerment have been recognized as a crucial factor in the economic and social development of the country and, to put these new beliefs into practice, traditional laws were reformed to allow a prosperous and sustainable future for all our people.

Activities once considered taboo, such as allowing women to drive, and sacred laws, such as demands for a male guardian, were abandoned or amended, and women were allowed to exercise freedom and control over their own lives. Women have been appointed to prominent government positions both locally and globally, and public and private sectors were urged to employ more women. Restrictions on gender mixing have been alleviated, and technical educational and training opportunities were expanded to include women.

Consequently, societal attitudes toward women's capabilities have radically changed. For example, in the past when a woman dared to speak up, she was characterized as "ill-mannered," but today doing so is considered courageous. Determination in the past was judged as stubbornness, while today it is encouraged and called perseverance; assertiveness, formerly deemed aggression, is now viewed as self-confidence.

Notwithstanding the great opportunities available for women, there are still more advancements to be made, because of the years of institutionalized neglect and marginalization. And while we have an incredible base of young talented women, they will need time and experience to polish their character and build their knowledge. Nevertheless, the future for Saudi women is brighter than before and full of promise. They just need to take responsibility for their lives and stay the course.

Economic necessity and social pressure have finally crumbled the ancient walls that confined women's autonomy and individuality. In no way does this mean that all the ancient walls have been demolished—far from it. True, many external barriers, such as customs and systems, have been reformed through the application of prolonged determination and persistence. But a much harder task is surmounting innate invisible walls that were bolstered by secondhand beliefs and centuries of social programming. That left a road ahead strewn with obstacles and hurdles for women who struggled to make something of themselves during that era of isolation, and its legacy can still do damage.

Women, as well as men, who seek meaning and fulfillment in life should be wary of inner walls that limit perspectives on the available possibilities around them. If you are not mindful of their tricky influence, they will ensnare you in self-doubt and undermine your power to manifest your dreams.

They will silence the little voice inside and refute anything extraordinary outside their boundaries.

They will hook you on an addiction to external validation and approval, so that your soul continues to be caged.

They will leave you to wonder why you are not at peace with yourself, despite any achievements and abundance.

Following my retirement, I was approached by several public and private companies and government organizations to participate in projects for economic development or serve as a member of their boards of directors. My extensive experience in Human Resources was in high demand in the country as we continue to reform policies and build the workforce for the future. Moreover, the private and public sectors were seeking accomplished businesswomen to assume key positions in their organizations, many of which were introducing diversity into their boardrooms and decision-making teams. Women's empowerment has become a global trend, if not a legal requirement in some cases, in an effort to also improve corporate governance and business results.

Although I am no longer interested in the corporate world or any formal appointment that might impinge upon my free time, I realize it would not be appropriate to hide away with all the knowledge I have stored. Young women need to see examples of other successful female leaders to encourage them to pursue their dreams. For this reason, I agreed to join the boards of a few organizations from various industries, at least for a short time. Eventually, I will remove myself from the business community as more women become ready to assume positions of power.

Happy as I am to share what I know and contribute to our economic growth, I find it necessary at this stage of my evolution to maintain autonomy and manage my time in line with the flavor of the day. My days are devoted to what excites me, such as reading, writing, traveling, practicing yoga, meditating, and oil painting—a hobby I started in 2004 through a self-study of the work of old masters and renowned artists. This nourished my passion for art, and painting became a calming way to transcend the world around me. Given the need for uninterrupted stretches of time, I avoided any work engagements that would disrupt my rhythm.

I hope my story will inspire some young people to believe in themselves, think for themselves, and rely on their innate capacity to find their authentic place in this magical life. My journey took me to the corporate stratosphere to help me search for meaning and identity. While I am grateful for the opportunities and experiences, I came to realize that my identity is not about reaching high positions or becoming a somebody.

"The game is not about becoming somebody, it's about becoming nobody," said Ram Dass, and how liberating that is.

As for what the future holds, the possibilities are unlimited, and I remain open to receive.

AUTHOR'S NOTE

My portrayal of events and people as found in this book is derived from actual personal experiences as they touched my life. They reflect the emotional and intellectual perceptions that these events created, and my reflections are not intended to render judgment on other people's behaviour. I am in no position to be acquainted with their inner motives and foundations; my words simply reflect thoughts and feelings from one perspective, my own, at a particular time and place.

ACKNOWLEDGMENTS

"No one can whistle a symphony," said Yale professor of divinity studies Halford E. Luccock. "It takes a whole orchestra to play it." That is very true in my case. I could not have done it all by myself.

I may be the main player in this story, but my achievements would not have been possible without all of those I encountered along the way. Family, friends, colleagues, acquaintances and even adversaries, every one of them contributed something to the magical discoveries that led me here.

First and foremost, I am grateful for and to my mother, Shaha Al-Dughaither, God bless her soul. I would not be who I am today without her unconditional love and encouragement to see the unlimited opportunities around me. She helped me believe in myself and claim my individual place in this life, and her influence continues with my every breath.

My late father, Mohammed Al-Ghoson, was the silent observer in the background of this journey, giving me space to lead my life and venture into the world freely, make my own mistakes and victories, and grow from my lessons.

Bibi, my grandmother Lulwa Al-Zuhair, and grand aunt Habayeb, Latifa Al-Zuhair, contributed their endless love and care, and inspired me with their strength and independence. God bless their souls.

My sisters and brothers, Muntaser, Ateka, Mazen, Asma, Mona, Fatema, Fahad, Aljohara and Nasser, their spouses, and my many nieces and nephews, all such a vital part of my life, stood by me, cheered my successes, and allowed me to lean on them in times of need.

A special thanks to my relentless editor, Stephen M. Silverman, who poured all his energy, passion and knowledge into refining the text. He helped me close gaps in the narrative, strengthen arguments, improve the flow, and polish the expressions, turning the manuscript into a buoyant literary work. And a special acknowledgment to Linda Joyce Stolow, who brought Stephen and me together.

I am grateful to Abdi Assadi, my spiritual counselor, for his guidance, insights, and restoration of my energy and peace of mind. Abdi implanted the inspiration for me to write this book, encouraged me along the way, and helped me recognize and follow my inner guidance and intuition.

To my cousin Abdulhameed Al-Rushaid, his wife Hetaf Al-Shamsi, and their beautiful four children, Nouf, Faisal, Mai and Lama, thank you for your unwavering support throughout my journey, and for always standing by my side.

Grateful thanks to my cousin Ibrahim Al-Ojan for opening my mind to the world of literature and kindling the passion for reading.

Thank you, too, to all my loving Al-Dughaither cousins: Essam, Maysoon, Emad, Mohammad, Moayed and Reem for their kindness and generosity, and for always showing me their total love and concern.

To all my amazing friends, old and new, grateful thanks to each and every one of you for touching and enriching my world in so many ways. You have influenced my life on a level far more than is evident on the surface: Mashael Mohammed, Amani Al-Shahid, Nafisa Koheji and her son Yaser Wazzan, Sheikha Althakafi and Ali Bughaigis and their children, Soulafa Nassar, Roy Yarid and Samar Khazindar, Badia Bager, Maha Mansoury, Omaima Gabil, Nabila Abbas, Ghada Al-Ghamdi, Maha Al-Bassam, Osama Taqiu Eddin, Najia Edrisi, Waleed Al-Mulla, Mohammed Al-Rawaf, Yamila Rodriguez, Lamya Arrayadh, Barrie Doughty, Malcom Hinchcliffe, Reda Mansouri, Adel Al-Bassam, Serine Al-Sowayel, Najla Saud, Jamil Dandani and Basma Sabti, Carl Watson, Ancel Lewars. Hamad and Annet Ammari, Saud, and Helen Ammari.

To my domestic helpers, Ramoo, Chandra and Raja, who so carefully looked after me with unwavering dedication for four decades, there are simply not enough words to express my gratitude.

A big thank you to my publisher, Peter Harrigan, and all the team at Medina Publishing: Chris Capstick, Sherif Dhaimish, Jeff Eamon, Alexandra Lawson, Maya Smadi, Rachel Hamilton and Lesley Wright.

Finally, I offer my tremendous appreciation to all the people who enriched my journey at Saudi Aramco: Abdallah Jum'ah, Ahmad Nassar, Abdulaziz Khayyal, Amin Al-Nasser, Beryl Tunnicliffe, Adnan Juma, Saeed Naji, Hassan Johari, Scott Stanaland, Barrie Doughty, Charles Heaussler, Farid Khoja, Ali Tuwairqi, Ali Namlah, Nasser Nafisee, Fouad Therman, Hamed Saddoun, Samir Tubayyeb, Abdulaziz Hashimi, Khalid Al-Mulhim, Khalid Faddagh, Nabil Jam'a, Khalid Dabbagh, Mohammed Saggaf and Mohammed Qahtani.

And a heartfelt gratitude to all my colleagues in Executive and Corporate Management, Human Resources, and Training and Development.

ABOUT THE AUTHOR

Huda Al-Ghoson spent thirty-seven years working for Saudi Aramco, the world's largest oil producing and refining company and the largest corporation in the Middle East. She was the executive director of Human Resources, the first Saudi woman to achieve an executive leadership position at the company. Al-Ghoson holds degrees from King Saud University, in Riyadh, and the American University, in Washington, D.C., and undertook executive training programs at the University of Michigan, and Oxford. She sits on the board of directors of Saudi Telecom Company, BUPA Arabia, Credit Suisse Saudi Arabia, and the Institute of Public Administration, among other companies. *Forbes* magazine has ranked Al-Ghoson fourth in its list of most powerful Arab women in the field of executive management, while *Arabian Business* magazine, in presenting Al-Ghoson with its 2014 Arab Woman Award, named her one of the most influential figures in the energy domain. She divides her time between residences in Dhahran, Saudi Arabia and London. This is her first book.

INDEX

Roman numerals in *italics* refer to pages in the plate section